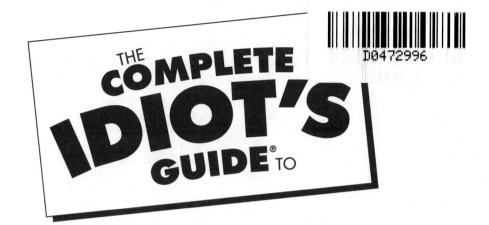

THE
COMPLETE
IDIOT'S
GUIDE® TO

African American History

by Melba J. Duncan

ALPHA

A Pearson Education Company

International Standard Book Number: 0-02-864312-7
Library of Congress Catalog Card Number: 2002115728

04   03   02   8   7   6   5   4   3   2   1

Interpretation of the printing code: The rightmost number of the first series of numbers is the year of the book's printing; the rightmost number of the second series of numbers is the number of the book's printing. For example, a printing code of 02-1 shows that the first printing occurred in 2002.

Printed in the United States of America

Note: This publication contains the opinions and ideas of its author. It is intended to provide helpful and informative material on the subject matter covered. It is sold with the understanding that the author and publisher are not engaged in rendering professional services in the book. If the reader requires personal assistance or advice, a competent professional should be consulted.

The author and publisher specifically disclaim any responsibility for any liability, loss, or risk, personal or otherwise, which is incurred as a consequence, directly or indirectly, of the use and application of any of the contents of this book.

For marketing and publicity, please call: 317-581-3722

The publisher offers discounts on this book when ordered in quantity for bulk purchases and special sales.

For sales within the United States, please contact: Corporate and Government Sales, 1-800-382-3419 or corpsales@pearsontechgroup.com

Outside the United States, please contact: International Sales, 317-581-3793 or international@pearsontechgroup.com

Publisher: *Marie Butler-Knight*
Product Manager: *Phil Kitchel*
Managing Editor: *Jennifer Chisholm*
Senior Acquisitions Editor: *Randy Ladenheim-Gil*
Development Editor: *Joan D. Paterson*
Production Editor: *Katherin Bidwell*
Copy Editor: *Michael Dietsch*
Illustrator: *Judith Burros*
Cartoonist: *Chris Eliopoulos*
Cover/Book Designer: *Trina Wurst*
Indexer: *Angie Bess*
Layout/Proofreading: *Megan Douglass, Sherry Taggart*

Contents at a Glance

Contents

Foreword

Melba Duncan's extraordinary book is a trip through the dungeons of American history—but it is also a journey that concludes in the sunlight of opportunity found by all those who are willing to stand up and claim their dreams. This must-read volume offers a compelling overview of nearly four centuries of African American challenge, spirit, and contribution. It should be mandatory reading for the student, the general reader interested in the rich legacy of the African American, and the history buff alike.

There are many books that have successfully documented the African American's experience. John Hope Franklin's book *From Slavery to Freedom* is the most comprehensive documentation of the African American's experience ever written; Kareem Abdul-Jabbar's *Black Profiles in Courage* informs us that many people of color through the centuries were noted for their explorations, achievements, and leadership—although standard works of history routinely ignored them. Now there is the remarkable book you hold in your hands, a worthy addition to the existing literature, and one of the most accessible books on the subject yet written.

This book offers an amazing and inspiring testimony to the spirit of a people who for 400 years lived in daily fear of intimidation, terrorism, humiliation, and death; a people who nevertheless found the strength to become great inventors, business men and women, scientists, military heroes, and artists; a people who transcended boundaries and limitations to define themselves and their nation. Melba's compulsively readable history once and for all eradicates the notion that this great people ever developed a tolerance for subjugation. They were—and are—always rising.

Enjoy the book!

—Horace Williams

Vice President of Government and Community Relations, the Pratt Institute

Co-founder (with Chase Bank, the Pratt Institute, and the United Way of Greater New York) of the Youth Service Coalition of New York

Project Coordinator, Myrtle Avenue Revitalization and Development Corporation (Brooklyn, New York)

Introduction

The Complete Idiot's Guide to African American History is an introduction to the extraordinary legacy of African American contribution in the United States. While I have not shied away from accounts of struggle and crisis, I have emphasized throughout this book the significant contributions and positive influences of African Americans to American society.

This society is freer, less violent, and more prosperous than it was during the years when slavery first took root here, and the contributions of African Americans in business, politics, science, and civil rights activism over four centuries must receive some credit for that fact. This nation is more democratic, more accepting of diversity, more supportive of equal opportunity, and more inclined to respect the rights of all its citizens today than it was in 1960, or 1920, or 1880, and that is in large measure because of the efforts of African Americans. This nation is less prone to internal strife and political chaos than it was in 1860, and that is due, to a larger extent than many realize, to the loyalty, service in arms, and commitment to the very idea of a United States of America shown by African Americans.

In a book such as this, it is essential to look at the hardships we have endured at the social, economic, and political levels. It is also essential, however, to look also at the many remarkable ways in which we have overcomethese hardships. I believe we cannot permit real grievances to overshadow our own extraordinary contributions in the past, the opportunities we find in the present, and the vision to which we hold firmly as we build the future.

The legacy of racial preference is, of course, still very much alive. Gaps remain in education, in socioeconomic stability, and in access to capital. "Logical" attempts to dispel preconceptions, stereotypes, or outright racial hatred have not had a great track record. What has worked well in the past, however, and is sure to continue working well into the future, is the creation of platforms of opportunity in the areas of entrepreneurship, education, and economic opportunity. Once economic parity is attained, racial hierarchies will diminish. The responsibility to make inroads in these areas, however, lies squarely on the shoulders of the African American.

History teaches that governmental structures will reflect the interests and values of dominant social groups. How, then, we ask, will change occur? What has been acceptable in the past—asking for individual freedom and agitating for tangible changes in laws or customs—must give way to new and different forms of expression.

The initiative for change must come from within our own community. Our actions should conform to *our* self-interest. Our agenda should be to inspire, and, where necessary, to raise unpopular issues and make unpopular choices. Attaining African American control of the economic, educational, public safety, criminal justice, and political institutions in African American communities is one such set of issues.

Ultimately, only we are responsible for the content and quality of the lives of our families and our communities. And ultimately, only we are responsible for adherence to the only motive that supports large-scale change—positive or negative—in American society: the profit motive. Racial prejudice is not simply an emotional response; it is also an economically based response.

Self-interest must become the primary motive for creating competitive businesses and civic infrastructure in the African American community. Self-interest will bring to life the internal resources, the technology, the dormant connections to institutions of power. Self-interest, properly channeled, will convert private success into economic and political opportunity. Self-interest will help us to broaden our goals so that they extend beyond fighting *de facto* segregation (as necessary as that is) to building and reinforcing a legacy of profitable business development in our communities. Self-interest will help us to build businesses that respond to the needs of a diverse population.

Learning how to "live within the system" does not mean accepting the idea of compromise; it does not mean losing our values or our culture. It does mean that the African American community needs those of us who are entrepreneurs and executives to take initiative in assuming advisory and leadership roles. We must help to create competitive businesses that cater to diverse audiences and support civic infrastructure; we must help to translate private success into large-scale political power and economic opportunity. We must help communities focus on building social, economic, and political standards that will endure: education for every child, the closing of income gaps, the embrace of entrepreneurship and competition, and stability and well-being in our neighborhoods. We must also continue to build bridges that permit entry into all communities. I am not suggesting that we lose our core identity. I am suggesting that we embrace the ideal of communicating in ways that open the largest possible number of doors.

This book is a starting point for those who are interested in learning about the remarkable contribution African American people have made to our country. As always, African Americans will play a leading role in the effort of summoning our nation to its enduring greatness.

About This Book

This book is divided into five sections that will help you learn more about the remarkable African American story.

Part 1, "Dreams and Dreams Deferred: The Early History," gives you answers to questions about the first part of the African American story.

Part 2, "A House Divided: The Later History," gives you information about the story from the Civil War to the present day.

Part 3, "Power on the Inside: Spirit and Soul," shows you some of the institutions and traditions the African American community has used to support itself and sustain its vision.

Part 4, "Power on the Outside: Contributions to American Culture," celebrates examples of great cultural contributions, not to a narrowly defined racial group, but to the American experience as a whole.

Part 5, "The Road from Here," gives you an in-depth look at some of the obstacles, the opportunities, and the good work being done in today's African American community.

Extras

You'll probably want to take advantage of the little nuggets of information that show up throughout the text of this book. These will help you gain a deeper understanding of some element of the African American story. Here's what they'll look like:

FAQ

Here, you'll get answers to some of the most important questions about African American history and culture.

What's the Word?

This is where you'll find concise summaries of key terms that may not be familiar to you.

 **On the March**

This is where you'll find background facts or supporting information about some part of the African American community's drive for autonomy and self-determination.

 Obstacles and Opportunities

These boxes offer illuminating examples of both challenges and opportunities.

Acknowledgments

I thank Randy Ladenheim-Gil, Joan Paterson, and the entire team at Alpha. Grateful thanks also go out to Max Rodriguez, Brandon Toropov, Judith Burros for her original artwork, Gene Brissie, Glenn KnicKrehm, and all those who have been staunch supporters of the Duncan Group over the years: our clients, our candidates, and especially our colleagues: Ron Ries, David Harmon, Noreen Denihan, Diane Rush, Eden Playe; my dear friends Madeleine Moore, Adam Moore, Madelyn Bednar, Paul Simmons, and Ron Simmons; my sisters Joan Duncan and Clevette Duncan; and my daughter Michelle K. Devlin, who remains my inspiration. Without their help, support, and encouragement, this book would not have been possible. My thanks go out, too, to the many, many wonderful people with whom I have worked over the years, and I offer my apologies that space limitations prevent me from listing them all here.

Special Thanks to the Technical Reviewer

Thanks go to Max Rodriguez, founder and publisher of the *Quarterly Black Review*, who served as technical reviewer on this project.

Trademarks

All terms mentioned in this book that are known to be or are suspected of being trademarks or service marks have been appropriately capitalized. Alpha Books and Pearson Education, Inc., cannot attest to the accuracy of this information. Use of a term in this book should not be regarded as affecting the validity of any trademark or service mark.

Part 1

Dreams and Dreams Deferred: The Early History

The institution of slavery casts a long, ominous shadow over the landscape of American history. Its repercussions are still felt. As many observers have noted, communities of African descent in this country have known two and a half centuries of brutal, state-endorsed captivity; another century of legalized oppression and vigilante abuse; and only half a century of anything else.

To decide where we're going, it sometimes helps to know where we've come from. In this part of the book, you learn about the beginnings of the African American story—a story of the kind of self-determination and commitment that turns obstacles into opportunities.

Portrait of a People

In This Chapter

- ◆ Race and self-definition
- ◆ The "proper sphere" message
- ◆ The portrait: Walking the path of one's own choice

In July 1863, New York City exploded.

Bloody riots raged through the city for three long days that month; the immediate cause of the violence was the presence of a newly opened Union recruiting station. The station reminded white working-class residents of the city of federal recruiting efforts in support of the Northern cause in the Civil War; it also reinforced the reality of obligations under the recently passed Conscription Act of 1863, a law that had summoned deep resentment in New York and elsewhere.

Because of all this, historians would later describe the wave of destruction that engulfed New York as the Draft Riots. That curt label, however, hardly describes what took place in the North's leading city. The anarchy in New York remains, to this day, the deadliest civil disturbance in the history of the United States. Nowadays, many Americans are either unaware of what took place in New York City in 1863, or have an incomplete understanding of what really fueled the violence.

A Pattern of Intimidation

To understand what actually happened in New York, it's certainly important to know about the provisions of the *Conscription Act of 1863* that so infuriated poor whites. It's also essential, though, to understand how whites have worked consciously, unconsciously, or in the borderland of reason known as rage to find ways to control, manipulate, and intimidate African Americans. This process dates from the early 1600s, when the institution of slavery took root in North America, and continues up to the present day.

The huge, distinctly African American community that came to thrive despite this long-running effort at social manipulation was unlike any other in the country. It was a community that would suffer greatly, triumph greatly, and define itself by delivering a continuous challenge for America to live up to its own principles. It was a community that, as Martin Luther King Jr. would argue nearly a century later in launching a bus boycott in Montgomery, would force future generations to stop, think, and conclude that a great people had brought fresh meaning to human civilization. That community, the African American community, is the subject of this book, which offers an American history of Africans in America .

What's the Word?

The **Conscription Act of 1863** authorized the drafting of soldiers into Union military forces during the Civil War. The Act provided loopholes for wealthy men, who could avoid service by paying a fee or hiring others to serve.

Sending a Message

The Draft Riots of 1863 were race riots, and in terms of lives lost, they were the worst in American history. And that, of course, is saying something.

By whatever name it is given, urban unrest related to racism has been a common feature of American life for nearly a century and a half. We have been, in a real sense, a nation at war with itself for all that time.

What were the major American race riots? There have been plenty to choose from, but here are the most frequently noted civil disturbances with racial dimensions.

More Than a Century of Racial Strife

New York City	1863
Coushatta, Louisiana	1874
Pana, Illinois	1899

New Orleans, Louisiana	1900
Atlanta, Georgia	1906
Springfield, Illinois	1908
East St. Louis, Illinois	1917
Houston, Texas	1917
Various parts of Texas	1919
Washington, D.C.	1919
Elaine, Arkansas	1919
Tulsa, Oklahoma	1921
Detroit, Michigan	1942
Beaumont, Texas	1943
Harlem (New York City)	1943
Columbia, Tennessee	1946
Athens, Alabama	1946
Cicero, Illinois	1951
Chattanooga, Tennessee	1960
Jacksonville, Florida	1960
Harlem and Bedford-Stuyvesant (New York City)	1964
Rochester, New York	1964
Jersey City, New Jersey	1964
Paterson, New Jersey	1964
Elizabeth, New Jersey	1964
Dixmoor, Illinois	1964
Philadelphia, Pennsylvania	1964
Watts (Los Angeles), California	1965
Chicago, Illinois	1965
Chicago, Illinois	1966
Lansing, Michigan	1966
Waukegan, Illinois	1966
Atlanta, Georgia	1966
Roxbury (Boston), Massachusetts	1967
Tampa, Florida	1967
Buffalo, New York	1967
Newark, New Jersey	1967
Cairo, Illinois	1967

continues

More Than a Century of Racial Strife   (continued)

Durham, North Carolina	1967
Memphis, Tennessee	1967
Detroit, Michigan	1967
Cambridge, Maryland	1967
Over 100 American cities (following the assassination of Martin Luther King Jr.)	1968
Cleveland, Ohio	1968
Gary, Indiana	1968
Miami, Florida	1968
Hartford, Connecticut	1969
Springfield, Massachusetts	1969
Jacksonville, Florida	1969
Augusta, Georgia	1970
Miami, Florida	1970
Asbury Park, New Jersey	1970
Hartford, Connecticut	1970
Daytona Beach, Florida	1970
Brownsville (New York City)	1971
Idabell, Oklahoma	1980
Miami, Florida	1980
Miami, Florida	1982
Miami, Florida	1989
Los Angeles, California and other U.S. cities (following the acquittal of officers videotaped beating motorist Rodney King)	1992

Of all of these, the New York riots of 1863 had the highest death toll—at least 400 and perhaps considerably more. It is worth noting that the list above does not include slave uprisings (some scholars estimate that there were roughly 250 of these before the end of the Civil War) or massacres of African Americans that were not accompanied by periods of civil disturbance.

In the race riots of 1863, as in those prior, the violence was heavily white-on-black. It might be more accurate to think of what happened in New York as civil unrest whose most prominent form of expression was a mass execution of African Americans by whites. (A side note: African American rage fueled U.S. race riots only from about 1960 onward; prior to that, these urban disturbances were driven by whites.)

"Know Your Place"

The 1863 riots took place in a Northern city still rejoicing over the recent Union victory at Gettysburg, which proved to be the turning point in the Civil War. The violence was not, in other words, a product of racism that could be blamed on the "Southern way of life." This hate-filled bloodshed was, rather, part of an ongoing, one-way pattern of "communication" from whites in all parts of the country to African Americans as a whole. The message was simple: Know your place, and do not attempt to advance beyond it.

Although the medium for conveying the message would change, it would continue to be sent over the next century and a half … a period when African American presence in urban areas would dramatically increase and the inner city and the urban underclass would become significant parts of American life.

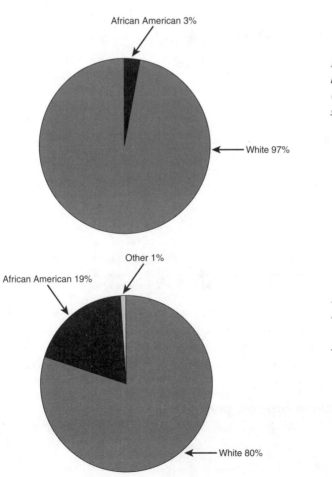

African American 3%

White 97%

Ethnic composition of 10 largest U.S. cities, 1900 (based on U.S. government statistics).

Other 1%

African American 19%

White 80%

Ethnic composition of 10 largest U.S. cities, 1950 (based on U.S. government statistics).

Population chart, 1990 (based on U.S. government statistics).

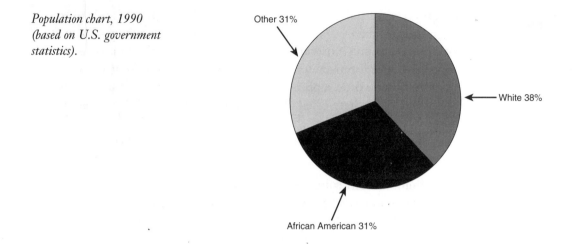

Other 31%

White 38%

African American 31%

 Obstacles and Opportunities _____

The most popular explanation of the 1863 Draft Riots points out that potential draftees into the Union Army deeply resented the fact that wealthy citizens could legally evade the draft by paying the government $300, or by locating a paid substitute. This explanation doesn't account for a critical social element of the riots. The rioters were Irish immigrants whom white native-born Americans loathed. Working-class Irishmen in 1863 New York saw the Conscription Act as a legal manipulation that forced them to face death for a cause that benefited two groups they despised. Those groups were the war profiteers who were growing rich on fat federal contracts, and the African Americans with whom the Irish competed fiercely for New York City's lowest-level jobs.

Three Days of Murder ... with a Message

After laying waste to the main recruiting post, mobs of furious rioters made their way to the homes of some of the wealthiest citizens in town and embarked on a campaign of terror and destruction. Actual war profiteers were comparatively hard to track down, though, so the mob turned its attention to the Civil War's more easily identifiable group: African Americans.

The riots quickly turned into a campaign of white murder and intimidation of African American civilians. Its purpose was now impossible to miss: to make absolutely sure that African Americans were so terrified that they would accept, without complaint, the role of lowest-ranking social group in New York City. To accomplish this objective, huge white mobs marched through the streets of the city, sabotaging factories and encouraging the workers within to join the growing ranks of the white crusade. The throngs took over street after street of America's great city and roamed with an ominous unity in search of faces of color.

They beat, shot, hanged, set ablaze, or drowned as many African Americans as they could find.

They turned an orphanage for African American children into an inferno.

They beat to death aged men of color who, on their own, couldn't possibly have posed any threat, economic or otherwise, to the aims of white working men.

They slaughtered, when they could find them, African American children, little ones who certainly understood nothing of the great issues of the day—such as who would or wouldn't be paid for cleaning out public toilets.

They danced before the mutilated bodies of those they had cut down, and swore that they would never die to free "niggers."

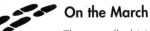 **On the March**

The so-called New York City Draft Riots raged for days until Union troops arrived on the scene to restore order. The soldiers were returning from the recent Union victory at Gettysburg.

The "Proper Sphere"

A critical goal of the mobs in New York was to see to it that African Americans "stayed in their place."

Many people, out of fear, hatred, ignorance, or a combination of the three, still assume, often without realizing exactly what they are doing, that there is such a thing as a "proper sphere" for African Americans—a realm of living defined *for*, and not by, African Americans. Without this continuously reinforced mental foundation, there would have been no plantation system, no racially motivated assaults (in New York or elsewhere), no segregation, and no need for a civil rights movement. There would today be no gap between white median family income and African American median family income, no racial unrest in the cities, and no shortage of top-level executives in the nation's largest companies.

But this is America. And the "proper sphere" mindset is, as it has been since long before the country's founding, an enduring and ominous part of our cultural landscape.

The so-called Draft Riots took place in the mid-nineteenth century. This is the early twenty-first century. It has been some time (though not as long as some might imagine) since sane whites gathered in mobs to glorify the execution of innocent African Americans, or used the word "nigger" in public as a verbal weapon, or casually slaughtered children to make a social point. And yet the essentials of the mental process that made the carnage in New York possible remain, in many corners, unchanged. This mental process is, in fact, an enduring, and persistently ignored, feature of American history. This is the process of thinking that attempts to define a "place" in which African Americans are to "stay"—and is, in fact, a cornerstone of a mythical "white" racial construct.

It is in the transcendence of these preconceptions that the African American community has composed an inspiring and constantly shifting image of itself: A portrait of a people capable of anything, a people whose "proper sphere" is self-defined, the largest and highest sphere possible for each individual.

> **On the March**
>
> The term "Negro," common for centuries in the United States, declined in use beginning in the early 1960s. One reason for the change was an influential resolution passed in 1959 by the African Nationalist Pioneer Movement in New York City; the resolution rejected the word as an example of "African people (having) been divided and enslaved by Europeans." Today, the terms "African American" or simply "African" have gained wide acceptance.

The Ongoing Struggle for Self-Definition

More consistently and for a longer period of time than any other ethnic group of Americans, African Americans have had to endure the dehumanization of having others (usually whites) attempt to define their status, social roles, capacities, and aspirations. The story of this country is filled with formal and informal efforts to ensure that this imaginary "place" is identified and that African Americans stay in it.

The century just passed is full of examples of such "proper sphere" thinking that played out in countless settings, and (predictably) to the disadvantage of African Americans. Physical violence has, as later chapters of this book will show, been used to reinforce this "proper sphere" principle over and over again. Here are just a few instances of the other ways African Americans have been sent the message to "stay in their place."

Abuse of the Criminal Justice System

In a shameful legal odyssey beginning in 1931, nine young African American men who came to be known as the Scottsboro Boys were convicted of raping two white women on a train. The evidence was inadequate ... but the desire of all-white southern juries to "send a message" to African Americans throughout the South was substantial.

The nine defendants were convicted; all were sentenced to die or to serve heavy sentences in prison. Legal problems with the case led the United States Supreme Court to reverse the convictions—not once, but twice. At a second trial, one of the alleged rape victims recanted her charges.

Five of the accused went free in 1937, but the Alabama state government simply refused to admit that there had been a miscarriage of justice for the remaining men. The case became a symbol of southern—or was it American?—judicial arrogance.

On the March

In 1976, the last known "Scottsboro Boy" received a formal pardon from the state of Alabama.

Three of the Scottsboro defendants were released in the 1940s; in 1948, one escaped from prison to safety in Michigan. (The State of Michigan refused to extradite the escapee to Alabama.)

As the Scottsboro case suggests, African Americans have been historically victimized by the American criminal justice system, and their unequal treatment at the hands of white police officers and juries has been a long-running source of passionate anger. African American males, in particular, have been subjected to so much institutionalized harassment and abuse from law enforcement officials over the years that a grim variation of DWI (Driving While Intoxicated) has emerged in the African American community: "Police love to make arrests for DWB: Driving While Black."

In a much-quoted 1966 study, Harry Kalven and Hans Zeisel examined the effect of racist attitudes on judicial performance and jury verdicts. They interviewed a large number of white jurors and found striking evidence that factors well beyond the defendant's guilt or innocence influenced jury decisions. One white juror shared his opinion in particularly blunt terms: "Niggers have to be taught to behave. I feel that if he hadn't done (what he was accused of), he'd probably done something else probably even worse and that he should be put out of the way for a good long while."

Anyone tempted to conclude that this approach to deciding cases is a habit of the distant past should consider the police-protective approach the Simi Valley, California, jury took in delivering the first Rodney King verdict. An all-white panel of jurors acquitted a group of white officers who had been videotaped delivering a brutal beating to King, an African American motorist. The verdict led to riots that claimed the lives of 58 people.

In his superb book *Black Robes, White Justice* (New York: Lyle Stuart, 1987), New York Supreme Court Justice Bruce Wright reports that, in New York in 1989, a white doctor convicted of raping an African American former patient was sentenced to probation. In the same year, in a different part of New York, an African American doctor who had been found guilty of raping white women was sentenced to serve six consecutive life sentences.

Abuse of the Civil Justice System

Today, it is easy to celebrate the victories of the civil rights movement in areas like voting rights, access to public accommodations, and desegregation in publicly funded school systems. It's important to remember, however, that these "advances" were simply demands for fundamental rights. What made the victories remarkable was that they were achieved within a civil justice system that had for nearly two centuries been starkly and unashamedly racist—a system openly dedicated, in countless ways, to keeping African Americans "in their place."

For most of the twentieth century, for instance, American courts upheld racially restrictive real estate covenants—ensuring that white neighborhoods would remain white, and that African Americans would remain relegated to substandard tenement neighborhoods or other enclaves. This legal sanction of countless free-form discriminatory selling practices made it easy to perpetuate a system that denied African Americans and other minorities equal rights in housing.

Such covenants are without legal force today. Many observers, however, see disturbing parallels between the goals of the mostly improvised system that denied African Americans equal access to housing in, say, Florida—and the goals of the equally untidy system that denied African Americans equal access to the ballot in the 2000 presidential election in the same state. Each system, critics argue, featured racist control of a process that only appeared bias-free; each served to send the same ominous message: "We control this particular game; know your place in it, and do not attempt to advance beyond it."

White Racism (Spoken and Unspoken)

Today, most white professionals, politicians, and civic leaders know it is unacceptable to express racial prejudice openly. But whether the words are spoken or not, the "proper sphere" mindset remains. (In the hiring arena, the internal message may go as follows: "We already have a black [fill in the blank].")

For every legal and social advance made by African Americans, there has been some form of white backlash. Sometimes the reaction has been loud, sometimes it has been quiet, and sometimes it has not been spoken at all, or communicated only in code words. But it has always been there, and its underlying message has always been the same: "They have advanced far enough; it is time to draw the line now." That African Americans have no say in defining what is "far enough" is predictable.

White backlash to African American achievement is sometimes expressed in condescending, paternalistic, or surrealistically self-deluded terms. Consider the following pious mouthings from 96 southern congressmen opposing the Supreme Court's landmark 1954 school desegregation, *Brown* v. *Board of Education:*

> This unwarranted exercise of power by the court, contrary to the Constitution, is creating chaos and confusion in the states principally affected. It is destroying the amicable relations between the white and Negro races that have been created through ninety years of patient effort by the good people of both races. It has planted hatred and suspicion where there has been heretofore friendship and understanding. (From the *Declaration of Ninety-Six Southern Congressmen,* March 12, 1956.)

This is white "proper sphere" rhetoric at its most polished—and its most shameless. According to the *Declaration,* friendship and understanding reigned in the south between African Americans and whites … *until* the Supreme Court decided, after nearly a century, to see to the implementation of the Fourteenth Amendment to the United States Constitution in the nation's public schools.

What does "proper sphere" rhetoric sound like in the modern era? Because most white people have learned to curb their tongues, the words, when they are actually spoken, often come from crude and ignorant people. In 1987, Los Angeles Dodgers executive Al Campanis made headlines with an on-air assertion that African Americans lacked the "necessities" to become successful managers in major league baseball. In a similar vein, CBS commentator Jimmy "the Greek" Snyder lamented, the following year, that further appointments of African Americans to coaching positions in major sports would mean that "there's not going to be anything left for white people." Both men were fired and received intense negative media coverage as a result of their remarks. Their words helped confirm—if

On the March

Not long after Los Angeles Dodgers executive Al Campanis was fired for racist blather suggesting that African Americans didn't have what it takes to manage in the big leagues, African American manager Cito Gaston (apparently unaware that he lacked the "necessities" for strategic thought) led the Toronto Blue Jays to two consecutive World Series championships.

confirmation was necessary—that white racism was indeed alive and well in the United States.

Campanis and Snyder, in their off-the-cuff remarks, made it clear what many whites were thinking. The fact that most such sentiments now go unspoken does not change the reality that, even without obvious bloodshed, and even with the passage of nearly a century and a half, the riots in New York are still raging in the American mind.

The Great National Drama

During his 1988 presidential campaign, the Reverend Jesse Jackson was the subject of a critical magazine profile (in a publication whose name, I must admit, has long since escaped me). The writer of the piece built his first paragraph on the point that, for Reverend Jackson, all of American history and politics simply revolved around the issue of slavery. The implication was that this viewpoint implied some lack of balance or perspective in Jackson's candidacy for the highest office in the land.

The more closely one looks at American history, though, the harder it is to escape the conclusion that it does in fact resonate outward, like circles in a pond, from the central fact of slavery. There are innumerable implications to that great American primal sin. Those implications are, whether we like it or not, the great national story.

The chapters that follow offer, I hope, enough evidence to support this notion—and to give a broad overview of the struggles and triumphs of the African community in America. This book is meant to be an introduction to the extraordinary history and culture of the African American community's ongoing effort to define itself, rather than let others do the defining.

This book is only an introduction. Its goal is not to tell the whole story of the African in America. The whole story can probably never be told, and it certainly can't be contained within the covers of a single book. My aim is to encourage readers of all ethnic backgrounds to become interested enough in the ongoing drama of the African American people to want to find out more about that drama. You will find a list of additional resources at the end of the book that will help you do just that.

The American Dream

There is a common expression: "The American Dream." Today, we've grown perhaps a little too accustomed to thinking of that dream as having only a financial or materialistic dimension. The actual American Dream has to do with having the right to decide what your own proper sphere is … without permitting anyone else to decide that all-important matter for you.

Ultimately, the real American Dream has nothing to do with upward mobility or household appliances or social status. The real American Dream is a good deal closer to the ideals set out by (and not, of course, lived up to) by some of the great thinkers of the Enlightenment—the founding fathers of our nation.

It is one of the tragedies of our imperfect republic that the inspiring dream of autonomy, of political awareness, of an inherent right to life, liberty, and the pursuit of happiness, was initially meant to be turned into reality only for white males. It fell to Dr. Martin Luther King Jr., to demand compellingly that America recognize an obligation to live up to its dream—to demand for all citizens, not grudging concessions, but the fundamental right to empowered self-definition that is the bedrock of the ongoing American national experiment.

Obstacles and Opportunities

The Enlightenment, a movement in late eighteenth-century Western thought, emphasized rationality, progressive humanitarianism, and the logic of science. Thinkers within the movement saw the ideal state as a rational institution founded on natural law, embracing human freedom as a birthright of humanity. Such ideals did not, however, persuade one of the great thinkers of the Enlightenment, Thomas Jefferson, to liberate his own large contingent of enslaved Africans.

Hey, You!

One of my favorite stories of self-definition is set in New York City and serves as a kind of counterpart to the gruesome events of the 1863 riots. The event took place nearly a century later, and is as small in scale as the tale of the epic slaughter in New York is incomprehensibly vast. But both events illuminate the same issue.

In 1952, a white woman walking the streets of Manhattan concluded for some reason that an African American man was following her. She appealed to the white officers in a passing squad car for help in escaping this menacing figure. The officers dutifully pursued the man and called out, "Hey you!"

The man, who was *not* stalking the woman but simply making his way to a friend's house, informed the officers that he had a name.

Unimpressed by this fact, the officers reminded the pedestrian that he was dealing with police officers. The man smiled, removed his wallet, flashed a badge, and informed the officers that *they* were dealing with a superior officer. He was Billy Rowe, New York City's newest deputy police commissioner, and the first African American in the nation to hold such a post. The officers withdrew sheepishly.

This book offers many, many angles meant to add up to a single portrait of an extraordinary people: a people committed to identifying their own sphere in life. The first image of that multi-layered portrait should be, I think, that of Billy Rowe striding purposefully past those bewildered white officers, walking (happily, one imagines) the path of his own choice.

The Least You Need to Know

- ◆ The bloody 1863 riots in New York City were meant to send a message to blacks: Know your place and don't attempt to advance beyond it.

- ◆ Countless other American traditions and institutions have sent, and continue to send, the same message.

- ◆ African Americans have continually risen beyond this tired message, and continue to do so today.

- ◆ There are many angles on the African American experience, but they combine to form a single portrait of a people—a people committed to identifying their own sphere in life.

Chapter 2

Slavery: What Happened When

In This Chapter

- ◆ The political role of slavery in the United States
- ◆ How slavery started
- ◆ How slavery defined the country
- ◆ Why slavery made America come apart at the seams

Trying to separate the story of the United States of America from the story of the institution of slavery in the country is a difficult and probably impossible task. In this chapter, you get a look at the most important historical elements of this distinctly American holocaust—a bloody, brutal, and utterly divisive tradition that defined the nation.

Slavery predated the legal existence of this country. It continues to exert a powerful influence on the cultural and social life of the United States nearly a century and a half after its formal abolition. Before the United States was, slavery was shaping the country; after slavery was gone, it remains.

We may never come to terms with it completely. In this chapter, you find out about the political implications of the institution of slavery in the United States, and you'll learn how and when the international slave trade operated.

Slavery: A Global Timeline

Slavery didn't begin in the United States. It didn't end with the American Civil War, either. (The United Nations continues, to this day, to work toward a formal worldwide ban on slavery; a 1966 study written for the U.N. found evidence that the practice was still active in parts of Africa and Asia.)

Below, you'll find a condensed timeline of slavery as it was practiced around the world in the period leading up to the American Civil War.

Timeline of Slavery

circa 6800 B.C.E.: The first urban settlements emerge in Mesopotamia. Captured enemy soldiers are forced to labor in support of municipal projects. Translation: with technology, cities, and the rise of a soldier class, there also arose slavery.

circa 2600 B.C.E.: Egyptian slave-capturing missions are commemorated on the walls of temples.

circa 120 C.E.: Perhaps half of the population of Rome consists of slaves.

circa 500 C.E.: Victorious Anglo-Saxons enslave Britons in large numbers.

circa 1000 C.E.: Slavery is common in the European agricultural economy, but it gradually becomes less common in Europe, whereas serfdom becomes more prevalent. (Serfdom is the process by which peasants are bound to a piece of land from generation to generation in service of a lord or noble.) In the Byzantine empire and in Islamic lands, slavery remains an accepted institution.

circa 1380: Ravaged by the plague, Europe finds itself short on workers. Slavery makes a comeback.

circa 1440: Portuguese expeditions initiate the practice of raiding Africa for slaves to export to Europe and the Americas. This is the beginning of a violent, ruthless, and highly profitable industry that will thrive for more than four centuries.

1619: The first enslaved Africans arrive in Britain's North American colonies. Virginia begins to build its agricultural economy on slave labor; other southern colonies will follow suit.

1769: Father Junipero Serra founds his first mission in California; the missions compel large numbers of Native Americans to forced labor, using a system similar to serfdom.

1777: Vermont is the first state to approve a formal ban on slavery within its borders. Over the next two and a half decades, Pennsylvania, Massachusetts, New Hampshire, Connecticut, Rhode Island, New York, and New Jersey will enact some kind of legislation or constitutional amendment ensuring emancipation.

1781: Emperor Joseph II forbids serfdom within the Hapsburg empire.

circa 1780: The global slave trade is at its height.

1789: The progressive, humanist, philosophical, and intellectual movement known as the Enlightenment helps to fan a growing condemnation of the African slave trade. On August 26 of this year, the National Assembly of the revolutionary French government declares that "Men are born and remain free and equal in rights."

Early nineteenth century: Slavery in the northern United States, never particularly profitable, has vanished, for all practical purposes. Northern shipping interests, however, continue to take part in the slave trade.

1803: Denmark explicitly forbids trade in African slaves.

1807: The British parliament bans the use of British ships in the slave trade, and forbids its colonies to take part in the trade.

1808: The U.S. Congress bans the importation of slaves on the first of January of this year. The date is the earliest permitted by the U.S. Constitution. (Illegal importation of slaves into the United States continues after this date.)

1813: Although its ships have never engaged in the slave trade, Sweden makes its view of the trade clear by formally banning it.

1814: The Netherlands forbids its ships to take part in the slave trade.

1820: Spain enacts limitations on its involvement in the slave trade.

continues

1825: Slavery is outlawed in Argentina, Peru, Chile, and Bolivia.

1834: Parliament formally bans slavery throughout the British Empire.

1848: Following the revolution in France this year, slavery is formally abolished in all French colonies.

1860: Abraham Lincoln's election to the presidency prompts a southern secessionist movement. (Lincoln was elected on a platform opposing the admission of new states permitting slavery.)

1861: Czar Alexander II of Russia frees the country's 50 million serfs.

Slavery, American Style

The American experience of slavery as an institution before the Civil War is filled with all the trauma, contradiction, and betrayal of a great tragedy. What follows is a short summary of the key plot points of that tragedy.

A contemporary illustration of captives being sent into bondage.

(Source: Library of Congress)

Indentured Servants—Not

In 1619, the first African captives arrived in the colony of Virginia. The evidence indicates that the very first Africans were regarded as indentured servants, but by the middle of the seventeenth century a tradition of lifelong labor for enslaved Africans had been firmly established, particularly in the South.

Snapshot: Life and Death on a Slave Ship

In 1972, salvager Mel Fisher and other treasure-hunters stumbled across the sunken wreckage of the *Henrietta Marie*, a slave ship that was lost to the ocean in 1700 after having just delivered perhaps 300 African men to lives of slavery in the Americas.

FAQ

What was indentured servitude? Those in indentured servitude were bound to labor for another person for a certain number of years to pay off a monetary debt or other obligation. When the obligation was repaid, the indentured servant was freed.

In the years since the discovery of the *Henrietta Marie*, treasure seekers and scientists have been retrieving artifacts from the wreckage (See "Last Voyage of the Slave Ship *Henrietta Marie*," Jennifer Steinberg, *National Geographic* magazine, August 2002). Their discoveries have painted a chilling picture of the immense and hellish human toll of the global slave trade. The ship is the oldest slave-trading vessel ever recovered, and one of very few to be located in U.S. waters.

Here are some of the conclusions we can now draw about the *Henrietta Marie* (and the many ships like her).

Sold to New Captors

Scholars believe that many of the slaves who were transported to North America and Europe in ships like the *Henrietta Marie* met their fate because they had fallen prisoners to rival tribes in Africa. Their enemies sold them to slave traders for such European goods as beads, spoons, and iron bars.

Keeping the Cargo Fed

The Africans on board the *Henrietta Marie* were fed two meals each day. A massive copper cooking cauldron was raised from the sea in 1972; it was apparently used to prepare boiled yams and beans.

A Long and Deadly Journey

Captives spent roughly three months at sea making the journey from West Africa to Jamaica. As a slaver, the *Henrietta Marie* completed two such trips and delivered 450 Africans to captivity in the New World.

Their wrists held in place by iron shackles, the captives were herded into crowded holds like beasts. The conditions were unspeakable, and it is not surprising that an estimated 20 percent of the prisoners perished on the journey.

African men and women who died en route were tossed overboard for sharks to devour.

The Declaration of Independence (of White Males)

In 1776, as the ink was drying on the recently signed Declaration that proclaimed "All men are created equal," all 13 former British colonies permitted slavery as an institution. States restricted the rights of slaves by means of "slave codes" designed to perpetuate the institution.

Sale and inspection of a Negro.

(Source: Library of Congress.)

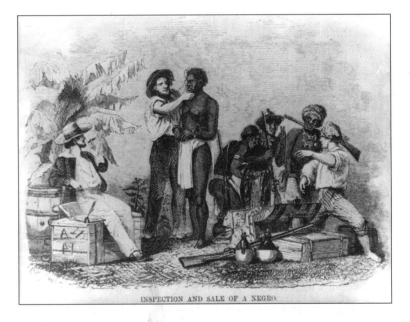

INSPECTION AND SALE OF A NEGRO.

The Northwest Ordinance

An important precedent was set with the passage of the Northwest Ordinance, which forbade slavery in the regions that later corresponded to the states of Wisconsin, Michigan, Illinois, Indiana, and Ohio.

Taken together with a wave of northern emancipation measures originating in the state of Vermont in 1777, the Northwest Ordinance established a pattern: slavery in the southern states, and no such legal institution in the northern states.

The Constitution and Its Loopholes

In 1788, the U.S. Constitution was ratified. Today, many think of the Constitution as a document guaranteeing, at least in theory, equality of opportunity to all American citizens, regardless of race. At the time of its implementation, however, the U.S. Constitution featured a number of clauses that directly contradicted this idea.

The U.S. Constitution, as ratified in 1788 …

- Forbade Congress from prohibiting the importation of slaves for the following 20 years.

- Mandated that a "person held to service or labor" in one state be "delivered up on claim of the party to whom such service or labor shall be due."

- Enacted an uneasy compromise designed to end a long debate over whether to count slaves in population totals that would affect taxes and representation in Congress. Slaves, who had no rights whatsoever under the Constitution, were each counted as three fifths of a person for the purpose of these totals. The clause was the first of a long line of uneasy official compromises between white southerners and white northerners regarding slavery.

Obstacles and Opportunities

In 1793, Congress passed the Fugitive Slave Law to enforce the U.S. Constitution's demand that runaway slaves be returned to their masters; the law permitted those who owned slaves to cross state lines in order to regain physical control of their escaped "property." Some Northern legislatures passed laws ensuring pursued slaves the right to trial by jury and the right to give testimony in court in these disputes.

Excluded from "We the People"

In short, the American Constitution as initially written and ratified gave enslaved men and women no reason to rejoice in the newly organized nation's founding principles.

As the American Civil Liberties Union has noted in its article "The Birth of the Bill of Rights," by Ira Glasser, there were chasms of inequality from the very first days of the American Constitutional system. "For the first 78 years after it was ratified," the ACLU notes,

> … the Constitution protected slavery and legalized racial subordination. Instead of constitutional rights, slaves were governed by "slave codes" that controlled every aspect of their lives. They had no access to the rule of law; they could not

go to court, make contracts, or own any property. They could be whipped, branded, imprisoned without trial, and hanged.

—"The Birth of the Bill of Rights," *Visions of Liberty*, Ira Glasser, Arcade Publishing, 1991.

End of the American Slave Ship but Not of Slavery

Congress finally put an end to the practice of importing slaves in 1807, with the ban taking effect the following year. However, the choice to make international traffic in human beings illegal did nothing to stem the nation's domestic trade in slaves in states where slavery persisted.

In the North, opposition to slavery was growing louder, thanks in part to the efforts of the Quakers, a pacifist religious group who had fought hard to outlaw slavery on moral grounds in Britain and took the same stand in the United States.

The Missouri Compromise

The nation's uneasy political balance was sustained—for a time—by the Missouri Compromise.

Under the arrangement, the free state of Maine entered the union at the same time as the slave state Missouri, and the institution of slavery was formally forbidden in a region of the (massive) Louisiana Territory north of the 36 degrees, 30 minutes line of latitude.

Rebellion in the South, Opposition in the North

The fateful year of 1831 saw two important displays of opposition to the institution of slavery in the United States.

In Massachusetts, abolitionist William Lloyd Garrison launched *The Liberator*, which would quickly become the most influential newspaper of the latest phase of the anti-slavery movement. Garrison led a new and vocal effort to condemn slavery as evil and banish the institution of slavery outright. This stood in stark contrast to previous anti-slavery campaigns, which had tended to focus on emancipation measures that paid slave owners for their slaves, or to develop colonies for American slaves in Africa. Garrison, a gifted propagandist, regarded such measures as insufficient, and took on the entire southern economic and political system.

Also in 1831, in Virginia, a brilliant, self-educated slave named Nat Turner led a violent revolt against whites. After killing 55 of them, Turner and his adherents were captured, and the rebellion fizzled. (There had been other plans to rise up against slaveholders, notably those of Gabriel Prosser in 1800 and Denmark Vesey in 1822; both of these were discovered and snuffed out before they were launched.)

Turner was, not surprisingly, put to death. In the aftermath of the attacks, violence against enslaved Africans reached staggering proportions, and southern legislatures enacted still more repressive measures within their slave codes.

Battle lines were drawn.

 Obstacles and Opportunities

Nat Turner was a pious, charismatic Virginia slave preacher with a gift for oratory. He concluded that he had been chosen by God to lead his people out of captivity and secretly recruited a group of about 60 freed and enslaved men to help him lead what he believed would turn into a massive uprising against white slave owners. Their bloody assaults against the family of the man who owned Turner, and against other whites in the area, did not serve as the spark to the larger revolt Turner had envisioned. Instead, the attacks galvanized southern whites, led to brutal reprisals against freedmen and enslaved Africans, and forced southern anti-slavery groups to operate in secret.

The Divisions Deepen

The nation's ongoing internal conflict over the slavery issue, already intense, grew even more so following the Supreme Court's 1842 decision in *Prigg* v. *Pennsylvania*.

This decision upheld a slaveholder's right to retrieve runaway slaves, and declared Pennsylvania's anti-kidnapping statute to be unconstitutional. The court also held, however, that the task of carrying out the Fugitive Slave Law was a federal matter that did not require action or support from state officials.

Over the next decade, a number of northern state legislatures passed laws explicitly forbidding state employees from taking part in the return of accused runaway slaves. The question of a slave's status in Federal territories would be revisited in the Supreme Court's 1857 Dred Scott decision, today regarded as one of the low points in the history of American jurisprudence.

Obstacles and Opportunities

In the infamous Dred Scott decision (1857), the United States Supreme Court held that a) Scott, a slave who had moved with his master from a slave state to a free state (and later to a free territory) had no right to sue for his freedom; b) that Africans in the United States, whether slaves or not, had no civil rights under the U.S. Constitution; and c) that neither Congress nor territorial governments had any authority to prohibit slavery in the territories. The decision was denounced by northern anti-slavery groups.

Yet Another Uneasy Compromise

When Congress signed off on the Compromise of 1850, it secured for the two poles of the white governing elite their last few years of white-knuckled coexistence.

California was permitted to join the Union as a free state; fugitive slave laws were redrafted to address Southern sensibilities; and the territories of Utah and New Mexico were permitted to determine the question of whether or not to permit slavery on the basis of popular referenda. The Compromise of 1850 also forbade the trade of slaves in Washington, D.C.

At the time, the Compromise of 1850 was seen—by whites, at least—as a final resolution. It was supposed to be the last and best attempt to maintain national unity and restore something resembling balance between powerful political interests in the South (whose entire social, cultural, and economic system was dependent on slavery) and those in the North (where abolitionist sentiments were growing). But it left the institution of slavery intact in the South.

On the March

As part of the Compromise of 1850, trade in slaves was outlawed in the District of Columbia. The institution of slavery, however, would persist for a few years more in the nation's capital.

The final political resolution of the slavery issue, as it turned out, would be a good deal bloodier. A vision of the epic conflict to come in the Civil War went on display in Kansas later in the 1850s.

A Precursor Battle

In 1854, Senator Stephen Douglas came up with a novel idea for drawing settlers to a new portion of the country and establishing a transcontinental rail line: the

Kansas–Nebraska Act. The Act, which passed into law, created two new territories. As the price of obtaining southern support, the law held that the question of whether slavery will be permitted in the new territories would be decided by popular vote. Thus, this portion of the legislation officially revoked the earlier guideline forbidding slavery in the northern tier of the Louisiana Territory.

It was a ghastly mistake. The law turned the freshly minted territory of Kansas into a bloody battleground, as pro- and anti-slavery groups battled for dominance, property, and political control. Within two years, the fighting had left 200 people dead and caused millions of dollars in property damage; within four years, rival legislatures in Kansas—one pro-slavery, one anti-slavery—were each claiming to represent the people of the territory.

America was coming apart at the seams.

African American Contributions

1539: Africans accompany the explorer DeSoto as he surveys the Mississippi River.

1565: Africans help to found St. Augustine, Florida.

1732: Benjamin Banneker, later to win fame as a scientist and inventor, is born in Maryland.

1745: Jean Baptiste Pointe duSable founds the riverside trading post that will become Chicago, Illinois.

1760: Jupiter Hammon, probably the first African American poet, publishes "An Evening Thought."

1789: John Berry Meachum, later to win praise as an abolitionist and educator, is born in Missouri.

1803: Five African Americans are part of the Lewis and Clark expedition; one of them—York, a scout, trader, and trapper—plays a critical role in the mission's success.

Don't Stop Here!

In this chapter, you've looked primarily at the political ramifications of slavery. In the next chapter, you'll see how it directly affected the individual human beings involved.

The Least You Need to Know

- Slavery predates the legal existence of the United States and, despite its formal abolition following the Civil War, haunts the country to this day.

- The global slave trade was profitable for white Americans who engaged in it from the middle of the seventeenth century until at least the beginning of the nineteenth century.

- Southern economy, culture, and political institutions were heavily reliant on slavery; by the beginning of the eighteenth century, however, the institution had vanished in the North.

- Opposition to slavery—in the form of open revolt and agitation by those who wanted to abolish the institution—became impossible to ignore around the middle of the nineteenth century.

- A series of uneasy compromises between South and North on questions relating to slavery marked American political life in the period before the Civil War.

- Nevertheless, America was falling apart at the seams by the middle of the nineteenth century.

Chapter 3

Slavery: The Human Toll

In this Chapter

- ◆ An unknowable human price
- ◆ Voices from the American holocaust
- ◆ Religious justification for American slavery

In this chapter, you get a glimpse of the staggering human toll that the institution of slavery took in the land that eventually became the United States of America.

An Incalculable Human Loss

We will never know the true cost of the human tragedy that was launched with the African slave trade. What we do know is that even drawing a broad outline around its likely dimensions is a disturbing experience.

Current estimates suggest that a total of perhaps 12 million Africans were imported to the New World as slaves. That figure stuns the mind, but it is not complete.

Many scholars believe that roughly one third of all Africans intended for the slave trade died before they were placed on ships. This is not an unreasonable estimate, considering that many of them were captured warriors who would have resisted such a fate. In addition, conditions on the ships were so appalling that it is entirely possible that another third of this huge population died before reaching the New World. The source for these estimates is the National Underground Railroad Network to Freedom Program.

The layout of a slave ship.

(Source: Library of Congress)

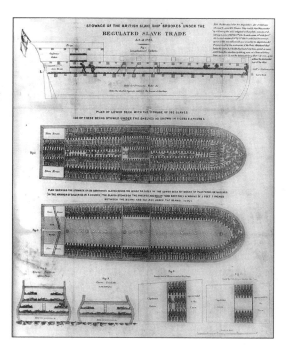

The Underground Railroad

The Underground Railroad provided fugitive southern slaves with help in their (illegal) journeys to free states; it was a loosely connected alliance of American anti-slavery activist groups whose brave members risked their lives to help others. Although the term "Underground Railroad" only came into use in the mid-1840s, similar operations had been conducted for years before that. Members of the Society of Friends, or Quakers, were prominent supporters of these dangerous campaigns; the most famous "conductor" on the Underground Railroad was Harriet Tubman (see Chapter 15). The National Underground Railroad Network to Freedom Program operates under the National Parks Service to "extol the historical significance of the Underground Railroad in the eradication of slavery and the evolution of our national civil rights movement." Visit the Network on the World Wide Web at www.cr.nps.gov/ugrr.

The best guess, then—and it is only a guess—is that something like 36 million Africans either met their deaths as a result of the slave trade or were sold into captivity between 1450 and 1850. This shocking number does not, of course, reflect the abuses inflicted on any of the descendants of the original Africans who fell prey to slave traders.

The deck of the ship Wildfire.

(Source: Library of Congress)

FAQ

What was life like on the slave ships? Olauda Equiano, an enslaved African who eventually wrote a narrative about his hellish experiences, described it in this way: "Now that the ship's cargo were confined together, it became absolutely pestilential. The closeness of the place, and the heat of the climate ... almost suffocated us. The shrieks of the women and the groans of the dying rendered it a scene of horror almost inconceivable ..."

America's Long-Running Holocaust

The picture that emerges, then, is one of institutionalized racial violence, inhumanity, abuse, and murder on a scale that many white Americans, to this day, simply do not allow themselves to consider.

Certainly the manifest abuses associated with the slave trade—in terms of economic exploitation, or wanton cruelty, or the darkest uses of available technology—rank alongside the worst human rights travesties of the most infamous dictators of the twentieth century. Having acknowledged that, one must then factor in the reality that these practices persisted, not for a few years under a single despot, but for more than four centuries in a profitable program of human conquest endorsed, for most of its duration, by the highest secular and religious powers.

Reproduction of a newspaper advertisement of a slave sale.

(Source: Judith Burros)

Slavery was a sustained American holocaust. The vast majority of its victims' voices will never be heard. Those few that have survived are harrowing indeed.

"Bought and Sold in the Market Like an Ox"

Consider, for instance, the account of Henry Bibb, whose *The Life and Adventures of an American Slave* was published in 1851:

> A slave, may be bought and sold in the market like an ox. He is liable to be sold off to a distant land from his family. He is bound in chains hand and foot; and his sufferings are aggravated a hundred fold by the terrible thought that he is not allowed to struggle against misfortune, corporal punishment, insults and

outrages committed upon himself and his family; and he is not allowed to help himself, to resist or escape the blow, which he sees impending over him.

I was a slave a prisoner for life. I could possess nothing, nor acquire anything but what must belong to my keeper. No one can imagine my feelings in my reflecting moments, but he who has himself been a slave.

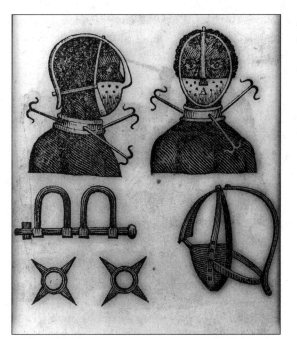

Mechanical slave control devices.

(Source: Library of Congress)

An English Specialty

The Portuguese, the Spanish, the Dutch, and the English were all deeply involved in the New World phase of the slave trade in its early years, but it was the British traders who came to dominate the market in human beings in North America.

English merchants established relationships with African chiefs to obtain imprisoned enemies. As the market grew—and it grew dramatically—kidnapping expeditions became more and more common for the slave traders. (The foundation for kidnapping of another sort was laid in the 1660s, when Virginia held that children of enslaved mothers were themselves enslaved, thus establishing a practice of owning, splitting, and selling African families.)

"The Groans and Cries of Many"

I was early snatched away from my native country, with about eighteen or twenty more boys and girls, as we were playing in a field. We lived but a few days' journey from the coast where we were kidnapped … I was soon conducted to a prison, for three days, where I heard the groans and cries of many, and saw some of my fellow-captives. But when a vessel arrived to conduct us away to the ship, it was a most horrible scene; there was nothing to be heard but the rattling of chains, [the] smacking of whips, and the groans and cries of our fellow-men. Some would not stir from the ground, when they were lashed and beaten in the most horrible manner.

—Ottoba Cugoanoa, "Narrative of the Enslavement of a Native of Africa," published in *The Negro's Memorial; or, Abolitionist's Catechism, by an Abolitionist*, Thomas Fisher (London: Hatchard and Co., 1825)

Those who survived the harrowing journey to the New World were subjected to more dehumanizing treatment on the auction block—often not just once, but as many times as the financial requirements of white slave owners dictated. As one enslaved man seeking liberty recalled, slave traders would "make us hold up our heads, walk briskly back and forth, while customers would feel up our hands and bodies, turn us about, ask us what we could do, make us open our mouths and show our teeth … Sometimes a man or woman … was taken, stripped, and inspected more minutely."

Auctions North and South

Slave auctions were not, of course, limited to southern cities in the early colonial period. Because of the national focus on southern slavery, it is often overlooked that New York and New Jersey were the largest slave holding states in the North. The very first slave auction took place in the Dutch settlement of New Amsterdam, which would eventually become New York City. Wherever they were conducted, they had three prominent features: they objectified the person on display; they tended to separate families and leave immense emotional and psychological wounds; and they made money for white slave owners.

As one former slave, Sylvia Cannon, recalled when she was interviewed by the Federal Writers' Project in 1937:

> I seen 'em sell plenty of colored people away in them days, because that [was] the way the white folks made a heap of their money. Course, they ain't never tell us how much they sell 'em for—just stand 'em up on a block 'bout three feet high, and a speculator bid 'em off just like they was horses. Them what was bid off didn't never say nothin', neither. Don't know who bought my brothers, George and Earl.

At this point in the transcript, the Federal Writers Project interviewer adds the notation, "She cried after this statement."

The largest slave auction in American history appears to have been held at a Savannah, Georgia, racetrack on March 3, 1859. It was (like so many such events) initiated by a white slave owner with heavy debts to pay. The supposedly humane arrangement under which the sale was conducted stipulated that the captives, housed in horse stalls for the event, were to be sold "in families." As a practical matter, this did not guarantee that those sold would not be separated from their loved ones.

At this particular auction, husbands remained with wives, and mothers remained with very young children, but no other family ties were respected. This meant, for instance, that 12-year-old boys were separated from their parents, and that brothers and sisters were sold to separate owners. The auction took two days; at its conclusion, 436 people had been sold on the block. Many had begged (in vain) to be sold with their loved ones. The auction was known by those who were subjected to it as the "Weeping Time."

The Plantation Economy

Rich whites owned slaves, but the institution of slavery was deeply woven into the entire Southern economy, culture, and lifestyle. (There was, it should be noted, a small number of freedmen and never-enslaved African Americans who became slaveholders.)

The following is a brief overview of some of the most common destinations and working environments for enslaved Africans in the South.

- ◆ **Coffee, tobacco, indigo, and rice plantations.** The success of these staple crops, along with that of sugar, helped to establish a plantation economy, and to make the importation of more and more slaves from Africa an economic priority in the South.

♦ **Sugar plantations.** Following the United States' purchase of the massive Louisiana Territory from France in 1803, sugar production surged and southern plantation owners purchased huge numbers of slaves to produce crushed cane for use in a variety of products, including molasses and rum.

♦ **Cotton plantations.** Many early settlers in the colonies grew cotton, and used slaves to complete the tedious work of picking, ginning (deseeding), and baling the cotton. Following by-then established tradition, field slaves worked the crops; house slaves attended to the plantation owner and his family. Thanks in large measure to the invention of the *cotton gin*, plantation owners found themselves in a position to produce—and sell—much more cotton than ever before, and demand for slaves skyrocketed.

What's the Word?

The **cotton gin** was a device that enabled a single man with a single horse to separate roughly fifty times as much raw cotton from its seeds as had been possible beforehand. The machine, whose invention is credited to a Northerner named Eli Whitney, revolutionized southern agriculture, and brought the cotton plantation to a position of extraordinary economic importance in the South. According to *Black Stars: African American Inventors* (Otha Richard Sullivan; John Wiley and Sons, 1998), Whitney was actually "improving the idea of the slaves who used a comblike device to clean cotton."

By the middle of the nineteenth century, the raw cotton industry, which had always been heavily dependent on the forced labor of slaves, was a mainstay of the southern economy. Anyone curious about the experience of working as a field slave in such a plantation can consult (among many such narratives) the book *Twelve Years a Slave* by Solomon Northrup (London: Sampson Low & Son, 1853):

> The hands are required to be in the cotton field as soon as it is light in the morning, and, with the exception of ten or fifteen minutes, which is given them at noon to swallow their allowance of cold bacon, they are not permitted to be a moment idle until it is too dark to see, and when the moon is full, they often-times labor till the middle of the night.

Good Master, Bad Master

Apologists for the institution of slavery (of which there are, amazingly, still a few among white supremacist groups) often make the point that some white masters were far more cruel than others, and that any number of masters were regarded as benevolent by their own slaves. While this is true as far as it goes, it is also true that the power dynamic inherent in being owned by another human being makes labels like "benevolent" essentially meaningless.

Even slaves who lived and worked in the "best" situations faced the constant fear of forced separations from their families, being sold into worse conditions, or being forced to endure both fates at the same time. All that needed to happen to turn a "benevolent" relationship into a nightmare few today can conceive was for a white master to fall on hard times—or decide for some other reason that benevolence was no longer affordable.

On the March

"Ibo's Landing," an American folk tale from the slavery era, tells of a group of Africans who refused to be delivered into bondage. After realizing that their captain has no intention of setting them free, eighteen captives declare, "No! Rather than be a slave here in America, we would rather be dead." In some versions of the story, the captives, chained together, plunge overboard together. In others, they fly away. (See *In the Time of the Drums*, Jump at the Sun Books, 1999.)

Sold Down the River

It is worth noting here that the common idiom "to be sold down the river"—meaning to be betrayed—has its roots in America's slave holocaust.

To understand the term completely, one has to understand that living and working conditions for enslaved men and women became steadily more inhuman the further one progressed down the Mississippi River. When a slave owner threatened, overtly or otherwise, to sell a slave down the river (and words were hardly necessary to convey such a threat), the power relationship between the two parties was quite clear. The slave owner's point of view can be summed up as follows: "Keep me happy, or prepare yourself for a fresh hell each and every morning you wake up, for the rest of your life."

This was the reality of life for the vast majority of the enslaved in the American South while slavery was a way of life in the United States.

On the Run

Not surprisingly, many slaves ran away. Their white owners often went to considerable lengths to recover them.

Billy and Quamina

RUN AWAY, at the 30th of May last, from John Forbes, Esq.'s plantation in St. John's parish, TWO NEGROES, named BILLY and QUAMINA, of the Guinea Country, and speak good English. Billy is lanky and well made, about five feet 10 or 11 inches high, of a black complection, has lost some of his upper teeth, and had on when he ran away a white and grey cloth jacket … Quamina is stout and well made, about five feet 10 or 11 inches high, very black, has his country's marks on his face… Whoever takes up said Negroes, and delivers them to me … or to the Warden of the Work-House in Savannah, shall receive a reward of $20, besides what the law allows. Davis Austin

—From a 1774 handbill

The tortures and privations of slave life on a plantation were enough to make anyone contemplate an escape attempt. Moses Roper, in his book *Adventures and Escape of Moses Roper* (1838), wrote:

> Mr. Gooch, the cotton planter, he purchased me at a town called Liberty Hill about three miles from his home. As soon as he got home, he immediately put me on his cotton plantation to work, and put me under overseers, gave me allowance of meat and bread with the other slaves, which was not half enough for me to live upon, and very laborious work. Here my heart was almost broke with grief at leaving my fellow slaves. Mr. Gooch did not mind my grief, for he flogged me nearly every day, and very severely.

> Mr. Gooch bought me for his son-in-law, Mr. Hammans, about five miles from his residence. This man had but two slaves besides myself; he treated me very kindly for a week or two, but in summer, when cotton was ready to hoe, he gave me task work connected with this department, which I could not get done, not having worked on cotton farms before. When I failed in my task, he commenced flogging me, and set me to work without any shirt in the cotton field, in a very hot sun, in the month of July. In August, Mr. Condell, his overseer, gave me a task at pulling fodder. Having finished my task before night, I left the field. The rain came on, which soaked the fodder. On discovering this, [Mr. Condell] threatened to flog me for not getting in the fodder before the rain came. This was the first time I attempted to run away, knowing that I should get a flogging. I was then between thirteen and fourteen years of age.

A good number of those who were recaptured no doubt wondered whether they might have been better off if they had been shot on sight instead of returned to the plantation. Roper goes on to report that runaway slaves who were returned to captivity always faced a "more rigorous system of flogging," and psychological battles—attempts to "break" slaves who tried to flee—were common. After a while, Roper's punishments for his repeated attempts to win his freedom included being tied naked for a flogging ... by the master's wife.

In the Name of Christianity

Scriptural justification for torture, for forced labor, for the dissolution of families—indeed, for slavery as a whole—was common from the very earliest days in colonial churches.

Theological support for white domination of the enslaved Africans was enthusiastic. One Reverend Alexander Campbell, for instance, held that "There is not one verse in the Bible inhibiting slavery, but many regulating it. It is not, then, we conclude, immoral."

And President of the Confederate States of America, Jefferson Davis intoned solemnly in his inaugural address that slavery was "established by the decree of Almighty God ... it is sanctioned in the Bible, in both Testaments, from Genesis to Revelation ... it has existed in all ages, has been found among the people of the highest civilizations, and in nations of the highest proficiency in the arts."

On the March

Revulsion at the institution of slavery was common among some Christian believers as early as the American Revolution, but organized efforts to force the emancipation of enslaved Africans did not become a crusading theme in white northern religious life until the 1830s.

Such appeals to the authority of the Hebrew and Christian scriptures held the attention and respect of countless white churchgoers in the North and the South for over 300 years. The African slave trade had been encouraged and supported by major European Christian denominations; it was maintained and given moral authority by Christian preachers in the New World as the colonies emerged into distinct political entities.

With that kind of moral authority—and with scholarship indicating that the ancient Israelites inherited, adopted, and reformed preexisting customs of slavery still years in the future—the practice of buying, selling, and exploiting human beings proceeded apace. In the critical early years of the practice, a huge number (and probably a majority) of American Christians saw slavery as fully consistent with the highest tenets of their faith.

FAQ

What was the most cited scriptural passage "endorsing" slavery? It was probably Genesis 9:25-27: "Cursed be Canaan! The lowest of slaves will he be to his brothers. He also said, 'Blessed be the Lord, the God of Shem! May Canaan be the slave of Shem. May God extend the territory of Japheth; may Japheth live in the tents of Shem and may Canaan be his slave." In this passage, Noah curses his own grandson Canaan and all Canaan's future descendants. Canaan and his progeny were regarded, conveniently, as Africans, thereby rendering any abuse of enslaved Africans by whites as more or less divinely ordained. This interpretation remained influential—and in southern circles, decisive—for centuries.

Exodus and the Psalms

For their part, slaves tended to identify with the stirring narrative in the book of Exodus concerning Moses' delivery of the Hebrew people from the captivity and slavery imposed by the Egyptians.

Small wonder that the white preachers hired to minister to *slave congregations* in the South learned to maneuver around the story, and around troublesome passages from the Psalms such as 71:2: "Deliver me in thy righteousness, and cause me to escape: incline thy ears unto me, and save me."

To learn more about the remarkable evolution of African American faith traditions, see Chapter 12.

What's the Word?

Slave congregations were groups of African American worshippers who eventually developed a distinctive new strain of Christianity. Forbidden (in theory) to learn to read, enslaved faith communities developed Christian rituals involving African elements such as storytellers, call-and-response traditions, dancing, chanting, and ecstatic singing. Not surprisingly, services often centered on the story of Moses' deliverance of the Hebrews from the Egyptians, as recounted in the Book of Exodus.

African American Contributions

(Early 1820s:) Harriet Tubman is born in Maryland.

1834: Henry Blair receives a patent for his corn-planting machine. He is the first African American to receive a patent.

1848: Mammy Pleasant helps to found San Francisco.

1849: Waller Jackson is one of a number of African Americans to travel "around the horn" to prospect for gold in California.

1858: William Wells Brown publishes *The Escape;* he is believed to be the first African American playwright.

The Least You Need to Know

♦ Perhaps 36 million Africans died as a result of the slave trade.

♦ Slave auctions split families for the economic benefit of rich white plantation owners.

♦ By the middle of the nineteenth century, the economy of the American South was built squarely on a foundation of slave labor.

♦ This economic system was maintained by violence, repression, and systematic abuse, and was reinforced by means of religious justification from white pulpits.

Chapter 4

Portrait of a Rebellion

In This Chapter

- ◆ The *Amistad* rebellion
- ◆ Why it was important
- ◆ How it changed America

In late August 1838, seagoing men were passing rumors of a strange pirate ship that prowled the eastern seaboard of the United States. This ship was supposedly under the control of black pirates, presumably escaped slaves.

The vessel shadowed legitimate trading ships ominously, making strange zigzag patterns as it trailed the merchant ships. If one got too close to it, trouble would no doubt follow.

Actually, the ship was a slaver that had been taken over by the enslaved Africans who had once been its captives. They were not pirates. They wanted only to go home.

Black Mutiny

The zigzagging vessel was the *Amistad*, a Spanish slaver whose mutinying "cargo" of several dozen African captives had killed at least two of their captors.

Were they men—or were they property?

Obstacles and Opportunities

The *Amistad* captives had been kidnapped and transported to Cuba from Africa in violation of Spanish law barring slave trafficking. The Cuban enforcement of this statute was, however, notoriously lax. Bribes and a little careful night navigation were usually all that were necessary to get captive Africans into Cuba. Once captive Africans were smuggled onto the island, they could be provided with false papers suggesting that they were Cuban-born slaves. This is what happened to the *Amistad* captives. The violation of Spanish law was an important point in the resolution of the case. American law had formally prohibited importation of slaves since 1808; this statute, too, was frequently evaded by slave traders.

Why the *Amistad* Still Matters

In recent years, the *Amistad* affair has taken on greater and greater significance for those seeking an understanding of African American history and culture. I have decided to devote a chapter to it here for five important reasons:

- The *Amistad* case serves as a kind of pivot-point between the uneasy racial compromises of the Constitution and the later tumult of the Civil War.

- The case was a landmark event in the development of the American abolitionist movement. It proved to abolitionists that they could successfully appeal to the conscience of northerners.

- As a result, the case affected racial attitudes in the North, and in so doing presaged the momentous conflict of the Civil War. Although most southerners regarded the *Amistad* controversy as abolitionist propaganda, the Africans at the center of the case won considerable sympathy among northerners. This fact presented President Martin Van Buren with another variation on the endless, exquisitely difficult dilemma of governing a nation that was half-free and half-enslaved. The *Amistad* episode is among the most revealing of a still-young America's social and political fault lines.

On the March

The *Amistad* case was, before the Dred Scott case of 1857, the most important American news story involving the status of enslaved Africans. The controversies and passions it inspired were important previews of later national debates on questions such as the status of those enslaved, states' rights, and the morality of slavery.

- The case highlighted a number of pressing questions that had been (and would continue to be) left unresolved by the American legal system. Among these questions were the following:

Were freed slaves citizens of the United States?

Were those enslaved to be regarded solely as property, or did they possess any natural rights whatsoever?

To what degree can one human being (say, an officer of the U.S. Navy) claim salvage over another (say, a captive who has launched a rebellion on a slave ship)?

◆ Finally, the *Amistad* case offers a compelling story of freedom lost and won. It made (and still makes) great copy, which is why abolitionists did everything they could to fill the newspapers of the day with the story—and why Hollywood eventually decided to make a big-budget movie out of it.

A Strange Northward Journey

When his attempt to be captured by the British had failed, the *Amistad*'s white navigator steered an erratic course northward toward the United States, hoping to be intercepted by some official vessel there.

He had succeeded, for some time, in convincing the Africans who now controlled the ship that he was following their orders and heading for Africa. During the day, the ship's white navigators sailed east—toward the sun—as the Africans, led by a charismatic ringleader known as Cinque, demanded. At night, however, the ship changed course.

Naval officers of the U.S. brig *Washington* found the ship anchored near Montauk Point, New York. There Cinque (who apparently had come to realize he was being played for a fool by the two whites he had spared) ordered the ship to a stop—and made an attempt to spend some of the ship's gold pieces on board for food and water.

While the ship—much the worse for wear and tear—stood anchored, Lieutenant Thomas Gedney boarded it and got the Spaniards' side of the story. After a brief period of confusion, he apprehended the Africans on board as well as those who had gone ashore. He then headed away from New York (a free state) and toward Connecticut (where slavery was, as of 1839, still legal). He attempted to claim the captive Africans as salvage property. Gedney's claim to

FAQ

Were there other slave-ship mutinies? The *Amistad* was not the only slave ship of the era to bring about an international incident as the result of a mutiny. In 1841, captive Africans took over an American slave ship called the *Creole* and sailed it into the Bahamas. Representatives of the British government set the mutineers free, based on the royal government's emancipation laws.

take possession of the mutineers on the *Amistad*, however, failed, and they were eventually charged with piracy and murder.

The ensuing legal wrangle—and the question of whether the Africans, who had been illegally brought to Cuba, were slaves—would captivate America and the world.

Joseph Cinque.

(Source: Judith Burros)

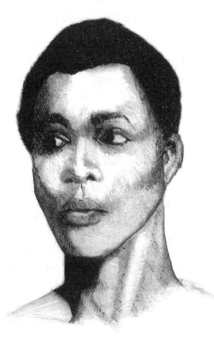

Piracy and Murder—or Self-Defense?

The two Spaniards who had survived the mutiny on board the *Amistad* aimed to have their ship and its human cargo returned to them by the American courts. Eventually, the Spanish government joined in the demand; the Spanish wanted the *Amistad* mutineers tried for piracy and murder. Abolitionists, who saw the uprising as a clear case of self-defense (and who also knew a good news story when they saw one) fought Spanish efforts to win control of the mutineers and sought to find a way to return the captives from the *Amistad* to Africa.

At the center of the controversy was a critical question: Were the mutineers murderers, or had they acted in appropriate self-defense? To answer that question—from the point of view of the American courts, at least—one had to determine whether the captives on board the *Amistad* were slaves. (No slave, under the prevailing U.S. law, had a right of self-defense against a master.)

The entire wrangle became a major headache for the administration of President Martin Van Buren, who was trying to win reelection by maintaining the fragile balance between the northern and southern wings of the Democratic party. (This was, of course, a balancing act that many a future Democratic presidential candidate would be forced to undertake in the decades to come.)

The Biggest Story of the Day

The dispute played out for month after month—serving the "what-the-nation-is-talking-about" role that might today be associated with an inescapable media event like the Florida election fiasco of 2000, a long-running celebrity scandal, or a major business upheaval. Cinque, the leader of the uprising, received what would today be described as heavy media coverage. Abolitionist papers emphasized his dignity and patience; papers hostile to the mutineers' cause portrayed him as a crazed, blood-thirsty beast.

According to the testimony of the mutineers, they had been kidnapped, denied adequate provisions, chained together, and packed into a tiny hold. Four of them had been whipped. Led by Cinque, the Africans had risen up against the Spaniards shortly after a cook had made the strategic error of informing the captives that they would eventually be beheaded and eaten alive.

If the remark was meant as a jest, it was a costly one for the Spaniards. Convinced that they had nothing to lose, the captives used nails to pick their locks, found a supply of cane knives, killed the captain and the cook, and took over the ship. (Two members of the crew jumped overboard and were, apparently, never heard from again.)

Once the Africans were apprehended by the U.S. Navy, they were placed in captivity once again, and with questionable legal justification. For an extended period, they occupied a legal limbo because American law couldn't quite determine how to classify them.

A Challenge to the American Legal System

The American legal system didn't have an immediate answer to the question of the day: Should the *Amistad* mutineers be permitted to return to Africa as free men to Africa, as the abolitionists wanted … or should they be handed over to the Spanish authorities to face trial, as the Spanish government demanded? The White House, however, had its answer.

President Van Buren, eager to keep his coalition in the Democratic Party intact, sought at first to position the *Amistad* affair solely as a foreign policy question—one that could be resolved quickly, and with as little offense to southerners as possible, by simply handing the Africans over to the Spanish. As the legal challenges from anti-slavery forces escalated, however, and Van Buren realized that he could not make the issue go away before the 1840 presidential election, he decided to use a variety of delaying tactics to ensure that the long legal battle was not resolved until after the election took place.

This is why it took until early 1841—long after Van Buren had lost the presidential election to William Henry Harrison—for the Supreme Court to decide the fate of the *Amistad* captives.

A White Man's Nation?

The *Amistad* case is fascinating for a number of reasons, one of which is the light it casts on racial perceptions among whites in the United States before the Civil War. There were many attitudes, of course, but the following quote from the decade of the *Amistad* affair, from Judge Andrew T. Judson, can serve as a representative example. Judson was a Connecticut official who claimed to oppose slavery, but who once argued before a jury that …

> [the United States of America is] a nation of *white men*, and every American should indulge that *pride* and *honor*, which is falsely called prejudice, and teach it to his children. Nothing else will preserve the *American name*, or the *American character*. Who of you would like to see the glory of this nation stripped away, and given to another race of men? [Emphasis in original.]

Judson was, in short, one of the majority of white northerners who considered the immediate abolition of slavery, or the idea of the "amalgamation of the races," to be the kind of dangerous extremism that was likely to lead to the end of the Republic. His views reflected the mainstream of northern thought during the period. As a judge, however, Judson would go on to play an important role in the long-running legal dispute that centered on the *Amistad* captives. He delivered a ruling that *refused* to return the captives to Spanish authorities in Cuba. It was appealed.

Enter John Quincy Adams

Former President John Quincy Adams, now a Congressman from Massachusetts, had been an informal advisor to abolitionists on the *Amistad* matter for many months. He expanded his role in the controversy after determining that there was (as he confided to his diary) "an abominable conspiracy, Executive and Judicial, against the lives of these wretched men."

Adams was born into a family known for its commitment to principle and public service, and was raised in the expectation that he would serve his nation at a high level. His father was the legendary John Adams, second U.S. president. In 1824, the younger Adams (by then a former senator and the current secretary of state) fought a breathtakingly close and bitterly disputed election contest with Andrew Jackson that ended up in the House of Representatives. The House awarded the election to Adams.

Historians have not been particularly kind to the younger Adams's presidency, citing his aloofness and his inability to build coalitions. Jackson defeated him soundly when he ran for re-election in 1828. Yet those who believed that the former president's career was over after his defeat were in for a surprise. Adams sought and won election to the House of Representatives in 1830, and the following year he began the final phase of his remarkable political career as the most prominent spokesman for the anti-slavery faction in the lower chamber of Congress.

Adams was not an abolitionist, but he loathed the institution of slavery, and devoted the balance of his life to opposing it. By the time he was approached to offer legal advice to the legal team representing the *Amistad* captives—and, eventually, argue the case before the U.S. Supreme Court—he was in his seventies, and had not represented a client in court in more than 30 years.

The closing argument he delivered was, however, the finest hour of his career.

Excerpts from John Quincy Adams' defense of the Amistad captives before the United States Supreme Court:

"I know of no other law that reaches the case of my clients but the law of Nature and of Nature's God, on which our fathers placed our national existence."

"[The] American government [has] consistently adopted the design of delivering [the *Amistad* captives] up, either as *property* or as assassins…. Was this justice?"

[In reference to a treaty between Spain and the United States stipulating that recovered merchandise "be taken care of and restored entire to the true proprietor":] "A stipulation to restore human beings *entire* might suit two nations of cannibals, but would be absurd, and worse than absurd, betweeen civilized and Christian nations."

continues

[In response to a claim from the Spanish that they were due "merchandise, rescued from pirates and robbers":] "The merchandise was rescued [by the U.S. Navy] out of its own hands, and the robbers were rescued out of the hands of the robbers! ... [Is] any thing more absurd than to say these forty Africans are robbers, out of whose hands they have themselves been rescued? Can a greater absurdity be imagined in construction than this, which applies the double characters of robbers and of merchandise to human beings?"

"[The Spanish have demanded that the president of the United States] turn himself into a jailer, to keep these people safely, and then into a tipstaff, to take them away for trial among the slave-traders..."

"Has the fourth of July become a day of ignominy and reproach?"

Set Free

After nearly two years of abuse, delay, wrongful imprisonment, and frequent and humiliating public display, the *Amistad* captives finally received something remarkable: an approximation of justice from an American Supreme Court heavily dominated by Southern justices. The Court set them free.

Here is a summary of the main points of the Supreme Court's decision:

◆ The Spaniards had not proved their claims to ownership of the Africans. (The importation of slaves into Cuba from Africa had been illegal for some years.)

◆ Since the Africans were not and had never been slaves, they could not have been thieves or pirates. (On this line of argument, the court followed the defense's claim that the Africans had acted in self-defense; as a result, the court issued an implicit warning to those illegally trafficking in slaves that American courts would not protect them if their "cargo" mutinied.)

◆ The court also decreed the U.S. Navy's seizure of the *Amistad* to be "highly meritorious." (In this part of the decision, the court chose to ignore the documented fact that the ship had sailed to Connecticut, where slavery was still legal, in an attempt to claim a price for the *Amistad*'s human cargo.)

For the African captives of the *Amistad*, the ruling was the long-delayed conclusion of a prolonged nightmare. After a few more logistical delays and strategy sessions, the

Africans who had survived kidnapping, torture, and the vagaries of the American legal system sailed back home for Africa on November 27, 1841.

The Other Side of the *Amistad* Decision

For Africans in America, the picture was not quite so appealing.

On the positive side of the ledger, the abolitionist movement had definitely gained momentum, and the sympathies of the North had been awakened, at least for a time, to some of the injustices of the institution of slavery. Also on the positive side, the American legal system had upheld the right of freed Africans to defend themselves. (Many had feared that the court would be unable to bring itself to acknowledge that freed Africans had any rights whatsoever.)

And yet, despite the apparent triumph and the victorious headlines in abolitionist newspapers, there was an ominous side to the Supreme Court's ruling. In finding for the captives, the justices had based their reasoning on their own determination that the Spanish government had failed to prove that the *Amistad* captives were slaves. They had *not* embraced Adams's argument that the Africans were free by virtue of natural law.

By following this line of reasoning, the court had actually reinforced existing U.S. law on slavery. Those who *were* legally slaves *could* be retained in captivity indefinitely— and, presumably, starved, tortured, and abused as the *Amistad* captives had been.

Though some white northerners had begun to look a little more skeptically at the institution of slavery, the enslavement of Africans continued in the South. With the help of able counsel, the *Amistad* mutineers had simply maneuvered around the human travesty of American law as it stood in the 1840s; they had not reformed it in any way.

Prelude to a Bloodbath

The question of whether to honor a Spanish claim for financial compensation for losses in the *Amistad* affair was a political football that remained in play from 1841 (the year the captives left for Africa) until 1860 (the year before the American Civil War began). The *Amistad* dispute was, in fact, a prelude to a longer and bloodier dispute that had the issue of slavery at its heart: the American Civil War.

On its own terms, however, *Amistad* was a dispute about a basic human requirement: freedom.

Make Us Free

We want you to ask the court what we have done wrong. What for Americans keep us in prison. Some people say Mendi people crazy; Mendi people dolt, because we no talk American language. Merica people no talk Mendi language; Merica people dolt? ... Some people say, Mendi people got no souls. Why we feel bad, we got no souls? We want to be free very much. ... Dear friend, we want you to know how we feel. Mendi people think, think , think. Nobody know what he think; teacher he know, we tell him some. Mendi people have got souls. We think we know God punish us if we tell lie. We never tell lie; we speak truth. What for Mendi people afraid? Because they got souls.... Cook say he kill, he eat Mendi people—we afraid—we kill cook; then captain kill one man with knife, and cut Mendi people plenty. We never kill captain, he no kill us ... All we want is make us free.

— From a letter dictated by the *Amistad* captive Kale published in the March 25, 1841, *Emancipator* (an abolitionist newspaper)

The Least You Need to Know

- The *Amistad* affair forced the American legal system to define the status of a number of Africans who had been kidnapped and illegally brought into Cuba. They mutinied and ended up in the United States.

- The leader of the uprising was a charismatic African named Cinque who received what would today be described as major media exposure.

- The episode, which was a huge news story, revealed fault-lines in the American political system that would lead to open conflict between North and South.

- Former president John Quincy Adams argued on behalf of the *Amistad* captives before the United States Supreme Court.

- Although the high court freed the *Amistad* mutineers, its ruling actually reinforced existing American legal principles regarding slavery.

Part 2

A House Divided: The Later History

In the middle of the nineteenth century, a momentous conflict engulfed the nation. At its heart, whether the combatants always realized it or not, was the momentous question of whether human beings ought to enslave other human beings.

The Civil War was the great pivot point of American history, but it did not turn the United States into a colorblind nation. In this part of the book, you learn about the struggles and triumphs of the African American community from the 1860s onward.

Discord and Decision: The Civil War

In This Chapter:

- ◆ The momentous conflict
- ◆ The Emancipation Proclamation
- ◆ The end of slavery

In this chapter, you learn about the bloody and momentous conflict between North and South that took place in the United States between 1861 and 1865.

The war had a number of causes: regional rivalries, the seething conflicts arising from the abolitionist movement, a series of bitter political clashes over whether slavery would be permitted in newly admitted states, and a basic disagreement over the relative authority of the federal government and the states. All these contributing factors to the war, however, led back to a single fault line: the existence of slavery as an institution in the United States.

Patchwork political deals in 1820 and 1850 (known as the Missouri Compromise and the Compromise of 1850, respectively) had been arranged to maintain the country's fragile political balance. Both compromises, however, left the institution of slavery itself intact. The nation would endure four years of often-hellish conflict on the ground before it found the political will to confront, and finally eliminate, the institution of slavery.

Fredrick Douglass Calls It as He Sees It

In 1852, the year of the publication of *Uncle Tom's Cabin*, the escaped slave, abolitionist author, and gifted orator Frederick Douglass addressed an Independence Day gathering in Rochester, New York, with the following words:

> Fellow citizens, I will not enlarge further on your national inconsistencies. The existence of slavery in this country brands your republicanism as a sham, your humanity as base pretense, and your Christianity as a lie. It destroys your moral power abroad, it corrupts your politicians at home. It saps the foundations of religion; it makes your name a hissing and a byeword to a mocking earth. It is the antagonistic force in your government, the only thing that seriously disturbs and endangers your Union. It fetters your progress, it is the enemy of improvement; the deadly foe of education; it fosters pride; it breeds indolence; it promotes vice; it shelters crime; it is a curse of the earth that supports it; and yet you cling to it as if it were the sheet anchor of all your hopes.

Frederick Douglass.

(Source: Ohio Historical Society)

Slavery was indeed disturbing and endangering the Union. Its days as a legal institution, however, were numbered.

What's the Word?

Uncle Tom's Cabin was a novel by Harriet Beecher Stowe, published in 1852. Though it included racist stereotypes (the contemporary disparaging term "Uncle Tom" derives from the novel's portrayal of a submissive slave), Stowe's anti-slavery story was highly effective in winning sympathy for the abolitionist cause in the North. The book was extraordinarily popular and was adapted into a hit stage play.

Ladies Whipping Girls.　Page 109.

Period illustration of a lady whipping a slave girl.

(Source: Library of Congress)

A Raid in Virginia

Seven and a half years after Douglass spoke those words, an abolitionist friend of his by the name of John Brown gathered 21 followers and mounted a raid on a federal arsenal in Virginia. Brown's aim was to distribute weapons to slaves and launch a rebellion. He took the arsenal briefly, but was captured the next day, and no rebellion materialized. Brown's effort polarized the ominously divided nation even further. Many abolitionists (including Douglass) were at pains to distance themselves from Brown's tactics, but as his trial unfolded, his dignity and religious faith won significant

What's the Word?

Secession is the act of a region or state removing itself from a federal union. The choice of Southern governments in 1860 and 1861 to secede from the United States sparked war. (No provision for a state's leaving the Union exists in the U.S. Constitution.)

sympathy for the abolitionist cause in the North. Whites in the South, however, regarded Brown with contempt and hatred.

Brown was hanged for treason in December of 1859. He had believed himself to be God's instrument in helping to bring about a fiery war that would produce an end to slavery. Just over a year later, following the election of Abraham Lincoln as president, the question of *secession* would initiate conflict between the North and the South. It would take some time—and no small amount of prodding from abolitionists like Douglass—before the North acknowledged the prohibition of slavery as a goal of the conflict.

A slave auction in Virginia.

(Source: Library of Congress)

Timeline: The Civil War

1860: Abraham Lincoln is elected president; his "radical" view that the Union should admit no further states permitting slavery horrifies the South. (Lincoln's views on race relations would, however, brand him as a white supremacist by twenty-first century standards.) The outcome of the election begins talk of secession in the South, and on December 20 South Carolina announces that it is no longer part of the Union. Eventually, 11 southern states secede and form the Confederate States of America.

1861: Lincoln is inaugurated. Southern forces fire on the federal garrison at Fort Sumter, South Carolina; the conflict begins in earnest. Early victories go to the South.

1862: Ulysses S. Grant secures a victory at Fort Donelson. The Union's Peninsular Campaign meets with defeat at the hands of General Robert E. Lee; Lee's forces are dealt a setback at Antietam. Congress abolishes slavery in the District of Columbia; Lincoln issues the Emancipation Proclamation. Union armies are defeated at Fredericksburg.

1863: Draft riots in New York City rage for four days. Lee's forces are defeated at Gettysburg, and the momentum shifts decisively to the North. Grant's Vicksburg campaign concludes successfully, securing control of the Mississippi for the Union. African American Sergeant William H. Carney, of the Fifty-Fourth Massachusetts Volunteers, receives the Congressional Medal of Honor for valor under fire.

1864: Grant maneuvers Lee's forces toward the Confederate capital, Richmond, Virginia, and assaults Petersburg. Congress authorizes equal pay, health care, arms, and equipment for African American troops. Sherman is victorious in his Atlanta campaign, and leads a devastating march across Georgia to the sea. Lincoln is reelected.

1865: Confederate defeat at Five Forks leads to the evacuation of Richmond. Lee, with no retreat possible, surrenders his army to Grant at Appomattox, Virginia. Though sporadic fighting continues, this surrender is usually regarded as the end of the war. Lincoln is assassinated on April 14.

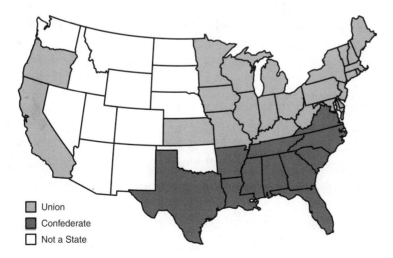

The North and the South during the Civil War.

- Union
- Confederate
- Not a State

The Emancipation Proclamation

President Abraham Lincoln issued the Emancipation Proclamation on September 22, 1862—to take effect on January 1, 1863. As its name implies, the executive order declared freedom—specifically, of slaves—and authorized the deployment of freedmen as Union Troops. The key words were …

> on the first day of January, in the year of our Lord one thousand eight hundred and sixty-three, all persons held as slaves within any State or designated part of a State, the people whereof shall then be in rebellion against the United States, shall be then, thenceforward, and forever free.

The proclamation named the rebellious entities as the southern states of Virginia (but not West Virginia), North Carolina, South Carolina, Georgia, Mississippi, Alabama, and Florida, and the western states of Arkansas and Texas. Finally, the order declared that "such persons [i.e. slaves] of suitable condition, will be received into the armed service of the United States."

The Road to the Proclamation

Lincoln did not come to the Proclamation either quickly or easily. While he was on record as opposing slavery, he did not want to make a move that was independent of Congress, whose support he needed for the war. Also, as the Union went to a war footing, Lincoln was also concerned that four states in the buffer zone between North and South—Delaware, Kentucky, Maryland, and Missouri—might go over to the Confederacy if slavery was declared illegal.

Of course, economics as well morality was at issue. Lincoln and other Northerners knew that slaves were the backbone of the Confederate economy. If they were freed, many would simply leave the plantations on which they were being used. Those who chose to remain would demand wages or insist on other compensation. The North could count on upsetting the economics of the South in a major way by any Proclamation.

Congress finally made its own move on the question in July 1862. It acted not out of ethical considerations, primarily, but from sheer military necessity. The Union needed more troops. So Congress passed legislation authorizing the freedom of any southern slave who left the Confederacy to join the Union armed forces.

Despite its limitations, the Proclamation was important politically, militarily, and historically. It was and continues to be, after all, a national document. It put an American president on record as against slavery. It loosened the underpinnings of the southern economy and gave a moral *raison d'être* to the war itself. What was called the "civil war" and the "war between the states" now became a war of liberation. And the proclamation set in motion expectations, on the parts of slaves and white abolitionists, that more gains would be registered in time.

Immediate Effects

By legitimizing the citizenship of blacks, and simultaneously inviting their participation in the war, Lincoln ensured his side of more troops at a time when the number of white volunteers was decreasing. In fact, African Americans served in the Union armed forces to the extent of approximately 200,000 volunteers by the war's end. While it is true that these soldiers were segregated into African American units and largely led by white officers, nonetheless their contributions were highly significant. The North could not have won the war without their participation.

By reframing the conflict as a war against slavery, through the Proclamation, Lincoln also neutralized the participation of England and France as combatants on the side of the South. While their dependency on the Confederacy's cotton might have inclined them to join the southern cause, the Union's formal introduction of the slavery issue made it impossible for them to do so. A majority of their own people was philosophically opposed to slavery, making support of the South politically unfeasible at home.

The Proclamation was, in other words, a master stroke from a consummate politician.

Long-Term Effects

Ultimately, what did the Emancipation Proclamation mean—for slaves, whites, and the United States as a whole?

For African Americans it was a clear, supportive, ground-breaking political statement. While it was restricted in scope, and more carefully articulated than most people imagine, it was still a documented pronouncement by a sitting President of the United States. (Only after Lincoln's death would a Constitutional amendment prohibit slavery.)

For the Union, the Emancipation Proclamation had a clear, substantial short-term effect in providing the extra military manpower the North

? FAQ _____

Did the Emancipation Proclamation formally end slavery in the U.S.? No—that was the Thirteenth Amendment to the Constitution (1865). However, the Proclamation laid the foundation for the later amendment, which held that "[n]either slavery nor involuntary servitude, except as a punishment for crime whereof the party shall have been duly convicted, shall exist within the United States, or any place subject to their jurisdiction."

needed to win the war and preserve the Union. The popular image of Lincoln single-handedly freeing thousands of downtrodden African American slaves with a stroke of the pen is a significant distortion of what actually happened, but the Emancipation Proclamation nevertheless opened an important door and made possible later legal advances for African Americans—and countless other Americans of all races.

A Limited Emancipation

It is often overlooked that the Emancipation Proclamation made no attempt whatsoever to free slaves held in border states that had remained loyal to the Union. The document also did nothing to change the legal status of slaves in areas of the South that Union forces already controlled. The decree actually freed only individuals in territory that was in active rebellion "as a fit and necessary war measure for suppressing said rebellion."

Ultimately, the Emancipation Proclamation is best regarded as a psychological benchmark—the moment at which the Federal government formally embraced the notion that slavery was worth forbidding. That realization had, of course, been a long time coming.

African American Troops on the March

There were so many African American men involved in the war on the Union side after Lincoln issued the Emancipation Proclamation that a so-called Bureau of Colored Troops was formed to recognize and organize African Americans fighting in the war. Known as United States Colored Troops, these men, mainly former slaves, eventually made up 144 infantry regiments, 13 heavy artillery regiments, 7 cavalry regiments, and 1 light artillery regiment. The state of Louisiana mustered the most troops overall: 24,000 men.

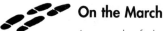 **On the March**

Among the fighting men abolitionist Fredrick Douglass recruited for the Union cause were his sons, Charles and Lewis. Both served in the Massachusetts 54th.

The Fifty-Fourth

The 54th Massachusetts Regiment, made up of more than 500 African American soldiers (mostly from Massachusetts and Pennsylvania) and led by Col. Robert Shaw of Boston, a white man, was immortalized in the 1989 film, *Glory*, starring Morgan Freeman.

On the battlefield, the regiment suffered severe casualties in a vain but brave attack on Fort Wagner in South Carolina. Killed outright were 34; wounded were 146; and recorded as captured or missing, 92. The July 18, 1863, assault featured a frontal charge up a beach without cover. The 54th managed to get over the fortifications before being thrown back. Col. Shaw was among those who died trying to prove to doubters that African American men could and would fight with as much valor as white men.

However, the brave soldiers of the 54th Massachusetts were certainly not the only African Americans who fought in the war. While many people erroneously believe that the Civil War was fought by white people to free the slaves, in fact approximately 180,000 African Americans served in the Union Army and 18,000 more in the Navy. They were in the cavalry and the infantry, in engineering and seamanship.

When desperate Confederate generals appealed to Jefferson Davis to offer slaves their freedom if they would fight for the South, the President of the Confederacy initially, and adamantly, refused. By the time the war's direction forced him to reconsider, the South was well on the way to defeat.

Other Important Battles Involving African American Troops

On October 27 and 28, 1862, the first battle involving African Americans troops was fought at Island Mound, Missouri. Elements of the First Kansas Colored Volunteer Regiment, composed mainly of former slaves from the state, overcame Confederate soldiers. The after-action report of Maj. Richard Ward records his admiration for the 64 African Americans in his command. During the battle with Confederate troops from the island, he noted that, "the enemy charged with a yell toward [Sgt.] Gardner's little band of twenty-five men …. Nothing dismayed, the little band turned upon their foes …. The enemy cried out to the men to surrender but they told them never. I have witnessed some hard fights, but I never saw a braver sight than that handful of brave men fighting 117 men who were all around and in amongst them. Not one surrendered or gave up a weapon."

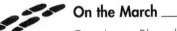 **On the March**

Gen. James Blunt, the Union commander, wrote of the First Kansas Colored Volunteers, "I never saw such fighting as was done by the Negro regiment …. The question [whether] Negroes will fight is settled …."

This same regiment, along with others, also participated in the Battle of Honey Springs on July 17, 1863, just days after the Battle of Gettysburg. They joined some 3,000 other Union troops against 6,000 Confederates, mainly from Texas. Groups of Native Americans fought on both sides. Although outnumbered, the North was ultimately victorious, as Confederate forces had trouble keeping their powder dry in the rainstorm that ensued. The Union Army virtually drove the Confederates out of the Indian Territory, now Kansas, suffering only 79 casualties against its opponent's 637. The paternalistic, arrogant assumption among whites that African Americans could not or would not fight effectively was quickly disproved.

On April 12, 1864, Maj. Gen. Nathan Forrest led 2,500 Confederate troops in an attack on 292 African American soldiers and 285 white soldiers at Fort Pillow, near Memphis. Eventually the Confederates overwhelmed the fort. The Union soldiers who survived fled down a ravine behind the fort. Here the Rebels caught them in a withering crossfire. They followed up by shooting even those who surrendered, with hands raised, the freedmen because they were African Americans, the whites because "you fight with niggers." "Remember Fort Pillow" became a Union battle cry thereafter, especially for African American troops.

> **On the March**
>
> First Sergeant Powhatan Beaty of the Fifth U.S. Colored Troops performed service above and beyond the call of duty when he took command of Company G at the Battle of Chaffin's Farm. All the officers were dead or wounded. Beaty rallied the surviving troops and led them in a successful charge, for which he received the Medal of Honor.

On September 29 and 30, 1864, in the Battle of Chaffin's Farm and New Market Heights outside of Richmond, Virginia, 13 Colored Infantry units were involved, along with numerous white regiments. The Union Army attacked Confederate forts at dawn on September 29. The Colored Division of XVIII Corps charged uphill against one fort, in the face of sustained fire. They had horrendous losses. After a two-day battle, which resulted in casualties of over 4,000, the Union Army managed to establish itself successfully in the area, while tying down large numbers of enemy troops. Fourteen African Americans received Medals of Honor for their bravery in this engagement.

Individual Accomplishments

Although unsung enlisted men did most of the close, brutal fighting, some African Americans also served as commissioned officers, even if in small numbers (120, to be specific). They served as doctors and chaplains as well as commanders, and became first and second lieutenants, captains, and even majors.

Eight African American sailors won Medals of Honor. Twenty-nine African American soldiers received the award.

One African American who stood out as a war leader was a woman. Harriet Tubman, famous as a "conductor" on the Underground Railroad, served the Union Army as a scout, nurse, cook, and spy. On June 2, 1863, she also led an attack on rice plantations along the Combahee River in South Carolina, destroying thousands of dollars worth of food and goods and freeing close to 800 slaves. The Second South Carolina Colored Volunteers, under the overall command of Col. James Montgomery of Kansas, served as her troops. In her honor they altered an old spiritual to "Swing Low, Sweet Harriet [instead of "chariot"], comin' for to carry me home."

Racism Endures

Despite the Emancipation Proclamation, African American soldiers and sailors encountered real-world discrimination in pay, clothing, food, and respect throughout the war. Nonetheless, they participated in significant ways in 449 engagements, where they clearly demonstrated that despite racist innuendoes, they could fight as well as any white man.

Looking backward, African American soldiers may well have found a model in Crispus Attucks, who led, fought, and died in the Boston Massacre of 1770. Looking forward, with the gift of prophecy, they might have glimpsed the Tuskegee Airmen and other African Americans who would became famous for their deeds in future wars of the United States.

African American Contributions

1861: William C. Nell is named postal clerk in Boston, Massachusetts, thereby becoming the first African American civilian federal employee.

1862: Mary Jane Patterson is graduated from Oberlin College. She is the first African American woman to receive a degree from an institution of higher learning.

1863: Abraham Lincoln appoints Henry M. Turner as the nation's first commissioned African American chaplain.

1864: William Appleton sees action at New Market Heights, Virginia, and eventually receives the Congressional Medal of Honor. He is one of 21 African Americans to receive the award for meritorious service during the Civil War.

1865: African American businessman John Hones helps to bring about the reversal of discriminatory laws in Illinois.

The Least You Need to Know

♦ Abolitionist John Brown led a raid on a Virginia arsenal in the hope of launching an armed rebellion among slaves. No such rebellion occurred, but the raid was an important precursor to the later conflict between North and South.

♦ Although he held views that would today earn him the label white supremacist, Abraham Lincoln's election to the presidency on a platform opposing extension of slavery to newly admitted states led to secession by South Carolina and other southern states.

♦ The seceding southern states formed the Confederate States of America.

♦ A bloody civil war between Union and Confederate forces followed in 1861.

♦ Lincoln's Emancipation Proclamation, written in 1862, did not end slavery in and of itself, but it was a shrewd political move that made later advances possible, including the Thirteenth Amendment to the Constitution (which did prohibit slavery).

♦ African Americans fought valiantly in the conflict, and helped to ensure the Union victory in 1865 … but they faced discrimination in pay, clothing, food, and respect throughout the war.

Chapter 6

Emancipation (Not)

In This Chapter

- Overt manipulation of the legal and political systems
- Back-room dealings
- White terrorism

For a time after the Civil War, African Americans who lived in the South held property, and won elective office. They exercised rights, in other words, that had been guaranteed under the newly amended United States Constitution. By the end of the presidential administration of Civil War hero Ulysses S. Grant in 1877, all those gains had been lost, and white southerners had resumed positions of political power and economic control with such ruthlessness that the abolition of slavery seemed a mere technicality.

White supremacists used three weapons to put African Americans "in their place." These weapons were overt legal action, behind-the-scenes manipulation of the political system, and terrorism (that is to say, planned campaigns of violence against innocent civilians).

In this chapter, you'll get a look at how these tools were employed in the period following the Civil War in an attempt to destroy the spirit, aspirations, and practical options of African Americans. The historian Howard

Zinn called the bleak situation faced by African Americans during this period as "emancipation without freedom." He was right.

Overt Legal and Political Measures

The formal gutting of the sweeping social and electoral reforms that followed the Civil War were among the most shameful events in American legal history. Here is a brief overview of some of the most prominent turnarounds.

No Land

A few months after assuming office, President Andrew Johnson (Abraham Lincoln's successor) overturned the federal government's program of distributing abandoned lands to freedmen. An attempt to divide confiscated land into 40-acre lots and distribute it among freed slaves and Union-sympathizing refugees received a good deal of attention, but it failed to win support in Congress.

The result: The lands of former slave owners went to an emerging white ruling class, and not to the freedmen who had worked them under pain of torture, separation from family members, and murder.

Watering Down the Fourteenth Amendment

The Fourteenth Amendment to the Constitution—obviously a measure intended to secure legal rights for African Americans—was ratified in 1868. It guaranteed all citizens due process and equal protection under the law.

Yet only five years after that ratification, the U.S. Supreme Court ruled that the amendment applied only to *federal* civil rights issues, and did not affect "civil rights heretofore belonging exclusively to the states."

No Civil Rights Law

In 1875, a comprehensive civil rights law went on the books. It guaranteed rights of equality of treatment in public facilities. In 1883, however, the U.S. Supreme Court ruled the law unconstitutional. The shift was part of a troubling legal trend.

In the very earliest cases considered by the Supreme Court involving interpretation of the Fourteenth Amendment, the justices construed it as forbidding any form of discrimination of African Americans sponsored or imposed by a state. The court's 1883 rejection of civil rights legislation, though, suggested a new set of judicial priorities.

Those priorities became even more obvious in *Plessy* v. *Ferguson*.

Plessy v. Ferguson

In this infamous 1896 decision, the U.S. Supreme Court examined the right of the state of Louisiana to operate a racially segregated public transport system.

Homer A. Plessy—the plaintiff—was one-eighth African American and seven-eighths white. He was placed under arrest for entering a Louisiana rail coach and refusing to relinquish his seat in the white section for one in the separate colored section. Louisiana law mandated racially distinct passenger compartments in rail transport. Plessy sued, arguing that the Louisiana law violated his constitutional rights.

The Supreme Court's ruling in the *Plessy* case gave the state of Louisiana everything it asked for, and Plessy got nothing. The court held that "separate but equal" facilities did not violate the Fourteenth Amendment's guarantee of equal protection under the law because—in the view of the court—the Constitution guaranteed only political, and not social, equality.

Obstacles and Opportunities

Plessy not only served to justify a half-century of segregation of public facilities in the South (see Chapter 7), but it also helped to legitimize the political consensus for supporting such legal hypocrisy.

The issue of segregation unified the white South as few others could. Loudly ensuring a commitment to separate—and clearly *unequal*—facilities for African Americans became Priority Number One for successful southern politicians. (The official ballot logo of the Democratic Party in Alabama, for instance, was a white rooster and the legend "White Supremacy"—a slogan that seemed somehow to hint at political, not merely social, inequality.)

**The Supreme Court Gives a Thumbs-Up to
"Separate But Equal" Accommodations**

Laws permitting, and even requiring, [the races'] separation in places where they are likely to be brought into contact do not necessarily imply the inferiority of either race to the other, and have been generally, if not universally, recognized as within the competence of the state legislatures.... If one race be inferior to the other socially, the Constitution of the United States cannot put them upon the same plane.

—From the majority decision in *Plessy* v. *Ferguson*

> ### But a Lone Dissent Foreshadows a Later Legal Breakthrough
>
> In respect of civil rights, common to all citizens, the Constitution of the United States does not, I think, permit any public authority to know the race of those entitled to be protected in the enjoyment of such rights …. [T]here is in this country no superior, dominant, ruling class of citizens. There is no caste here. Our Constitution is color-blind, and neither knows nor tolerates classes among citizens…. The thin disguise of 'equal' accommodations for passengers in railroad coaches will not mislead anyone, nor atone for the wrong this day done….
>
> —From the dissent of John Marshall Harlan, the only Supreme Court justice voting to strike down the Louisiana law at issue in *Plessy* v. *Ferguson*. This dissent laid the intellectual foundation for the Court's later decision to overturn *Plessy* in *Brown* v. *Board of Education* (1954).

Poll Taxes, Literacy Tests, and "White Primaries"

In order to gain readmittance to the Union after the Civil War, the states of the old Confederacy had to agree not to exclude African Americans from the election process. Agree they did—but white southern politicians, led by the ever-creative example of the state of Mississippi, developed a host of innovative legal traps, the practical effect of which was—hard to believe though this may be—the effective denial of voting rights to African Americans.

African Americans attempting to register to vote in the South were disqualified for any number of reasons. They were turned away because they could not summarize arcane sections of the state Constitution to the satisfaction of the registrar; because they had failed to pay poll taxes; because they could not pass elaborate "literacy" or "understanding" tests; and because they failed to meet a host of other farfetched standards that somehow didn't stop whites from exercising their voting rights in large numbers. State legislatures also arranged for special "white primaries" from which African Americans were excluded, a particularly blatant violation of constitutional principles.

These state laws made a mockery of both the recently enacted Fourteenth Amendment and the solemn vows of southern political leaders to enfranchise all citizens in accordance with the demands of the U.S. Constitution. The latest hypocrisies issuing from the state legislatures must have confirmed the darkest suspicions of newly freed

African Americans (and increasingly isolated northern liberals) that the law was merely another game played by whites, exclusively for the benefit of whites.

From Slavery to Serfdom

The Thirteenth Amendment formally outlawed slavery. Yet President Andrew Johnson helped southern states to reenter the Union with regulations in place that ensured working lives for African Americans that were, to say the least, deeply reminiscent of the lives they'd lived as slaves. (See the discussion of "black codes" in Chapter 7.)

Emancipation or no emancipation, African Americans found themselves bound by law to land they were prohibited from owning. They found themselves deeply in debt. They found themselves reporting to racist white storekeepers and planters who cheated them mercilessly. This may not have been slavery, but it was certainly a long way from freedom. If ownership of human beings was no longer permissible, the legal entrapment and exploitation of African Americans was still, apparently, the American way.

The laws were corrupt because the government had been reclaimed by racist white supremacists; the most economically powerful white northerners had, after 1877, gone along with the power grab. As Henry Adams, an African American Union veteran put it when testifying before Congress:

> "… the whole South—every state in the South—had got into the hands of the very men that held us slaves."

Behind-the-Scene Manipulation of the Political System

In 1867, African American voters held the numerical majority in the states of Alabama, Florida, Louisiana, Mississippi, and South Carolina. In 1868, African American voters provided the national margin of victory for the Republican presidential candidate, General Ulysses S. Grant. Within a decade, however, African Americans had been effectively remarginalized, and by 1900, laws were on the books in all the southern states, the direct or indirect effect of which was the segregation of African Americans and the denial of their right to vote.

Northern opposition to such practices had evaporated. Why?

The answer is to be found in the 1877 back-room deal that brought about the end of the Reconstruction era, ensured the withdrawal of federal troops from the South, and initiated the one-party, white-supremacist rule that endured in the south for nearly a century. This back-room deal took place in the Wormley Hotel in Washington, D.C., on February 26, 1877.

The fateful meeting was entirely without constitutional or legal precedent. It was, however, one of the most important conferences of the era. It demonstrated the willingness of northern elites to turn a blind eye to southern abuse of civil rights.

Hayes Caves In to the South

The meeting at the Wormley Hotel involved representatives of the Republican presidential candidate, Rutherford B. Hayes, and representatives of white Southern political interests.

In the election, Hayes had lost the popular vote to his Democratic challenger, Samuel Tilden. In an electoral-college dispute similar in externals to that which plunged the 2000 presidential election into chaos, three states possessing a decisive 19 electoral votes had not yet put forward their official slates of delegates. If Hayes could win these delegates, he would secure the presidency.

In order to get those votes—and a term in the White House that would otherwise have gone to his opponent—Hayes authorized his representatives at the Wormley to make a series of bargains. One of these agreements was that, upon entering the White House, Hayes would order the withdrawal of federal troops from the South, thereby removing the last impediment to a reversion of unchallengeable white control of the political process in the South.

Obstacles and Opportunities

The behind-the-scenes 1877 deal that secured the presidency for Rutherford B. Hayes and the Republicans did not re-establish the pre–Civil war economic order in the (decimated) South. It did, however, guarantee a new group of elite whites control of the political process, and it paved the way for a commercial reconciliation between (new) southern landholders and northern financial interests.

This was the so-called Compromise of 1877. Like the compromises that had come before—in 1820 and 1850—it was an agreement between white political bosses whose decisions had fateful and long-enduring repercussions on the lives of African Americans—people who had had no meaningful involvement in the quiet negotiations. As a practical matter, it was the African Americans who were compromised.

The back-room deal of 1877 was an example of the kind of sleazy high-level politics that severely undercut American claims to uphold often-stated democratic ideals and commitments to the faithful execution of the laws. When Congress convened a committee to sort out the final disposition of the disputed electoral votes of the election of 1876, the fix was in.

Hayes was the new president-elect. The troops would be withdrawn. And anyone who imagined that the white supremacists in the South would honor African American rights was to be rudely awakened in short order.

Totalitarianism in the South

So it was that northerners accepted the existence of a segregated, white-supremacist social system that systematically ignored the rights of its citizens. The result was a network of one-party state governments committed to a white-supremacist ideal—and to relentless abuse of supposedly democratic processes. In the twentieth century, such a governmental scheme would be labeled totalitarian. At the end of the nineteenth century, however, Americans chose to call it the "Solid South."

Terrorism

For the institution of slavery to have thrived in the United States, slave owners had had to use violence—or, more accurately, the threat of violence, reinforced constantly by its predictable, highly visual application against those enslaved. Precisely the same approach helped to secure the long reign of "emancipation without freedom" in the South.

White terrorist groups—chief among them the Ku Klux Klan—made sure African Americans lived in constant terror of random violence.

The Klan

The white supremacist organization known as the Ku Klux Klan had two formal incarnations. The first, dating from 1866, was led by the former Confederate Nathan Bedford Forrest; it focused on wounding, murdering, and otherwise terrorizing African Americans, and on maintaining a racially divided society in which whites dominated. That version of the Klan was formally disbanded in 1869, although Forrest's followers continued to work in informal networks to deny African Americans their voting rights.

The Klan formally resurfaced in 1915, inspired to carry out a much broader mission of hatred. In response to large-scale immigration from Europe, the Klan added Catholics, Jews, and southern and eastern Europeans to its list of undesirables. This incarnation of the Klan, which took advantage of a wave of native-soil patriotism during the World War I period, proved extraordinarily popular not only in the South, but in certain Northern areas as well. (The movement was an extremely powerful political force, for instance, in the state of Kansas in the early and mid-1920s.)

American Terrorism in the Aftermath of the Civil War

The following is a sampling of some of the outrages perpetuated by white suprema-cist groups against African Americans following the conclusion of the Civil War. It's important to bear in mind that these acts of violence were undertaken by pseudo-military organizations against innocent civilians for the purposes of bringing about a desired set of political, social, and economic changes. Thus, white supremacists in the American South offered object lessons in terrorism to the later hijackers, bombers, and suicide pilots of the twentieth and twenty-first centuries.

Bloody Doings in the South

Date	Event
July 1866	White mobs, led by local law enforcement, attack African American and white Republicans meeting in New Orleans. Forty people are left dead; the leader of federal troops in Louisiana refers to the event as a "massacre."
September 1867	Whites assault a group of African Americans who had embarked on a public march through Georgia. Nine African Americans die; a number of whites taking part in the march also receive injuries.
September 1867	At least two hundred African Americans are reported murdered in the Opelousas Massacre in Louisiana.
October 1867	Several more African Americans are murdered in Louisiana by white marauders.
August 1869	North Carolina's election process is effectively comman-deered by white supremacists whose tactics include politi-cal assassination and violence against African Americans.
April 1873	Over 60 African Americans die in the Colfax Massacre in Grant Parish, Louisiana.
December 1874	Seventy-five Republicans meeting in Vicksburg, Mississippi are murdered by white supremacists.
November 1875	The infamous "Mississippi Plan" successfully delivers con-trol of the state government to white supremacists, despite a black majority of voters. The plan includes massacres, staged riots, and a program of systematic intimidation of African American voters. (The plan will later be adapted for similar takeovers in South Carolina and Louisiana.)
September 1876	Thirty-nine African Americans and two whites are mur-dered by whites in Ellenton, South Carolina.

Date	Event
May 1879	Confederate veteran General James R. Chalmers attempts to stem African American migration by shutting down the Mississippi River to African American travelers. He vows to sink any boat that attempts to run his blockade.
1882	Reports of substantial numbers of lynchings of African Americans appear. They will continue for half a century.
1898	Eight African Americans are killed in civil disturbances in Wilmington, North Carolina.

It was a bleak time indeed to be an African in America.

By the turn of the century, African Americans may have been technically liberated from the formal bonds of slavery, but they were nevertheless caught in a web of discrimination, intimidation, and violence that added up to something very nearly as obscene. With the clear sanction of the United States Supreme Court, many state legislatures set about establishing a system of laws designed to ensure the perpetual humiliation, submission, and victimization of African Americans.

The laws—and the way of life they represented—came to be known by a catchy name: Jim Crow.

African American Contributions

1866: African Americans Edward G. Walker and Charles L. Mitchell are elected as state legislators in Massachusetts.

1866: George T. Downing, a successful African American businessman, helps to bring about legislation ending segregated schools in Rhode Island.

1869: Bose Ikard, one of many overlooked African American cowboys, settles in Texas and has a number of run-ins with Comanches. It's estimated that one third of all western settlers were either African American or Mexican; other important African American westerners (ignored for decades by Hollywood westerns) include Jesse Stahl, Nat Love, and Mary Fields.

1871: Frederick Douglass is appointed to the board of trustees of Howard University.

1875: Blanche Kelso is elected to the United States Senate from Mississippi. He is the first African American to be elected to the Senate and serve out a full six-year term.

The Least You Need to Know

- ◆ In a brief period following the Civil War in which reforms seemed to be taking hold, African Americans found themselves in a condition of "emancipation without freedom."

- ◆ White supremacists used overt manipulation of the legal and political system to reclaim power and subjugate African Americans.

- ◆ They also used back-room dealings to engineer a withdrawal of federal troops from the South and ensure the return of white rule.

- ◆ Terrorism was another common weapon used to undermine the rights of African Americans and ensure that they lived in fear of whites.

The Jim Crow Laws

In This Chapter

- ◆ The Jim Crow period and the legal subjugation of African Americans after the Civil War
- ◆ How Jim Crow started
- ◆ What it did
- ◆ Why it hasn't really ended yet

Suppose you sat a young person down and posed a riddle.

Imagine you said to that young person—a teenager, say, or perhaps someone in his or her early twenties, something like the following. "I'm thinking of a particular country. In this country, within living memory, laws were passed making it a crime to allow white nurses to treat black male patients; or to teach black and white schoolchildren in a single class; or to live in the same room with someone of another race (with or without the benefit of a marriage license); or to permit black amateur sports teams to step onto the same field of play as white amateur sports teams; or to permit blacks and whites to use the same public drinking fountain. What country am I thinking of?"

A good many young Americans might answer, "South Africa." They might explain their answer on the basis of the infamous apartheid laws that instituted a rigid segregation in that racially divided country from the late 1940s to the early 1990s. Another answer, however, can actually be found a good deal closer to home.

The laws we're discussing were passed in the United States of America—not so very long ago. They were a national disgrace, and they did lasting social, economic, and psychological damage to the African American community.

What's the Word?

Apartheid was the set of brutally oppressive racial-segregation laws instituted in South Africa prior to the long-delayed emergence of majority rule in that country in the early 1990s. The apartheid laws made South Africa an international pariah.

FAQ

Why were the Jim Crow laws known by that name? No one is entirely certain how the state laws enforcing racial segregation and denying equal access to opportunity and voting rights came to be known as Jim Crow laws. What we do know is that "Jim Crow" was a popular "black" character played by white actors in minstrel performances, and that the substandard railroad cars set aside for African American passengers in the South were known as Jim Crow cars.

America's Apartheid

America's *apartheid* laws went by another name. They were called Jim Crow laws.

A majority of American states had some form of legal racial-segregation program. These laws helped to ensure that, for most of the twentieth century, millions of African Americans lived in deprivation, and in fear in private—separate and unequal.

Jim Crow defined, codified, and protected the nation's entrenched racial prejudices, beginning in the late nineteenth century. The reach of these discriminatory laws was definitely *not* limited to the South, although that was where the worst abuses took place. Jim Crow laws saw to it that …

- Intermarriage was legally prohibited.

- Public accommodations had separate entrances and facilities for African American and white users. Very often, as in the case of restaurants and cinemas, African American citizens were simply prohibited access to white facilities.

- Business owners and educators who might otherwise have chosen to operate in a nondiscriminatory way were threatened with stiff fines if they chose to do so.

There were many other legal applications of segregationist ideals, but these were the most common and the most widely enforced.

A "colored only" entrance to a southern movie theatre.

(Judith Burros.)

What Jim Crow Was Designed to Do

The Jim Crow system's clear purpose was to offer constant and undeniable evidence that African Americans would be required by law to regard themselves as second-class citizens—forever. The true aim was not just the separation of the races (that was the expressed intention), but the long-term social and psychological intimidation of African Americans (the unexpressed—and still unspoken—intention).

Obstacles and Opportunities _____

Don't assume that the term *Jim Crow* refers only to legal measures. As a practical matter, the term "Jim Crow" refers to both the formal and informal dimensions of the program of disenfranchisement, discrimination, and public humiliation African Americans faced from about the 1880s on in the South and elsewhere in the United States.

The Constitution Gets an Overhaul: America Decides to Ignore It

Three Civil War amendments to the U.S. Constitution were meant to secure personal freedom and political rights for African Americans.

The Thirteenth Amendment formally prohibited slavery.

The Fourteenth Amendment defined American citizenship, required the states to honor the same due-process guarantees in criminal proceedings that were required of the federal government, and forbade the states to "deny to any person within its jurisdiction the equal protection of the laws."

The Fifteenth Amendment guaranteed that "the right of citizens of the United States to vote shall not be denied or abridged by the United States, or by any State, on account of race, color, or previous condition of servitude."

All three amendments were effectively undermined or flouted by social and legal machinations during the Jim Crow era. Many African Americans were slaves in all but name under the sharecropper system that emerged after the Civil War. Rights under the Fourteenth Amendment were steadily usurped by white-supremacist state legislatures, backed up by the U.S. Supreme Court. The African American right to vote was systematically voided in a variety of creative ways by white lawmakers and election officials.

Jim Crow's Forebears

The Jim Crow system—which is usually regarded as lasting from the 1880s to the time of the passage of federal civil rights legislation in the 1960s—was only the continuation of years of officially sanctioned racial segregation in the United States.

There were ample precedents for the laws and practices that took root in the South and elsewhere in the latter portion of the nineteenth century. Unlike some of its precursors, though, Jim Crow stuck around for quite a while.

 On the March

> The Black Codes, an important precursor to the Jim Crow laws, were in effect in the South immediately after the Civil War. They varied by state, but they typically forced recently "freed" slaves to work at specific occupations, set out penalties for unemployment, and regulated such issues as marriage and property rights. (South Carolina, for instance, required African American men to obtain a license and a certificate from a local judge if they planned to work at any other pursuit besides agriculture.)
>
> Federal officials overturned the Black Codes in 1866. Anyone who imagined that this step represented the end of the American legal system's abuse of African Americans, however, was in for disappointment.

The Rise of Jim Crow

To recap: For a brief period after the Civil War African Americans really did enjoy a taste of the rights promised them under the Thirteenth, Fourteenth, and Fifteenth

Amendments, and under federal laws like the Civil Rights Act of 1875. (This period was known as *Radical Reconstruction.*)

But, as you'll recall, powerful racist politicians, based both in the North and South, saw to it that the change was not a lasting one.

The Jim Crow period can be traced to the result of the bitterly disputed presidential election of 1876, which you'll recall from Chapter 6. After months of chaos, the outcome of the 1876 presidential election was finally determined in early 1877, thanks to the back-room deal that secured the White House for Rutherford B. Hayes and effectively ended Radical Reconstruction.

Thanks to works of fiction like *Gone with the Wind*, only one side's version of what happened during the period of Radical Reconstruction has really captured the popular imagination: the side that focuses on things like notorious, opportunistic Northern politicians and high taxes on Tara.

What was airbrushed over in Scarlett's story? A couple of minor details, including the first free exercise of the right to vote by African Americans in the United States, the establishment of a state-supported free school system, and the repeal of racially discriminatory state laws.

White southerners wouldn't stand for any of this. When it became clear that they couldn't win elections by making (implausible) promises to African American voters, they began a campaign of abuse and intimidation of African Americans that included, among other developments, the founding of the terrorist Ku Klux Klan group.

What's the Word?

The period of **Radical Reconstruction** refers to the time in southern history *after* the conclusion of the Civil War (1865), but *before* southern Democrats discontinued social and political reforms and began a broad program of systematic repression of African American southerners (roughly 1875). See Chapter 6.

What's the Word?

The Civil Rights Act of 1875 guaranteed the "full and equal enjoyment of the accommodations, advantages, facilities, and privileges of inns, public conveyances on land or water, theatres, and other places of public amusement … applicable alike to citizens of every race and color, regardless of any previous condition of servitude." The U.S. Supreme Court later declared the Act unconstitutional. Congress would remain silent on the question of civil rights for the better part of a century.

Customs and Traditions—of Terror

After the end of the era of Radical Reconstruction in 1877 came a long period of northern tolerance for overt discrimination and violence against African Americans, typically couched in language of respect for (white) southern customs.

It was in this period of national acquiescence to racist "traditions" that African Americans first encountered a new set of formal rules and regulations designed to perpetuate white supremacy.

For the laws of the Jim Crow era to function, the vast majority of white Americans, North and South, had to go along with them. They had to make a conscious choice to accept legally sanctioned racial prejudice, blatant electoral abuses, and the clear, deadly signals the laws sent that virtually any abuse of African Americans would probably go unpunished.

White America went along for the ride. In one way or another, of course, it had been doing so for years.

Jim Crow Cars

Among the earliest pieces of Jim Crow legislation were those regulating enforcing the segregation of railway facilities. Public segregation of transport facilities was a fact of life in the South by the turn of the century, and a good many states outside of the South adopted equally discriminatory measures.

There are some contemporary references to the South's "colored-only" railroad cars as "Jim Crow cars." These cars were often poorly lit, unbearably overheated, and overcrowded. Passengers were frequently forced to share space with farm animals; whisky-drinking white male passengers sometimes passed through the cars long enough to share foul language and abuse.

Many African Americans protested; an 1882 editorial, for instance, indignantly urged southern railway systems to "toe the mark of progress." But that mark was being moved—steadily and predictably—backward.

The Supreme Court Signs Off on Jim Crow

Before long, state legislatures had passed a wave of discriminatory laws. In 1896, the U.S. Supreme Court formally endorsed these laws with its decision in *Plessy* v. *Ferguson*, discussed in Chapter 6. The decision was a critical formal endorsement of the entire Jim Crow cultural and legal structure. Others would follow.

On the March

Before Rosa Parks, there was Homer Plessy, a Louisiana carpenter. As part of an intentional constitutional challenge against Louisiana segregation law, Plessy stepped onto a train on the seventh of June 1892, and took a seat in the whites-only car. He declined to give up his seat and was placed under arrest. His case eventually reached the U.S. Supreme Court, which held not only that Plessy had not been harmed by the Louisiana law, but also that state-mandated racial segregation did nothing whatsoever to brand African Americans "with a badge of inferiority."

Today, *Plessy* v. *Ferguson* is widely regarded as one of the lowest points in the long history of the Supreme Court. The decision would not be formally overturned for nearly 60 years.

Did the U.S. Supreme Court ever rule on the question of Jim Crow–era racial segregation in schools? Yes. In *Cumming* v. *County Board of Education* (1899), the court held that separate educational facilities were permissible, *even when no facilities at all were available to African American students.*

Reading Between the Lines

Not all the Jim Crow laws made specific reference to racial issues. Many relied on selective application and enforcement to send the message that African Americans were relegated to second-class status and denied the right to vote.

Plenty of laws *did* draw racial lines, however, and reviewing their provisions today is an experience that freezes the blood in the veins. Read them yourself—and ask yourself how it must have felt to live in the United States in the first half of the twentieth century, when statutes like the following were the "law of the land."

♦ "No colored barber shall serve as a barber [to] white women or girls."

♦ "Any person … who shall be guilty of printing, publishing, or circulating printed, typewritten or written matter urging or presenting for public acceptance or general information, arguments or suggestions in favor of social equality or of intermarriage between whites and Negroes, shall be guilty of a misdemeanor and subject to fine not exceeding five hundred (500.00) dollars or imprisonment not exceeding six months, or both."

♦ "The marriage of a person of Caucasian blood with a Negro, Mongolian, Malay, or Hindu shall be null and void."

FAQ

Where can you learn more about the Jim Crow era? An excellent place to start is with the boxed set of two CDs called *Remembering Jim Crow*, a superb oral history of the period published by Duke University and The New Press. You can find out more at www-cds.aas.duke.edu or call 1-800-233-4830.

♦ "All railroad companies and corporations, and all persons running or operating cars or coaches by steam on any railroad line or track … for the transportation of passengers, are hereby required to provide separate cars and coaches for the travel and transportation of the white and colored passengers."

♦ "Separate rooms (shall) be provided for the teaching of pupils of African descent, and (when) said rooms are so provided, such pupils may not be admitted to the school rooms occupied and used by pupils of Caucasian or other descent."

Now, it's certainly true that the southern states passed laws that denied civil rights to African Americans and discouraged social contact between whites and African Americans. The first example you just read—the law prohibiting the hands of African American barbers from coming into contact with the fair tresses of white maidens—was passed in Georgia. And the second example—the one that attempts to set a big, fat, land mine beneath the surface of the First Amendment and blow it to bits in the name of segregation—was passed in Mississippi.

It's also true, however, that Jim Crow laws were not limited to southern states. The three statutes that followed in the list above—the ones regulating marriage, railroad facilities, and classrooms—were passed in Arizona, Maryland, and New Mexico, respectively.

 On the March

In 1944, the author Gunnar Myrdal published a book called *An American Dilemma*; it shone a spotlight on the abuses of the Jim Crow laws, and made them something of an international spectacle. Then, in 1954, came the thunderclap: The Supreme Court finally overturned *Plessy*, ruling in *Brown* v. *Board of Education* that state segregation of public facilities violated the Fourteenth Amendment. (For more on this decision, see Chapter 10.)

These and other developments, notably an ongoing series of sit-ins, boycotts, marches, and other forms of public demonstration helped to bring an end to the era of formal legal discrimination against African Americans.

That such laws were not only passed, but maintained, supported, and enforced, speaks volumes about the lethally discriminatory social environment in the United States in the first half of the twentieth century. That environment, as much as the formal legal language of the day, was the essence of the Jim Crow period.

? **FAQ** _____

How long was Jim Crow the formal law of the land? The long and shameful period of legal acceptance of the Jim Crow system continued from 1896 until the middle of the next century. The ongoing legal challenges of the National Association for the Advancement of Colored People resulted in two decisions that weakened *Plessy* (*Sweatt* v. *Painter*, 1949, and *McLaurin* v. *Oklahoma*, 1950) and one that formally overturned it (*Brown* v. *Board of Education*, 1954).

Laws Are Laws, People Are People

The passing of the period of formal legal abuse of African Americans is significant … but it can't really be said to have ended the era of Jim Crow.

That's because Jim Crow, as we have seen, was not simply a series of legal maneuvers, but a way of life. Changing laws is one thing; changing the attitudes that made those laws possible is quite another.

A recent oral history project produced by American Radio Works, *Remembering Jim Crow*, proved this point beyond a shadow of a doubt. As the broadcast made clear, it is quite possible—*today*—to talk to elderly people who look back on America's apartheid years with a variety of rose-tinted nostalgia that borders on the surrealistic. (Not surprisingly, all these people are white.)

The way of thinking about human beings that made the Jim Crow period possible in the first place cannot, unfortunately, be overturned with a Supreme Court ruling or an act of Congress. And because that way of thinking persists—quietly but pervasively—in certain communities in white America, it is a sad but undeniable fact the Jim Crow era has not yet concluded in the United States.

African American Contributions

1881: Andrew Jackson Beard patents the first of his specially designed plows. Sixteen years later, he will sell a patent for a railroad-coupling mechanism for $50,000.

continues

---

continued

1883: Jan Earnst Matzeliger receives a patent for his "lasting machine," which dramatically increases shoe production and reduces costs by 50 percent.

1884: Granville T. Woods, the "black Edison," receives the first of his many patents. His most famous invention is probably the third rail, a system he developed to enable an electric train to operate without an internal engine.

1885: Samuel David Ferguson is ordained as a bishop in the Episcopal Church.

1893: Frances Ellen Watkins Harper publishes *Iola Leroy, or Shadows Uplifted.* The volume is among the first novels published by African American women.

1895: Josephine St. Pierre Ruffin helps to found the National Federation of Afro-American Women.

1896: Mary Church Terrell is one of the founders of the National Association of Colored Women.

The Least You Need to Know

♦ Jim Crow was not just a series of discriminatory laws, but a pattern of white supremacist customs.

♦ The seeds of the Jim Crow period were sown in the aftermath of the disputed 1876 presidential election, the resolution of which resulted in the end of Radical Reconstruction.

♦ Jim Crow laws set a racial double-standard with regard to access to public facilities, housing, business operations, and many other areas of life.

♦ Jim Crow laws and attitudes were most pronounced in the South, but were in place in many parts of the United States.

♦ Social protest and unrelenting legal challenges from the National Association of Colored People helped to bring an end to the period of officially sanctioned discrimination and abuse of African Americans.

♦ Jim Crow was a way of life, not just a series of legal measures; although the laws have been erased, nostalgia for the customs of the era still remain in some quarters of white America.

Chapter 8

The Great Migration

In This Chapter

- ◆ The exodus from the South
- ◆ What caused the migration
- ◆ What happened as a result of the migration

As popularly used, the term Great Migration describes the movement of millions of African American southerners to the West and North that began in the early part of the twentieth century. However, there were really several migrations that combined to make up a larger exodus.

On the Move

The Great Migration has been explained as "the movement of the Black Belt from the South to the North." This definition oversimplifies things some-what—there remained large numbers of African Americans in the South—but it captures the general idea, namely that hundreds of thousands of African Americans left the South for political, social, and economic reasons.

The first wave of migration occurred in the 1870s, when large numbers of African Americans migrated to Texas, Kansas, and other western areas to escape the negative aspects of living in the Deep South. Another quarter of a million African Americans moved to the North between 1890 and 1910, while about 35,000 moved to the Far West (California, Colorado, and so on). Some people think of these population movements as a precursor to the Great Migration itself.

The departures increased dramatically in the years between 1914 and 1929, the period generally assigned to the Great Migration. During these years between 300,000 and 1,000,000 others resettled in the North.

On the March

After emancipation … [the Great Migration was] the great watershed in American Negro history.

—August Meier, *Negro Thought in America, 1880-1915* (Ann Arbor: University of Michigan Press)

On the March

There were several great population shifts out of the South involving African Americans; different historians sometimes use varying terminology to describe the various components of the migrations.

In fact, what happened in the years between 1914 and 1929 laid the groundwork for a pattern that would continue for much of the century. African American migration from the South remained strong through the 1960s, except during the Great Depression, when the trend slowed for a time.

With the onset of World War II, however, the tempo picked up once again. Three million African Americans moved out of the South during Phase II, from 1941 to 1970. They were relocating, typically, to major cities in the Northeast and Midwest. Chicago was one of the most common destinations.

The African Americans who left their homes during these years hoped to find better jobs and a new sense of actual (as opposed to theoretical) citizenship. They were searching for natural human freedoms for themselves, their families, and their new communities in the North.

Causes

As you'll recall from Chapters 6 and 7, there were dramatic but short-lived changes in the political power of African Americans during the second half of the nineteenth century.

By 1877, you'll recall, whites had taken back all the political offices—and assumed control of all the South's political institutions. Remember, too, that, in 1896 the Supreme Court held that segregation laws were not forbidden by the Fourteenth Amendment, in the landmark case of *Plessy* v. *Ferguson*.

Thus, racial segregation became the norm; African Americans were restricted to "colored" facilities clearly inferior to those reserved for white citizens. The formal adoption of segregation as a way of life sent an impossible signal to white supremacists.

It can hardly be a coincidence that close to 3,000 African Americans are known to have been lynched in the South between 1892 and 1903.

African Americans and progressive whites persistently drew the media's attention to the practice of lynching from the early twentieth century onward, and anti-lynching campaigns were a major focus of early civil rights activists.

Almost 3,000 African Americans are known to have been lynched in the South between 1892 and 1903.

(Judith Burros)

On the March _____

Lynching—summary execution by a mob, typically by hanging—was a brutal practice used to maintain white social control in the American South. (The practice takes its name from the abrupt vigilante "trials" of Tories and offenders conducted by Colonel Charles Lynch during the Revolutionary War.) The aim of the "classic" southern lynch mobs was not so much to punish individual African Americans, but to instill fear in entire African American communities. Many lynchings went unrecorded, but the statistics we do have suggest that, between 1882 and 1968, white supremacists in Mississippi, Georgia, and Texas were the leading practitioners of ritualized terror against African Americans. Increased visibility and brutality of southern lynch mobs accompanied a rise in influence of the Ku Klux Klan and helped to persuade many African Americans to leave the South.

The African American Press Sounds Off

Abuses against African Americans were exposed in newspapers like the *Chicago Defender*, an African American journal that published articles exposing the blatant racism of white southerners, political oppression, and the perpetual threat of lynching.

 FAQ

Why was Chicago such an important part of the Great Migration? Chicago already had a vibrant (and comparatively well-off) African American community. It was also the site of publication of the nation's most widely read African American newspaper, the *Chicago Defender*, which lobbied tirelessly for migration from the South. These and other factors combined to make it an important destination for African Americans moving north.

Robert Sengstacke Abbott founded the *Defender* on May 6, 1905. He openly denounced "segregation, discrimination, [and] disenfranchisement" in the pages of his newspaper. The *Defender* also called for African Americans to leave the South for Chicago, and frequently provided contact information for churches and other groups readers could contact for help. Thousands of African American southerners made contact with northern churches as a result of Abbott's work.

With the onset of World War I, the *Defender* became more visible and influential than ever. A memorable 1917 headline read: "Millions to Leave South."

What's the Word?

The ***Chicago Defender*** was the most influential African American weekly in the nation in the early part of the twentieth century. Launched in 1905 by Robert S. Abbot in a crude format with an initial investment of 25 cents, the *Defender* eventually reached an estimated audience of 500,000; roughly two thirds of its audience lived outside Chicago. Abbott's paper was suppressed in parts of the South, but was smuggled in nevertheless by an underground network of African American readers.

In Search of a New Life

The combination of these newspaper reports with word-of-mouth advice, active recruiting by northern labor agents, and promises of free transportation made migration attractive to many. In 1910, the North and the South were so dissimilar that they could have been two different countries. The southern states were economically backward. They had fewer schools and higher rates of illiteracy than their northern counterparts, who also boasted cultural attractions and booming industries.

Also, new farm machinery was being created, equipment that could perform the field work faster and more efficiently. This drove thousands of poor tenant farmers off the land and toward the cities. In 1915, a severe boll weevil infestation destroyed millions of acres of cotton, along with the jobs of those who raised and picked it.

Migration also increased with the advent of World War I, in response to the large number of unskilled factory job openings as manufacturers boosted production for the war. The hostilities kept European laborers from emigrating to the United States to fill these positions.

Recruiting scouts sent to the South found their job easy (once they'd purchased the "recruitment licenses" required by southern state governments). There was no shortage of volunteers. However, many agents took advantage of these willing workers. They insisted that African American laborers sign harsh and unfair labor contracts requiring back-breaking work and yielding poor pay.

FAQ

What was the boll weevil? The boll weevil was a highly destructive insect that entered the United States from Mexico. It battered the southern economy in the period between 1910 and 1920 by inflicting vast amounts of damage on the region's cotton crops. Many African Americans in the South suffered grievously in the resulting economic downturn, and left the South to seek greater economic opportunity in the North.

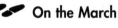 **On the March**

Growth of the African American population in northern cities was dramatic in the early part of the century. Indianapolis was typical: the number of African Americans in the city was just under 16,000 in 1900. By 1920, the figure was over 34,000. (Source: Indiana Historical Society.)

Key Events: The Great Migration

1883: The Supreme Court nullifies the Civil Rights Act of 1866.

1892: The Supreme Court upholds racial segregation; formulates "separate but equal" doctrine.

1900–1910: At least 846 lynchings are recorded; the vast majority of the victims are African Americans.

1915: The boll weevil wreaks havoc on agriculture in the South.

1917: United States enters World War I.

Effects of the Great Migration

Not surprisingly, the Great Migration had a big impact on the South. While W. E. B. DuBois saw the mass movement as the end of the South's old order of African American oppression, many white southerners took another view. "I do not know how the South can live without Negro labor," wailed one Georgia plantation owner. "It is the life of the South; it is the foundation of its prosperity."

On the March

Many southern whites concluded that any attempt to restrict freedom of movement was ill-advised. A number of leading southerners even argued that the wave of African American migration should initiate a campaign to improve the living conditions of southern African Americans.

Some progressive southerners tried to halt the migration by promising better pay and improved treatment. Other planters tried to keep African American workers by intimidation. Some whites even boarded northbound trains to attack African American men and women in an attempt to return them forcibly to their homes.

None of the enticements—benign or otherwise—could change the pattern. After centuries of abuse in the South, African Americans were (as the saying of a later era would have it) voting with their feet.

Demographic Shifts

The Great Migration changed the demographic structure of the nation. From the 1890s to the 1960s the African American population in the South fell from 90.3 percent to 60 percent; in the North, it grew from 9.7 percent to 34 percent. The percentage of African Americans living in the country plummeted from 90 percent to 27 percent, while the percentage of those living in cities soared from 10 percent to 73 percent.

On the March

Greater political power for African Americans was one obvious by-product of the Great Migration. Consider the case of Oscar DePriest, who left Alabama for Chicago and then embarked on a successful political career, winning seats on the county commission and the city council before winning election to the U.S. House of Representatives.

Changes and Challenges

African Americans turned to the "Promised Land" of the North in search of jobs and toleration, and many found them.

Unlike the South, the North was a place where African Americans could start their own businesses, live peacefully in their own neighborhoods, and even enjoy a measure of political power, provided they settled in the right cities and kept their expectations low. A fair number of those who had traveled to Chicago from the South eventually became successful entrepreneurs and prominent public figures in their new home.

It would be a mistake, however, to see the growth of the African American population in major northern cities as a spur to social unanimity among African Americans. There were sharp economic and educational divisions. Chicago's South Side "black belt," for instance, contained several neighborhoods demarcated by economic status. The poorest African Americans were to be found in the district's older, northern section; more prominent, established families resided in the southern section.

Dawn of the Urban Challenge

The Great Migration's dramatic expansion of African American communities in the North brought about urban tensions that have yet to be fully resolved.

Consider the case of Eugene Williams, who, on July 27, 1919, accidentally floated into a "whites-only" section of a public beach. A group of white men promptly murdered him; six days of horrific race riots followed, and 38 people died.

The Chicago race riots were not the first in the North in reaction to the Great Migration, and they would not be the last.

Obstacles and Opportunities

By 1921, a thriving African American commercial sector had emerged in Tulsa, Oklahoma. On June 1 of that year, an alleged assault by an African American man upon a white woman led to horrific civil unrest—and the systematic destruction by white rioters of the Greenwood District, which had come to be known as the "Black Wall Street." The riot was among the worst in American history; its human and economic impact has few parallels. Hundreds died, and losses ran into the millions (in 1921 dollars!).

They remain, however, among the most difficult to forget, in part because of the reporting of the *Chicago Defender*.

Bricks, Clubs, and an Oath

Monday morning found the thoroughfares in the white neighborhoods throated with a sea of humans—everywhere—some armed with guns, bricks, clubs and an oath. The presence of a black face in their vicinity was a signal for a carnival of death, and before any aid could reach the poor, unfortunate one his body reposed in some kindly gutter, his brains spilled over a dirty pavement. Some of the victims were chased, caught and dragged into alleys and lots, where they were left for dead. In all parts of the city, white mobs dragged from surface cars, African American passengers wholly ignorant of any trouble, and set upon them. An unidentified man, young woman and a 3 month old baby were found dead on the street at the intersection of 47th street and Wentworth avenue. She had attempted to board a car there when the mob seized her, beat her, slashed her body into ribbons and beat the Baby's brains out against a telegraph pole. Not satisfied with this, one rioter severed her breasts and a white youngster bore it aloft on pole, triumphantly, while the crowd hooted gleefully. All the time this was happening, several policemen were in the crowd, but did not make any attempt to make rescue until too late.

—*Chicago Defender* coverage of the 1919 race riots

A commission established to determine the causes of the carnage in Chicago found a series of urban problems that have stubbornly remained in American life in the years since. These problems included rigidly separated African American and white communities, substandard conditions and serious social challenges (including crime, substance abuse, vice, poverty, and broken homes) in the African American neighborhoods, and a legacy of alienation between African American and white sectors in the city.

In the years since the Great Migration, the same basic pattern has emerged in every major American city.

? **FAQ** _____

What was the Harlem Renaissance? This name describes a period of African American literary and artistic development, centered in New York City, that took place between the end of World War I and the middle 1930s. For more information on the Harlem Renaissance, see Chapter 18.

A Cultural Movement

When moving north, southern migrants did not forget to bring along their culture, which ultimately changed the environment of the northern cities. The songs and art that personified the Harlem Renaissance in New York City came with the Great Migration. Restaurants featured southern-style menus. Southern foods appeared in African American-owned groceries.

The Hard Reality of Life in the Cities

As with many attempts to locate the "Promised Land," the Great Migration had its share of disappointments.

For most migrants, the North was a step up from the South, but it was no paradise. As in the South, segregation in housing and hiring were the norm, and northern racism sometimes took on a brutality that equaled anything in Mississippi or Alabama. Most often, new arrivals could land only low-paying jobs as janitors, elevator operators, domestics, and unskilled laborers.

Often, employers established blatantly discriminatory promotional salary policies that kept wages down for African American workers. Many African American migrants opted to go on strike in order to secure better pay.

Every migrant lost something as soon as he or she boarded the train. Some left behind families and congregations. Others lost the respect of their southern relatives and ministers. However, despite the challenges, most of those who went north never returned.

On the March

The South was not alone in devising strategies for undercutting the civil rights of African Americans. White newspaper editorialists in the North regularly argued in favor of segregation of public facilities, voting restrictions, and laws against interracial marriages.

FAQ

What did the migration look like? In an extraordinary series of paintings, *The Great Migration,* the famous African American painter Jacob Lawrence illustrated the mass exodus of African Americans from the South. His parents were among those who migrated north. The paintings are now housed in the Museum of Modern Art in New York City.

African American Contributions

1903: W. E. B. DuBois publishes *The Souls of Black Folk.*

1909: Matthew Henson literally carries Robert E. Peary to the North Pole; the expedition captures the attention of the world, and Peary, rather than Henson, snags the biggest headlines.

1912: Garrett Augustus Morgan invents the gas mask, which was first used to protect firefighters. In 1925, he was granted the patent on a machine that now seems synonymous with the modern city: the traffic light.

1926: Dr. Carter G. Woodson launches Negro History Week.

The Least You Need to Know

- ◆ A massive wave of African American immigration from the South began in the first two decades of the twentieth century.

- ◆ Causes for this exodus included prolonged persecution of African Americans by white southerners, economic reversals in the South, and the demand for labor that followed American entry into World War I.

- ◆ The migration changed the demographic structure of the United States, giving rise to a heavy urban presence of African Americans in major cities.

- ◆ A pattern of racial alienation and social and economic inequity appeared in American cities in the wake of the migration; the pattern has persisted.

Chapter 9

A Challenge to a Nation

In This Chapter

◆ The conflict over social equality

◆ The rise of the NAACP

◆ Previews of struggles to come

In the five decades before the Reverend Martin Luther King Jr. led the 1954 Montgomery, Alabama, bus boycott—and helped launch what is now seen as the modern American civil rights movement—an earlier generation of African Americans bravely challenged racist institutions and practices north and south. These people made significant strides in defense of the rights of African American citizens, and their work on a number of fronts made the later campaigns of Dr. King and others possible.

In this chapter, you learn about some of the visionaries who issued prominent challenges to contemporary racial practices in America in the first half of the twentieth century. It was during this period that a great chorus of African American dissenting voices began, slowly at first, but with increasing momentum, to win both national notice and moral force.

The Great Debate: Social Equality

A driving force in the movement that arose in the early twentieth century in the United States was the conflict over the issue of seeking social equality for the group then known as "the Negro race." Two giants—Booker T. Washington and W. E. B. DuBois—took opposing views.

W. E. B. DuBois.

(Source: Library of Congress)

On the March

Shortly after the founding of the NAACP in 1909, three other groups merged to form the National Urban League. This new organization focused on the many challenges and obstacles faced by African Americans in U.S. cities. The Urban League's first executive secretary was Eugene Kinckle Jones.

The debate between the two men was an illuminating one. What we now know is that, in a capital-driven society, social equality without economic parity is impossible. In retrospect, we can conclude that both Washington and DuBois were right. DuBois's movement eventually gained prominence, but history supports Washington's viewpoint, and the argument continues today: social integration versus economic (self)-sufficiency.

For DuBois and for other African American leaders, the idea of accepting legal and social distinctions rooted in race was deeply offensive, as was the suggestion that work to overcome racial discrimination should be put off until some future state of African American economic influence emerged. In 1905, DuBois and William Monroe Trotter founded a group that came to be known as the Niagara Movement (so named because the group had been convened at an organizational meeting held near Niagara Falls). It was dedicated to the abolition of all racially discriminatory practices in the United States.

On the March

The great educator Booker T. Washington—founder of the now-famous Tuskegee Institute (in 1881)—argued persuasively that industrial training was a powerful resource in building economic self-sufficiency and a sense of self-respect among African Americans. He promoted a rigorous program of education in what would today be called the blue-collar professions. Washington drew intense criticism from African American thinkers, however, for his opinion on social equality: He argued that it was inappropriate for African Americans to struggle for social parity with whites before having achieved economic equality. The Harvard-educated writer and civil rights activist W. E. B. DuBois, among many others, ridiculed this approach, and insisted that a forceful campaign for social equality had to be a high priority for African Americans.

Three years later, following a race riot in Springfield, Illinois, DuBois' group of African American intellectuals decided to broaden their movement. They began reaching out to a number of like-minded whites, and eventually launched—on February 12, 1909, the one-hundredth anniversary of Abraham Lincoln's birth—a new organization dedicated to promoting racial equality, opposing segregation, and seeking justice for those who perpetrated racially motivated violence.

They called their new group the National Association for the Advancement of Colored People, or NAACP.

Organized Legal Action and Protest

The founding of the NAACP was, of course, a milestone in African American history, and in U.S. race relations. The group's founding approach—African Americans and whites uniting in opposition to discriminatory laws and social practices—proved popular, and the NAACP expanded rapidly. Its first meeting had been attended by just 53 people; within two years it boasted chapters in Chicago, Boston, and New York; a magazine, the *Crisis*, founded in 1910 and edited until 1932 by W. E. B. DuBois, became a national platform for civil rights issues.

? **FAQ**

What is the NAACP's dominant philosophy for securing legal and social advances for African Americans? The organization has consistently promoted nonviolent protest and the escalation of civil rights challenges within the existing American legal system. Over the years, the NAACP has drawn criticism from some corners for avoiding a more militant approach in addressing racial issues in the United States—but it has maintained its approach nonetheless.

A side note: There is, in various corners of the African American community, some disillusionment with today's NAACP; it's worth observing here that this disillusionment is often connected with the organization's undelivered promise of economic parity through social equality. Many feel that Booker T. Washington was, in fact correct: Social validation, in the final analysis, really is a byproduct of self-sufficiency.

Before *Brown* v. *Board of Education*

For many people, the NAACP is synonymous with legal action in such landmark civil rights cases as the 1954 *Brown* v. *Board of Education* case, which forbade segregation in public schools. The case was argued successfully by NAACP attorney (and future Supreme Court Justice) Thurgood Marshall. In the important decades before *Brown* was decided, however, the NAACP consistently challenged racial violence, injustice, and stereotyping on many fronts.

Here's a brief sampling of some of the struggles the organization undertook in its early years:

◆ **1910 onward: The organization mounted an increasingly vocal campaign to increase public awareness of lynchings in the south.** The NAACP was also a tireless advocate of anti-lynching legislation in the first half of the century. Considering the tendency of white lawmakers in Congress to ignore or *filibuster* laws providing for punishment of this particular brand of hate crime, the NAACP *had* to be tireless. An anti-lynching measure that had made it through the House of Representatives in 1922 was defeated by means of a filibuster led by southern senators; a proposal for a 1934 anti-lynching bill was shelved by the (supposedly progressive) New Deal administration of Franklin Roosevelt. The NAACP's persistent protest and lobbying efforts against lynching were, however, sustained and impossible to ignore. These efforts were a major factor in the eventual wave of national revulsion that helped to bring a long-overdue decline in this bloody southern "tradition."

What's the Word? _____

To **filibuster** is to indefinitely prolong "debate" about a given bill or measure that you do not have the votes to defeat on an up-or-down vote. Lawmakers engage in filibusters in the hope that their opponents will eventually withdraw the measure under discussion. For much of the twentieth century, white supremacist southern senators used the filibuster—a seemingly endless series of random speeches that continue until a motion to conclude debate is carried—to derail proposed anti-lynching legislation, voting rights bills, and many other measures.

- ◆ **1915: The NAACP protested against showings of the racist film *Birth of a Nation*.** The film's crude racial stereotypes and depiction of gallant white Confederate patriots overshadowed its technical innovations. Then as now, the organization spoke out against demeaning media stereotypes of African Americans and their lifestyles.

- ◆ **1917 onward: The NAACP helped to coordinate huge nonviolent mass protests**. One notable example was as the silent march in New York of ten thousand African Americans, which took place in this year. The event was held in protest of racially motivated violence, abuse, and discrimination.

- ◆ **1930: The NAACP made headlines with its loud opposition to racist judiciary appointments.** In this year, the organization challenged President Hoover's appointment of North Carolina Judge John J. Parker to the Supreme Court and launched a nationwide protest campaign. The nomination failed.

- ◆ **1933: The NAACP initiated a fateful challenge to the legality of segregation.** In a preview of later legal battles, the organization brought suit against the University of North Carolina for denying admission to Thomas Hocutt. The suit was unsuccessful, but it formed the NAACP's first move in a comprehensive legal assault on segregated public institutions and state-sanctioned discriminatory policies.

- ◆ **1936: The NAACP challenged unequal salary structures for African American teachers.** In a Maryland lawsuit, the organization initiated what would ultimately be a successful legal challenge to radically differing, racially discriminatory pay scales for public school teachers. Ironically, when white Southerners argued in favor of maintaining segregated school systems in the 1950s, they used the NAACP's victory on behalf of previously underpaid African American teachers as evidence that segregated school systems are inherently equal institutions.

◆ **1939: The NAACP's Legal Defense and Educational Fund was born.** The new outfit, headed by attorney Thurgood Marshall, was the launching-point for the most important civil rights cases of the century.

◆ **1941: The NAACP elevated its media skills to high art.** The Daughters of the American Revolution—an elite women's organization for descendants of those who helped win the Revolutionary War—announced that African American singer Marian Anderson would be forbidden from singing at Constitution Hall. NAACP leaders decided to make the most of the snub. They worked with First Lady Eleanor Roosevelt and Secretary of the Interior Harold Ickes to win approval from President Franklin Roosevelt for Anderson to give a free concert at the Lincoln Memorial. FDR loved the idea, and the NAACP had one of its most stirring public relations triumphs. Seventy-five thousand people showed up—among them some of the most prominent politicians, jurists, and diplomats in the country—to hear Anderson give a performance that is still regarded as incomparable. The leadership of the Daughters of the American Revolution, and racists everywhere, managed to look heartless … not to mention easily outmaneuvered in the court of public opinion.

 On the March _____

Eleanor Roosevelt gave up her membership in the Daughters of the American Revolution (DAR) when the group refused to permit the famed African American singer Marian Anderson to sing at Constitution Hall. The incident—and Anderson's later triumphant concert at the Lincoln Memorial—won sympathy and national acclaim for the African American cause … and a public relations nightmare for the DAR. (Of course, the incident also exposed supremacist elements within the highest levels of American society.)

◆ **1942 onward: The NAACP lobbied on behalf of African American servicemen.** African Americans in the American armed services faced systematic abuse and discrimination. Many were court-martialed unjustly. The NAACP's Legal Defense and Educational Fund worked to get racially motivated convictions overturned; where this was impossible, members sought to win more lenient sentences for victims of military racism.

A National Disgrace

Total reported number of lynchings in the United States for representative years, drawn from government figures:

1890: 85	1910: 67
1895: 113	1915: 56
1900: 106	1920: 53
1905: 57	

Terrorists, of course, did not go out of the way to bring their activities to the attention of law enforcement officials. (Leave aside, for the moment, the fact that many of the terrorists were government officials.) The actual number of lynchings in any of these years was certainly far higher than the number of those reported.

Other Voices, Other Challenges

The voices of the leaders and members of the NAACP were not, of course, the only voices raised in challenge to racial policies in the United States in the first half of the century. Other important events are detailed in this section.

Marcus Garvey's "Back to Africa" Movement

Marcus Garvey, a passionate and committed black nationalist, was born in Jamaica. He founded, in 1914, an organization he called the Universal Negro Improvement Association (UNIA); its aim was to promote solidarity among blacks and celebrate without apology the significant achievements of African history and culture.

Garvey was impatient with any notion that racial integration could be successful in the United States, or indeed in any nation where blacks did not constitute a majority of the population. He promoted a "back to Africa" vision that drew

 On the March

W. E. B. DuBois, like Marcus Garvey, sought to foster solidarity of blacks from many nations. In 1919, DuBois organized the second Pan-African Congress, which took place in Paris. In his later years (he died in Ghana, West Africa, in 1963), he embraced the global black liberation movement, among other causes.

both enthusiastic crowds and cynical opponents from within the African American community, most notably from the DuBois-led NAACP.

Marcus Garvey.

(Source: Library of Congress)

Garvey's nationalist movement and exuberant rhetoric won him a major following, and he was probably the most prominent African American leader in the country in the early 1920s. Many suspected (and Garvey insisted) that dark governmental forces were behind his later imprisonment for mail fraud; the conviction arose from accusations of participation in financial irregularities related to an all-black steamship firm, the Black Star Steamship Line, he had launched.

The company's three ships made travel and trade possible between their United States, Caribbean, Central American, and African stops. The economically independent Black Star Line was a symbol of pride for blacks and seemed to attract more members to the UNIA. Early in 1922 Garvey was convicted of mail fraud and given a maximum sentence of five years at the Atlanta federal penitentiary by Judge Julian Mack, also a NAACP member.

Whatever the truth behind the manipulations that led to his legal troubles, Garvey's movement faltered after he was deported to Jamaica in 1927 upon his release from prison. He never regained the public influence he had earlier enjoyed as a spellbinding public speaker and editor of the influential newspaper *Negro World.* However, in the United States Garveyism became central to the development of the African American consciousness and freedom movements of 1960s.

Because of his courage, his pride, his tenacity, his gift for oratory, and his relentless insistence on the autonomy, dignity, and beauty of his people, Marcus Garvey has often been cited as a precursor to the 1960s African American leader Malcolm X. Interestingly, Malcolm was born in the same year Garvey's movement began its nosedive, 1925.

Pickets During the Depression

Shortly after the stock market crash of 1929, an African American protest movement against stores that refused to hire African American staff arose in Chicago. Picket lines quickly spread to other major cities. The protesters' powerful slogan: "Don't Buy Where You Can't Work."

The operation continued, doggedly, for the duration of the Great Depression. Economic issues were of keen importance to African American communities in the troubled years following the crash; by 1937, it was estimated that over one quarter of all African American males were unable to find work.

The pickets were a portent of public protests to come.

The National Negro Congress

In 1936, delegates from over 500 different African American groups gathered in Chicago and formed the National Negro Congress, an umbrella group that would yield considerable political clout in the years to come. The group selected Asa Phillip Randolph, head of the Brotherhood of Sleeping Car Porters, as its first president.

Having successfully made the transition from "black labor leader" to "black leader," the energetic Randolph soon proved was not shy about making life difficult for white politicians. He was, in particular, a thorn in the side of President Franklin Delano Roosevelt, whose level of political commitment to the civil rights movement at that time could perhaps be described as "all talk unless absolutely forced to take action."

Randolph's determination—and, in particular, his obvious willingness to call a 100,000-person

 **On the March**

In the relationship between Randolph and Roosevelt, there emerged a new dynamic in American political life: persistent, face-to-face African American lobbying for White House concessions on matters of importance to the African American community. That pattern has continued to this day.

July 4 march on Washington that would have embarrassed the Roosevelt White House—led to a concession: an executive order forbidding racial discrimination in government projects and defense industries. The march was called off. A later president, John F. Kennedy, would attempt, without success, to get African American leaders to call off the 1963 March on Washington; when they refused, he made the best of the situation by insisting that he was in agreement with its aims.

The (Other) Bus Boycott

Long before the 1954 boycott of buses in Montgomery, Alabama, made national headlines, African Americans in New York City won concessions from a city transit system committed to racist practices. The year was 1941, and the issue was whether New York's bus companies would employ African American drivers and mechanics. African Americans stayed off city buses for four weeks, at which point the bus companies agreed to change their hiring practices.

CORE Is Born

In 1942, James Farmer founded the Congress of Racial Equality, better known as CORE. The group was devoted to nonviolent campaigns of "direct action" against racially discriminatory practices in public places, housing, and other settings. Although the group would win national attention in the early 1960s for its courageous Freedom Rides through the segregated south, its early campaigns were in the north. A 1942 sit-in, for instance, took place at the segregated Stoner's Restaurant in Chicago.

Two Calls for Change

By the time the mid-1940s rolled around, white America received two more challenges. They had far more in common than may have appeared at the time.

A Call for Change on the Diamond

In the spring of 1947, Jackie Robinson was called up from the Brooklyn Dodgers' minor league club in Montreal to try out for a spot on the big-league club's roster. He made the team, and posted a season that was as remarkable for its social implications as it was for its on-field excellence. A truly gifted athlete, and one of the most courageous Americans of the twentieth century, Robinson was due some respect. He rarely got it during a rookie season marred by crude outbursts (and worse) from racist teammates, opponents, and fans.

Robinson was not, as some have mistakenly assumed, the first African American player in the major leagues. (There was a small but visible number of African Americans in major league baseball in the 1880s and 1890s, notably a superb catcher by the name of Moses Fleetwood Walker.) Robinson was, however, something far more important than the first African American to play major league ball. He was the man who consciously demolished baseball's "gentleman's agreement" color line, a hypocritical form of on-the-field apartheid whose very existence was denied for half a century by the white baseball establishment.

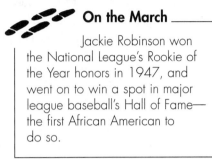

On the March

Jackie Robinson won the National League's Rookie of the Year honors in 1947, and went on to win a spot in major league baseball's Hall of Fame—the first African American to do so.

Baseball's shameful color line was not a "natural" occurrence; like all expressions of race hatred, it had to be invented by human beings and implemented by human beings. It was the handiwork, at least in its earliest days, of a virulently racist player-manager for the National League's Chicago White Stockings by the name of Cap Anson. It was Anson who, in the 1890s, declared that "gentlemen [did] not play baseball with niggers."

Enough whites went along with the idea for it to gain momentum—and for athletes like Josh Gibson, Satchel Paige, and scores of other gifted African American ballplayers to be denied the chance to exercise their talents at the highest level.

By 1947, Jackie Robinson—and millions of other African Americans—had had enough.

A Call for Change in the American Mind

Having served three years in the Army, including over a year in combat in the South Pacific, Isaac Woodward was, like the big-league prospect then toiling in the minor leagues, due some respect. Like Jackie Robinson, he wouldn't get it.

In 1946, by taking an unacceptably long time at a South Carolina rest stop, Woodward apparently annoyed the white driver of the Army bus he had been riding. The driver reported him to the police.

Not much later, the veteran who had served his country so honorably somehow found himself on the receiving end of a vicious beating. The blows to the face left Woodward permanently blind.

Woodward's plight received national publicity, thanks to the efforts of the NAACP—which used the travesty to lobby, once again, for effective civil rights laws. The African American soldier's suffering constitutes an important (and under-recognized) moment in African American history—in its way, as important as Robinson's breakthrough. Where Robinson would engender African American pride, Woodward's experience was emblematic of the unjust suffering of an entire people. It also served to symbolize the new African American dissatisfaction—a sense that enough was enough—that took root in the postwar period.

Millions of African American men had served in World War II in the defense, supposedly, of equality and democratic ideals. They returned home to find the same tired prejudices and social obstacles in place. And they were angry about it.

Membership in the NAACP skyrocketed after the war. A feeling arose in African American communities that more than enough time had passed, that more than enough wrongs had been endured, and that something actually had to change in the minds, and courtrooms, and public places of the United States of America.

African American Contributions

1925: Malcolm Little (later to be known as Malcolm X) is born in Omaha, Nebraska. He will rise to prominence as a fiery orator and an uncompromising voice for African American autonomy and dignity.

1927: Duke Ellington plays for the first time at the Cotton Club.

1929: Martin Luther King Jr. is born in Atlanta, Georgia. He will become the most important civil rights activist of the century.

1934: Claude Harvard, a Ford Motor Company engineer, invents an automated system for inspecting piston pins; Henry Ford arranges for Harvard to demonstrate the system at the 1934 Century of Progress Exposition in Chicago, Illinois.

1940: Dr. Charles Drew is named medical director of England's wartime plasma project. Drew eventually develops revolutionary techniques for preserving blood, and establishes the first blood bank, thus saving countless English and American lives during the Second World War, and laying the foundation for the modern blood bank system. Drew eventually becomes director of the American Red Cross.

1949: Frederick McKinley Jones receives patents for portable air conditioners he invented for traveling cargo vehicles (such as railcars and trucks).

The Least You Need to Know

♦ Booker T. Washington and W. E. B. DuBois differed sharply on the issue of whether African Americans should seek social equality with whites.

♦ Washington felt it was futile to do so before African Americans had developed economic autonomy; DuBois and others argued that the struggle for social equality couldn't wait.

♦ DuBois helped to found the National Association for the Advancement of Colored People (NAACP) in 1909; it became the nation's leading civil rights organization.

♦ Other voices calling for change in the first half of the century in the United States included that of the black nationalist Marcus Garvey.

♦ A pronounced change in attitude followed the conclusion of the Second World War; African Americans were impatient for change, and they joined the NAACP in large numbers.

Chapter 10

The Modern Civil Rights Movement

In This Chapter

- ◆ The importance of *Brown* v. *Board of Education*
- ◆ The courage of Rosa Parks
- ◆ The steadfastness and commitment of Martin Luther King Jr.
- ◆ The Civil Rights Act of 1964
- ◆ The impact of Bloody Sunday
- ◆ Remembering those who paid the ultimate price

Although years of struggle and agitation for progress had come before-hand, and much of consequence would follow in later years, the most critical phase of the U.S. civil rights movement occurred in just 14 years.

This tumultuous phase in American life occupied the decade and a half between two events of seismic social importance. The first of these events was the landmark Supreme Court ruling in *Brown* v. *Board of Education*; the second was the April 4, 1968, assassination of the Rev. Martin Luther

King Jr. These events were fitting beginning and ending points for an era that delivered both exquisite hope and exquisite agony.

The Federal Government

The landmark *Brown* decision signaled the intention of the federal government to live up to the promises of its own Constitution—and, by extension, to encourage the development of a new kind of country, with new priorities. The decision also highlighted the difference between legal victory and tangible social change.

The King assassination highlighted some of the more sickening risks of trying to remake the country's racial attitudes, and it also galvanized huge groups of Americans who might not have come together under other circumstances to express a shared moral outrage at racial violence.

A complete discussion of each of these events could occupy several books this size, and any attempt to capture all the important events of the intervening years in a single chapter is probably doomed to failure. The purpose of this part of the book is not to deliver the final word on the African American experience during the fateful period between 1954 and 1968, but simply to give you an introduction to the period and help you become familiar with some of the chief events.

If what follows encourages you to learn more on your own, this chapter will have served its purpose. See the appendixes for lists of books and websites that will tell you more about this remarkable period in American history.

> **On the March**
>
> Free at last, free at last. Thank God Almighty, we are free at last.
>
> —Rev. Martin Luther King Jr., citing a traditional African American hymn during his address at the August 1963 March on Washington

Time for a Change

Challenging racial prejudice in the United States in the 1950s was a daunting undertaking. While African Americans, in the main, again bore the brunt of the backlash, no single person, group, or institution put civil rights on the national agenda, and no one person, group, or institution saw to it that it stayed on the national agenda. Stay it did.

The changes in attitude and law that did occur came about as the result of a shared commitment from many, many people to take risks, highlight injustice, and press the cause for change. That commitment was not an easy one to make.

Reproduction of a segregationist flyer from the 1950s

(Source: Judith Burros)

It is easy to forget, in today's era of more cautious and covert discrimination, that the choice to add one's voice to the chorus for change was a choice that could—and not infrequently did—result in death. But those were the stakes between the years 1954 and 1968 in the United States of America.

Tens of thousands of people of all races risked not just their standing in the community, but also their lives, in the hope of building a coalition for racial equality that could not possibly be ignored. They succeeded in building that coalition—even if the highest ideals of the cause they promoted remain, in some cases, unfulfilled. (That may simply be the nature of high ideals.)

Activism for Equal Opportunity

The Movement (as it came to be known) was peopled not only by courageous African Americans, but also by college students and religious leaders of many races.

These activists employed the tactics of legal challenges, civil protests (including sit-ins, marches, and freedom rides), and other initiatives in their efforts to see that African Americans received equal opportunity and protection in the United States.

The Nonviolent Ideal

Not all who agitated for racial equality between 1954 and 1968 did so in the hope of promoting nonviolent social change. A significant portion of the civil rights movement was, however, devoted to the idea of peaceful challenges, rather than bloody resistance or attack, to change racist institutions.

A key factor in the success of the civil rights movement was the choice that radicalized African American organizations offered to cautiously slow-moving governmental policy-makers: the rhetoric of "Black Power" or the pacifism of Martin Luther King Jr.; the street rage of Malcolm X or the theology of Reverend King. Policy makers chose the leader representing peaceful change.

The primary advocate for this approach was Dr. Martin Luther King Jr. Two of King's major historical influences were Henry David Thoreau and Mahatma Gandhi. Thoreau had argued, in *Civil Disobedience*, that if enough people openly disobeyed unjust laws, those laws would fall. Gandhi had followed much the same approach in launching his "peaceful revolution" against British rule in India.

There were many components of the struggle for civil rights; the following events are some of the highlights.

Dr. Martin Luther King Jr.

(Source: Judith Burros)

Brown v. Board of Education

On May 17, 1954, the Supreme Court declared in a unanimous decision that the board of education of Topeka, Kansas, had to admit four African American children to a previously all-white school.

Overturning the "separate but equal" doctrine adopted in 1896 in *Plessy* v. *Ferguson*, the Court declared that "separate educational facilities are inherently unequal" and, as such, violate the Fourteenth Amendment to the U.S. Constitution, which guarantees all citizens "equal protection of the laws." The ruling, the result of years of work by the NAACP, had the impact of a lightning strike.

On the March

Thurgood Marshall was a giant figure in the American civil rights movement. He was legal director of the NAACP and lead attorney in the landmark *Brown* v. *Board of Education* case. Marshall was named to the Supreme Court in 1967 by President Lyndon Johnson, thereby becoming the first African American in history to sit on the high court. He was a member of the court for 24 years.

Thurgood Marshall.

(Source: Library of Congress)

The *Brown* ruling paved the way for large-scale desegregation—although it certainly did not bring desegregation about overnight. The winning attorney for the National Association for the Advancement of Colored People was Thurgood Marshall, who later became the nation's first African American justice of the Supreme Court.

> **Inherently Unequal**
>
> We conclude that in the field of public education the doctrine of 'separate but equal' has no place. Separate educational facilities are inherently unequal. Therefore, we hold that the plaintiffs and others similarly situated for whom the actions have been brought are, by reason of the segregation complained of, deprived of the equal protection of the laws guaranteed by the Fourteenth Amendment.
>
> —Chief Justice Earl Warren, in *Brown* v. *Board of Education* (1954)

Rosa Parks Takes a Ride

Worn out after a hard day's work, NAACP member and Montgomery, Alabama, resident Rosa Parks refused to give up her seat at the front of a public bus to a white passenger on December 1, 1955. According to law and long-established custom, African Americans were supposed to sit in the back of public buses. Police arrested Parks when she flaunted the law and the custom.

The Rosa Parks incident was, however, in no way spontaneous. Parks was part of a trained-for-civil-disobedience cadre of civil rights workers; her action was part of a pre-planned strategy to call attention to southern separatist policies. Rosa Parks was certainly not the first to refuse to obey such laws, or to be arrested for refusing.

On the March

Dr. Martin Luther King Jr., who had followed in his father and grandfather's footsteps to become a Baptist minister, helped organize the boycott of public transit in Montgomery, Alabama. It lasted for over a year and ultimately changed the law mandating segregated buses in Montgomery. In 1957, the Southern Christian Leadership Conference (SCLC) was born, and King was its first president. Later that year, he led a march of 57,000 people on the Lincoln Memorial, and emerged as the clear leader of the growing movement to win civil and legal equality for African Americans. In 1964, Dr. King received the Nobel Peace Prize.

Her case was, however, the cause for a new kind of reaction from the community. In response to Parks's arrest, African American leaders launched a bus boycott.

Thousands of African Americans walked to and from work, school, and errands for more than a year, until the city capitulated and the buses were desegregated. A young preacher from the area, the Rev. Martin Luther King Jr., was instrumental in the action's success.

The Little Rock Nine

The eventful year of 1957 saw a number of extraordinary events—among them, the founding of the Southern Christian Leadership Conference (SCLC) and King's early march on Washington. But the most remarkable events in the civil rights realm took place in Little Rock, Arkansas.

Arkansas governor Orval Faubus defied a federal court order to integrate the all-white Central High School in Little Rock, in accordance with the Supreme Court's ruling in *Brown* v. *Board of Education*. In fact, he called out the Arkansas National Guard to prevent the admission of nine African American students who had been carefully selected to be the first to integrate the school.

President Dwight Eisenhower was forced to send 1,000 paratroopers and federalize 10,000 members of the Arkansas National Guard to protect the students and uphold the law. When the students were duly admitted on September 25, 1957, a clear message was sent that the federal government would physically, as well as legally, support integration.

The Sit-Ins Begin

What would turn out to be a major, and highly effective, civil rights tactic made its debut on February 1, 1960, when four African American students from North Carolina Agricultural and Technical College in Greensboro sat down at a segregated lunch counter in Woolworth's Five and Dime and placed their orders. In so doing, they were breaking the law.

A crowd of white teenagers poured drinks on their heads and shouted obscenities. However, the students hung in. *The New York Times* covered the incident, which drew national attention.

Over the next few days, the four were joined by other students, white as well as African American. Soon there were similar nonviolent protests all over the South.

"The United States was not going to continue like it was …"

We did Woolworth's, McLellan's, Kress's, W.T. Grant. The theory was, "If you're going to live on us, you're going to be fair with us." Pretty quickly, Kress's goes out of business … Other stores began to change. Hudson Belk had the Capital Room Restaurant, which desegregated. K&W Cafeteria downtown changed …. (Eventually,) there was total agreement that the United States was not going to continue like it was on the race issue. Either they were going to be prepared to kill us all or something had to give. That time had come.

—The Reverend David Forbes of Raleigh, North Carolina, recalling his activity in the sit-in campaigns of the 1960s; quoted in the Southern Oral History Program (www.sohp.org).

The Freedom Rides

In the spring of 1961, the Congress of Racial Equality (CORE) set out to test the implementation of laws requiring the integration of interstate public transportation. Gathering groups of student volunteers and clergy, they sent them on bus trips through the south. Bigoted Alabamans set one bus on fire.

Police-instigated violence was common during the Civil Rights demonstrations in the south during the 1960s.

(Source: Judith Burrows)

However, by September, over a thousand "freedom riders" had participated in the effort, which was widely covered by the media.

James Meredith and Ole Miss

Although *Brown* v. *Board of Education* had been tested at the high school level, a successful challenge at the collegiate level had not yet been made in 1962. James Meredith took that challenge on when he tried to register at the University of Mississippi in Oxford in 1962.

President John F. Kennedy ordered him protected by federal marshals. The marshals safeguarded Meredith but could not control a huge riot that broke out, resulting in the deaths of two students. It took the National Guard to restore order and see Meredith enrolled.

On the March

Stokely Carmichael was one of the most important African American activists of the 1960s. He was chairman of the Student Nonviolent Coordinating Committee (SNCC), which drew support from a younger, and eventually more militant, group of activists than were found in Dr. Martin Luther King's Southern Christian Leadership Conference. Carmichael, who had long maintained a close relationship with Dr. King, nevertheless insisted on SNCC's independence, and eventually differed with him on fundamental issues (such as alliances with white liberals). Carmichael's emphasis on "Black Power," and his insistence that nonviolence need not be the guiding philosophy of the movement led to a rift with King. Carmichael eventually served as an official within the Black Panther Party and later advocated an international program of African liberation.

Medgar Evers Murdered

One of the darkest days in the civil rights movement's history occurred when one Byron De La Beckwith, a white racist, gunned down Medgar Evers, Mississippi's NAACP field secretary, on the doorstep of his Jackson, Mississippi, home. The charismatic 37-year-old leader died in his wife's arms as his children looked on and De La Beckwith sped away.

It took three trials and 30 years to put De La Beckwith in prison.

"I Have a Dream"

Rev. Martin Luther King Jr. gave his most famous speech at the August 28, 1963, March on Washington. Speaking from the Lincoln Memorial to a crowd of some 300,000 civil rights advocates of all ages and races, his largely improvised remarks were to become his most famous words: "I have a dream today …"

The Sixteenth-Street Bombing

Barely two weeks after King articulated his impassioned vision of peace, a bomb exploded at the Sixteenth Street Baptist Church in Birmingham, Alabama, during Sunday school. Four young African American girls died instantly.

Riots erupted in the city as African Americans expressed their anger. It wasn't until 2002 that the last of the suspects was convicted.

Freedom Summer, 1964

In the summer of 1964 civil rights groups banded together in a massive effort to register African American voters in Mississippi.

They sent college students and others all over the south knocking on doors. Some southern whites objected to what they called "outside agitators." On June 21 three young civil rights workers, one African American and two white, disappeared. Their bodies were found buried in a dam only after President Lyndon Johnson sent Army soldiers to look for them. (See "Remembering Those Who Paid the Ultimate Price" later in this chapter.)

> **On the March**
>
> The Civil Rights Act of 1964 prohibits discrimination in federally assisted government programs and protects the constitutional rights of people of *all races* in public facilities and public education.

Making the most of the legacy of the assassinated John F. Kennedy, President Lyndon Johnson signed the Civil Rights Act of 1964 into law, making segregation in public facilities and discrimination in employment illegal.

The Other Side of the Coin

While the majority of activists joined with white supporters in pursuing a course of litigation, sit-ins, and other nonviolent efforts, other forces were also at work. These were *separatists*, advocates of violent change, or both.

Stokely Carmichael radicalized the Student Nonviolent Coordinating Committee (SNCC). In Oakland, California, Bobby Seale and Huey Newton organized the Black Panthers to provide community services, breakfasts for the poor and elderly, educational programs; patrol African American neighborhoods; and monitor police treatment of people of color. They dressed in uniforms of black berets and leather jackets and were heavily armed. Their platform, known as the Manifesto (What We Need, What We Want), outlined the demands of a now radicalized African American citizenry.

What's the Word? _____

A **separatist** is someone who advocates the formal separation of racial or cultural groups.

You can find the Manifesto at: http://www.cla.wayne.edu/polisci/krause/Comparative/SOURCES/blackpanther.htm.

The charismatic preacher Malcolm X was converted to the Nation of Islam and the teachings of Elijah Muhammad while he was in prison. He was initially a black nationalist and separatist.

Malcolm X founded the Organization of Afro-American Unity, dedicated to promoting and supporting the notion of "Black Pride." After he broke with the Nation of Islam in 1965, and after declaring that he favored a more integrated vision for African Americans, Malcolm X was assassinated while speaking in Harlem. Three of the men arrested in the murder were later identified as members of the Nation of Islam. (Interestingly, Malcolm's assassination prevented him from undertaking his next project, a presentation of charges of U.S. crimes against humanity at the United Nations and the World Court.)

Malcolm's *Autobiography* (co-written with the author Alex Haley) remains an important piece of American literature.

Bloody Sunday

Outraged by the killing of a civil rights activist by an Alabama state trooper, the African American community decided to hold a march on Sunday, March 7, 1965. They planned to walk from Selma to Montgomery, to demand that Governor George Wallace take action to put a stop to police brutality. However, when the marchers reached the city limits, they found state troopers blocking their way.

As the demonstrators crossed the Edmund Pettus Bridge (which led out of Selma), the troopers ordered them to disperse. The troopers, however, did not wait for the warning to be heeded. They attacked the crowd of people, using tear gas, whips, and clubs. Fifty marchers were hospitalized.

"Bloody Sunday" received national attention. Numerous marches were organized in response. Rev. Martin Luther King Jr. led a march to the Selma bridge two days later (during which one protestor was killed), and another march from Selma to Montgomery on March 25.

Shortly thereafter, President Johnson addressed Congress on the recent violence and in support of civil rights legislation. The speech helped ensure the passage of the Voting Rights Act of 1965 on August 10. This legislation outlawed literacy tests and other such requirements intended to restrict African American voting.

 On the March

But even if we pass this bill the battle will not be over. What happened in Selma is part of a far larger movement which reaches into every section and state of America. It is the effort of American Negroes to secure for themselves the full blessings of American life. Their cause must be our cause too. Because it's not just Negroes, but really it's all of us, who must overcome the crippling legacy of bigotry and injustice. And we shall overcome.

—President Lyndon Johnson borrows a familiar line from the popular civil rights anthem during a critical 1965 address to Congress on civil rights.

King Assassinated

On April 4, 1968, Rev. Martin Luther King Jr. traveled to Memphis, Tennessee, to support a sanitation workers' strike. After an uplifting speech, he returned to the Lorraine Motel, where he was staying. Standing on the second-floor balcony with aides, he was shot and killed. Across the country, there were riots in 130 cities. Thousands attended the Nobel Peace Prize winner's funeral.

The eloquent and charismatic interpreter of the nonviolent principles of Mahatma Gandhi was mourned internationally. James Earl Ray pled guilty to the crime, was convicted, and died in prison.

With King's death, the civil rights leader with the broadest appeal was silenced. His passing marked the end of an era that had seen important improvements in civil rights—and continuing evidence of the violence and cruelty that lurked not far beneath the surface of mainstream racism in white America.

In the year Dr. King was assassinated, Governor George Wallace of Alabama—at that point still an unrepentant segregationist—mounted a presidential campaign that garnered 13.5 percent of the popular vote (amounting to nearly 10 million votes) and 46 electoral votes. Although progress had been made, racism was still going strong in the United States of America.

Remembering Those Who Paid the Ultimate Price

The national Civil Rights Memorial, in Montgomery, Alabama, commemorates those who gave their lives for freedom between 1954 and 1968. Among those honored at the memorial are ...

Emmett Till.   This 14-year-old boy's brutal 1955 murder followed reports that he had flirted with a white woman. The two men accused of the assault were acquitted by an all-white jury.

Addie Mae Collins, Denise McNair, Carole Robertson, and Cynthia Wesley. These were the four African American schoolgirls who were killed when a bomb went off at the Sixteenth Street Baptist Church in Birmingham, Alabama, on September 15, 1963.

James Earl Chaney, Andrew Goodman, and Michael Schwermer.   Chaney, who was African American, and Goodman and Schwermer, who were white, were Freedom Riders protesting Mississippi's poll tax, which was designed to keep African American citizens from exercising their right to vote. The three were placed under arrest by a deputy sheriff who handed them over to members of the Ku Klux Klan. Klansmen murdered the trio on June 21, 1964, in Philadelphia, Mississippi.

Viola Liuzzo.   Liuzzo was a Detroit homemaker who was motivated to help marchers at Selma after seeing television news reports of the events at the Edmund Pettus Bridge. She was shot by Klansmen while transporting marchers to Selma.

To learn more about the Civil Rights Memorial, visit www.splcenter.org.

African American Contributions

1955: Marian Anderson makes her debut at the Metropolitan Opera House; she is the first African American singer in the history of the institution.

1959: Lorraine Hansberry's *A Raisin in the Sun* opens on Broadway.

1964: Martin Luther King Jr. receives the Nobel Peace Price.

1967: Thurgood Marshall's nomination to the U.S. Supreme Court is confirmed by the Senate.

1968: Shirley Chisholm is elected to Congress.

The Least You Need to Know

◆ The period between 1954 and 1968 in the United States was a time of conflict, tumult, and agitation in the civil rights arena.

◆ This period coincides with the career of the most charismatic of the leaders of the civil rights movement, Dr. Martin Luther King Jr.

◆ African Americans united with others to agitate against unjust laws in education, voting rights, and public accommodations.

◆ Although there were significant victories in these areas, the ugly fact of racism in America remained, as evidenced by the murder of Dr. King and the popularity of the presidential campaign of George Wallace.

After Dr. King

In This Chapter

◆ Progress in the aftermath of the King assassination

◆ Prejudice continues in the United States

◆ Police brutality and rioting in Los Angeles

The period from the assassination of Dr. Martin Luther King Jr. on April 4, 1968, to the 1992 riots in response to the Rodney King verdict may be described as an interim period in the struggle for civil rights in the United States.

This was a time that featured various white political and legal challenges to advancements in racial equality (the Boston anti-desegregation protests; *Bakke* v. *Board of Education*, and California's Proposition 209, each of which challenged affirmative action programs; and the electoral adventures of Klansman David Duke) and few mass marches or protests. The period was also notable for a visible drain of African American community leadership into mainstream leadership positions. From the 1970s to the 1990s a preoccupation with private concerns, such as the growth of personal wealth, seemed more and more to overshadow broad social concerns in the country as a whole, and even in portions of the African American community. Even so, there were some significant civil rights milestones.

End of Segregation in Public Schools

On October 29, 1969, the Supreme Court ruled that school districts must end segregation "now and hereafter." With this unambiguous language, the Court, which now had Thurgood Marshall as a member, left no room for doubt or delay.

The Court was responding to a legal challenge from diehard anti-integrationists, who had learned—from civil rights proponents, no doubt—that the legal system could be used to support social objectives. The anti-integrationists, however, received a major defeat when the Court ruled unanimously that Mississippi (and, by extension, the nation) was obliged to integrate public schools "at once."

What's the Word?

Alexander v. Holmes County Board of Education is an important (and, today, curiously underrated) Supreme Court decision from 1969. It mandated immediate action in the segregation of public school facilities.

This was a dramatic change from the language of the 1955 decree implementing *Brown* v. *Board of Education*, which had required integration of educational facilities "with all deliberate speed." In many parts of the country, this was interpreted by local school boards as "when you feel comfortable getting around to it."

After retiring, Chief Justice Earl Warren explained the choice of the "all deliberate speed" language of 1955 in this way: "There were so many blocks preventing an immediate solution of the thing in reality, that the best we could look for would be a progression of action."

In other words, the Court left states (and the federal court system) leeway to move toward desegregation in 1955. The 1969 case, known as *Alexander* v. *Holmes County Board of Education*, finally made clear to all involved that, a decade and a half after *Brown*, time was up. There was to be no more legal justification for delay in the integration of public school facilities.

Alexander was a crucial decision—as important in effect as Brown was in principle. For some reason, however, the case has not received much attention from the mainstream media and the public school system in the years since it was delivered.

Paramount Importance

The question presented is one of paramount importance, involving as it does the denial of fundamental rights to many thousands of school children, who are presently attending Mississippi schools under segregated conditions contrary to the applicable decisions of this court. Against this background the court of appeals should have denied all motions for additional time because the continued operation of segregated schools under a standard of allowing 'all deliberate speed' is no longer constitutionally permissible. Under explicit holdings of this court the obligation of every school district is to terminate dual school systems at once and to operate now and hereafter only unitary schools.

—From the Supreme Court's unanimous decision in *Alexander* v. *Holmes County Board of Education* (1969)

The Fallout from *Brown* and *Alexander*

Alexander v. *Holmes County Board of Education* was the kind of resounding, unambiguous legal victory that might well have seemed unattainable only a few decades earlier to African Americans. At long last, the nation's highest court had sent a clear signal demanding immediate change from racist local authorities. One lesson of this period, however, was that legal redress was not the same thing as equal opportunity in the real world.

Having secured the legal right to equal, unitary educational facilities, African Americans saw many white communities respond with bitter resistance to the reality of racially diverse classrooms. The conflicts over desegregation proved, as though further proof were necessary, that the racial divisions in America's urban centers were still in place—and painfully obvious.

The challenge of desegregation was most pronounced in major cities, and it was probably clearest in Boston in the mid-1970s.

FAQ

Why were northern cities the focus of conflicts over busing? Northern cities were likely to be divided into very large neighborhoods (or, more accurately, subcities), in which either African Americans or whites lived. This meant that desegregating public schools in these cities required students to travel to schools far from their homes, a prospect that many white parents resisted bitterly.

1974: Boston's School System Flunks

In Boston in 1974, Judge Arthur Garrity set up a plan of mandatory school integration in reaction to the traditionally racist policies of educational officials there. The city—northern and with a tradition of progressivism—quickly splintered into violent subgroups as white families in Charlestown and South Boston fought bitterly against the notion of "outsiders" determining where and with whom their children would go to school. The polarizing social crisis that followed in Boston managed to bring out paranoia and stereotyping on both sides, and underlined the vast psychological distance that remained between white and African American groups in urban America.

The Garrity plan, which was derided by white critics as "forced busing", aimed to correct *de jure* (formally instituted) segregation, not *de facto* (incidental and unintentional) segregation. In other words, what Garrity was trying to remedy was Boston's long-standing policy of conscious, deliberate support and maintenance of segregation in the city's schools—segregation that deprived African American students of their right to a quality education.

What's the Word?

De facto segregation arises from existing neighborhood configurations or recent trends in demographics; the courts have avoided action against this kind of segregation. **De jure** segregation arises from the policies and decisions of officials; it is the deliberate, planned separation of the races. Only this second kind of segregation led to mandatory busing decrees in the United States.

Forced integration of the school system was supported by African Americans, by the legal system, and by key media outlets (notably the *Boston Globe*, whose offices were subjected to rifle assaults during the crisis). It was opposed—vigorously—by families where virtually no African Americans lived.

The Garrity plan turned school facilities into battlegrounds and school officials into crisis resolution specialists. Conflict on the streets and in school grounds was, in the years immediately following Garrity's initial decision in 1974, both common and bloody. How much effective teaching in subjects like mathematics and English actually occurred in this environment may be open to question, but it's hard to deny that African American students and families received a lesson in Northern bigotry.

Schools Under Siege

In his extraordinary book *Common Ground* (Vintage Books, 1985), J. Anthony Lukas tells of an assistant principal in the Boston system informing a group of besieged African American students that police had managed to sidetrack a group of belligerent white students. A group of buses gathered in an alley, positioned strategically to help the youngsters escape from the white mob by means of the fire stairs. Before long, though, the white students realized what was going on, and started screaming, "They're going out the side!"

The white boys turned, left the building, and headed for the alleys—but not in time to stop the buses' departure. Enraged, they flung stones at the departing school vehicles.

Clearly, entrenched racism was not simply a southern problem.

Making Diversity in the Classroom a Reality

It would take Boston—and many other American cities—years to come to terms with the notion of a racially diverse public school system. While that process unfolded, the city and the nation were subjected to scenes of chaos and social conflict that revealed how broad the fault lines between the races actually ran.

Emerging Leaders

This "interim period" (1968–1992) was less a time of organizational and social progress than of individual ascendancy by African Americans, mainly male. (But see Chapter 16 for a discussion of Shirley Chisholm, who became, in 1972, the first African American *and* the first African American woman to launch a significant major-party presidential campaign.)

A number of African American men assumed important leadership positions in main-stream America. Here's a brief overview.

Jesse Jackson

Once an important aide to Dr. Martin Luther King Jr., Chicago's Jesse Jackson founded Operation PUSH (People United to Save Humanity), the motto of which was "I am somebody!" Jackson also established the Rainbow Coalition, intended to bring activists of all races together.

Jackson was the first African American to make a mainstream run for the President of the United States, competing in the 1984 and 1988 races as a major Democratic can-didate. Although he has taken a somewhat lower profile since the 1988 campaign, he has continued to make national news with his ability to draw attention to social con-cerns such as crime, inequality of opportunity, voter registration, and teen pregnancy in America's inner cities. Jackson has also found ways to involve himself in a number of foreign-affairs issues.

> **On the March** _____
>
> When I was a child growing up in Greenville, South Carolina, the Reverend Sample used to preach ever so often a sermon relating to Jesus and he said, 'If I be lifted up, I will draw all men unto me.' I didn't quite understand what he meant as a child growing up, but I understand a little better now. If you raise up truth, it is magnetic.
>
> —Rev. Jesse Jackson, addressing the 1984 Democratic National Convention.

Although he has endured his share of scandal and controversy, Jackson nevertheless remains a charismatic and energetic spokesman for the civil rights movement and for various progressive causes. His son Jesse Jackson Jr. is a congressman from Illinois.

Louis Farrakhan

Louis Farrakhan emerged in the 1970s as a charismatic, telegenic, and controversial Muslim leader. Farrakhan headed up the Nation of Islam and won a reputation as a powerful spokesman for the Nation of Islam's separatist, Islamic vision for African Americans.

Farrakhan's frequent anti-Jewish statements made him unappealing to many, but his emphasis on self-sufficiency and personal responsibility was (and continues to be) well received in many quarters.

> **On the March** _____
>
> We cannot … keep on blaming white people for our shortcomings. We have to know our own sins … and repent of the evils that are destroying our own communities. … We must atone for the destruction that is going on: the fratricide, the death dealing drugs, and the violence that plagues us. The present generation of Caucasians, however, must accept the responsibility and the challenge to be participants in finding the solution that will correct the wrong that was done [to us] that has never been properly addressed.
>
> —Louis Farrakhan

Harold Washington

Harold Washington, elected the first African American mayor of Chicago in 1983, was one of a number of African American mayors elected in this period. Thomas Bradley of Los Angeles, who served from 1973 to 1993, was another. Atlanta boasted an African American mayor (Andrew Young, a former member of the Carter Administration) and so did New Orleans (Ernest Morial).

Washington served as mayor during a time of bitter racial division in the city of Chicago, and was frequently opposed by alderman Ed Vrdolyak, who controlled the city council. Redistricting in Chicago resulted in a sharp reduction in Vrdolyak's political power, however, and Washington briefly assembled a working majority in Chicago. He won reelection in 1987, but died shortly thereafter of a heart attack.

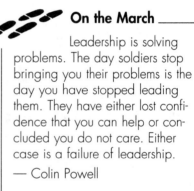

On the March

Remember me as one who tried to be fair.

—Mayor Harold Washington of Chicago

Colin Powell

On August 10, 1989, General Colin L. Powell, a decorated Vietnam veteran, was appointed Chairman of the Joint Chiefs of Staff, thereby becoming the first African American to serve as head of America's armed forces. He later played a key role in strategizing the victory of the U.S.-led coalition in Iraq.

In recent years, Powell has received attention as a potential presidential candidate, although he has yet to seek the office. (In 2000, President-elect George W. Bush nominated Powell as his Secretary of State; Powell was easily confirmed, making him the first African American to assume that position, as well.)

On the March

Leadership is solving problems. The day soldiers stop bringing you their problems is the day you have stopped leading them. They have either lost confidence that you can help or concluded you do not care. Either case is a failure of leadership.

— Colin Powell

Clarence Thomas

Clarence Thomas was confirmed by the Senate as the second African American member of the Supreme Court on October 15, 1991. He was appointed to take the place of Thurgood Marshall, who had announced his retirement.

The confirmation vote of 52–48 was the closest vote for a Supreme Court nominee in the twentieth century, and it reflected the controversy surrounding Thomas's appointment. During the confirmation hearings, allegations of sexual harassment were outlined in detail before the Judiciary Committee in nationally

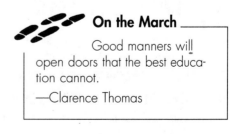

On the March

Good manners will open doors that the best education cannot.

—Clarence Thomas

televised hearings. The allegations came from Anita Hill, an African American and a Yale Law School graduate. Hill had worked for Thomas at the Equal Employment Opportunity Commission (EEOC). There was strong testimony on both sides of this issue, and the dispute cast a cloud over Thomas that has yet to disperse.

The African American Middle Class

The 1980s saw the rise of a new African American middle class in the United States. This group had benefited from social struggle, hard work, education, and personal commitment; it was, at the same time, strongly delineated from both white society and the African American inner-city "underclass."

Questions of cultural definition and the stratification of middle-class African Americans into a relatively isolated community arose; these questions have persisted in the years since. Many African Americans applaud the emergence of this group; others are frustrated at its apparent unwillingness to do more to help bring economic self-sufficiency to urban African American communities.

On the Tube: (Black) Father Knows Best

On the pop-culture front, a major landmark was the extraordinary success of *The Cosby Show*, a network situation comedy whose protagonist, played by Bill Cosby, was an upscale professional. The show celebrated the foibles of American family life first and foremost; that the family happened to be African American was secondary. It all seems quite natural now, but not so very many years before, African Americans had been marginalized (or, more commonly, completely ignored) on network television.

That white America accepted—and came to love—the fictional Huxtable family depicted on *The Cosby Show* is a cultural phenomenon worth noting. The days when racists could frighten sponsors into abandoning shows that featured nonsubmissive African Americans (such as Nat King Cole's variety program) were clearly long past.

A Looming Question

At the same time African Americans were gaining high-visibility leadership positions, pondering the consequences of economic progress, and becoming cultural role models, larger social questions were coming under consideration.

One of the biggest of these issues was affirmative action. Should groups of people (such as African Americans, members of other minority groups, and women) who have historically been discriminated against, be the focus of efforts to compensate for that past discrimination?

Controversy over *affirmative action* policies (which had been in place for some years in educational, business, and government settings) grew to impressive dimensions during the "interim period." Then as now, the topic was a controversial one, with some regarding formal efforts to ensure diversity and opportunity as a boon, and others regarding such efforts as an obstacle to the development of a "colorblind" society.

What's the Word?

Many people confuse **nondiscrimination** with **affirmative action**. Nondiscrimination is the removal of (illegal) discriminatory obstacles in employment, housing, education, or public accommodations. Affirmative action goes further; it involves making an active effort to recruit, hire, promote, or award contracts to individuals or groups who have been discriminated against in the past. Proponents of affirmative action argue that this "extra effort" is necessary to offset the effects of past discrimination, because even a neutral or nondiscriminatory approach is likely to perpetuate existing inequities.

The Rodney King Riots

A racial incident in California galvanized the nation's attention in the early 1990s.

Police officers in Los Angeles stopped the Hyundai of African American driver Rodney King after a high-speed chase through city streets in the early hours of the morning. Sgt. Stacey Koon and three other LAPD officers (Laurence Powell, Theodore Briseno, and Timothy Wind) struck King more than 50 times with metal batons before finally handcuffing him and calling an ambulance. From a nearby apartment, an amateur videographer, George Holliday had recorded the scene.

FAQ

What does a "normal" racist sound like in Los Angeles? A former L.A. police chief won attention as a possible candidate when he explained why African Americans were dying so frequently when placed under arrest by local law enforcement officials. "We may be finding," Darryl Gates said, "that in some blacks, when the choke hold is applied, the veins or arteries do not open up like in normal people."

Rodney King is assaulted by police.

(Illustration: Judith Burros.)

When Holliday's tape of the beating was shown on national TV, it caused widespread outrage among people of all races. The four police officers were indicted for excessive use of force; on April 29, 1992, an all-white jury acquitted the four police officers involved in the King beating.

Immediately, rioting broke in Los Angeles, and there were serious disturbances elsewhere. When the smoke cleared five days later, 54 people lay dead. The riots had the dubious distinction of having brought about one of the highest death tolls of any civil disturbance in the twentieth century.

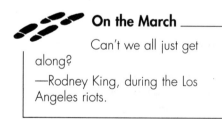

On the March

Can't we all just get along?
—Rodney King, during the Los Angeles riots.

On April 30, President George Bush announced that he had ordered the Department of Justice to investigate the possibility of filing charges against the LAPD officers for violating the federal civil rights of Rodney King. On August 4, a federal grand jury indicted the four officers. In their second trial, begun February 23, 1993, with two African Americans now on the jury, two of the police officers were acquitted and two convicted. No riots ensued.

In the wake of the rioting, some media reports focused on the sharply differing assessments of African Americans and whites when it came to governmental bodies, the police, and the criminal justice system. The "interim period" of the civil rights movement concluded with national consensus on racial matters seemingly limited to a single conclusion, one that could be dated back to the Great Migration: There was something deeply wrong in the inner cities of America. It was something that had been wrong for a very long time indeed.

African American Contributions

1969: Dr. Meredith Courdine receives the first of his 15 patents related to the electrogasdynamic (EGD) generator; the device's applications include air pollution measurement and reduction, power generation, and refrigeration.

1970: Engineer John P. Moon leaves his job at IBM. He joins forces with a number of fellow engineers to found National Micronetics Corporation, which manufactures ferrite recording heads for computers. Before long, demand for the heads surges, and the firm is an important—and profitable—early high-tech firm.

1977: Alex Haley's *Roots* airs as a miniseries and attracts record ratings.

1985: Oprah Winfrey's talk show is syndicated nationally.

1987: Colin Powell, a lieutenant general and a decorated Vietnam veteran, is named national security adviser to President Ronald Reagan.

1988: Doug Williams, the first African American to play quarterback in the Super Bowl, passes for 340 yards and leads the Washington Redskins to victory. Williams is named the game's most valuable player.

The Least You Need to Know

- ◆ The period following the death of Martin Luther King Jr. was marked by progress on the legal front and a muted interest among whites in civil rights issues.

- ◆ During this period, there was also a profound cultural change in the way many white Americans perceived African Americans.

- ◆ There was controversy regarding issues such as school integration and affirmative action.

- ◆ The acquittal of the officers accused of assaulting motorist Rodney King led to epic race riots and underlined the problems in America's inner cities and the enduring divisions between black and white.

A House United, a House Divided

In This Chapter

- ◆ Importance of the Million Man March
- ◆ Voting irregularities in Florida
- ◆ The Reparations question

The period between the riots arising from the Rodney King incident and the early years of the twenty-first century has seen both progress and despair.

While there have been some issues to inspire and galvanize African Americans on the national level, many observers have detected a decline in the sense of passion and shared purpose that marked previous years. There has also been a growing dissatisfaction about the lack of progress in improving the lot of African Americans who live in America's inner cities.

In this chapter, you'll find discussions of some of the highlights of this most recent period in African American history.

The Million Man March

On October 16, 1995, Nation of Islam leader Louis Farrakhan gathered hundreds of thousands in Washington, D.C., for a "day of reflection and atonement" where African American men could reaffirm their commitment to "unity, atonement, and brotherhood."

The rally was one of the largest demonstrations in Washington's history. Among those who joined Farrakhan on the steps of the U.S. Capitol were civil rights veterans Jesse Jackson, Rosa Parks, and Dick Gregory. Farrakhan led the crowd in pledges to "take responsibility for their lives and families, and commit to stopping the scourges of drugs, violence and unemployment."

Big Media Misses the Point

It's fair to say that the mainstream media, and white America in general, never really knew what to make of this march, or understood its importance. Farrakhan's leading role in the event seemed only to ensure that the press would find reasons to focus on peripheral issues, and not on the powerful appeals to accountability, self-improvement, commitment to the community, and personal responsibility that drew so many men to Washington that day.

That was a shame, because Farrakhan's explicit emphasis on the acknowledgment of error, on repentance, on personal growth, and on union with a higher power inspired contemporary African American men in a way that little else in their history had. His historic appeal certainly deserved more objective coverage from the media than it received.

The Clinton Pardon That Didn't Lead the Nightly News

On February 19, 1999, President Bill Clinton righted a grievous past wrong by post-humously pardoning Henry Flipper, the first African American graduate of West Point.

At West Point, Flipper routinely suffered the "silent treatment" from white cadets. After graduation, he won praise for leading African American frontier troops, known as Buffalo Soldiers, but in 1879 he was charged with embezzling.

The accusation was, by all accounts, an invention of white officers eager to punish Flipper for his friendship with a white woman. Flipper was eventually cleared of theft but found guilty of conduct unbecoming an officer. Discharged, he found success as a civilian and eventually became an assistant to the Secretary of the Interior. West Point now bestows an annual Henry Flipper award for bravery in the face of long odds.

Clinton's pardon was believed to be the first posthumous pardon ever awarded by the executive branch.

California Civil Rights Initiative Undoes Affirmative Action

On November 5, 1996, the California electorate passed Proposition 209, a constitutional amendment by initiative, by a vote of 54 percent to 46 percent. It is now Article I, Section 31 of the California Constitution.

In brief, the Initiative stated that "[t]he state shall not discriminate against, or grant preferential treatment to, any individual or group on the basis of race, sex, color, ethnicity, or national origin in the operation of public employment, public education, or public contracting." Essentially, the act banned affirmative action in state colleges and agencies, reversing a national trend.

A disappointed President Bill Clinton said of affirmative action, "Mend it, don't end it."

Julian Bond Speaks Out

Civil rights activist Julian Bond, the former Georgia state senator, director of the National Association for the Advancement of Colored People (NAACP), and present chairman of the NAACP Board of Directors spoke bluntly about racial issues during a speaking tour he conducted as the twentieth century closed.

The problem for contemporary African Americans, as Bond saw it, is still "white supremacy," but not in the traditional sense of the word. White supremacy today takes the form of a "vast affirmative-action program for whites." Bond also charges that an increasing white ambivalence and aloofness has undermined the African American struggle for equality, and accuses some whites of maintaining a "don't ask, don't tell policy" when it comes to racial discrimination.

Bond believes African Americans and whites should continue to work together to achieve racial justice. He outlines four broad solutions: continued litigation for improving the opportunities of African Americans; the cessation of racial profiling, "responsible for putting more blacks in prison"; fighting discrimination "in the streets and in the suites"; and the improvement of the nation's schools to prepare African American children for the twenty-first century. His position is a clear counterpoint to the California Civil Rights Initiative and similar efforts.

Obstacles and Opportunities

Racial profiling is the stopping, detaining, or questioning of a person based solely on his or her race, typically by police. Law enforcement officials who determine which individuals to pull over or search for contraband solely on the basis of skin color or ethnicity have been the subject of controversy and legal challenge in recent years. The American Civil Liberties Union keeps a file of horrific police abuses under the title "Driving While Black"; you can check it out at www.aclu.org/profiling.

Fiasco in Florida

Who said the days of excluding African Americans from the polls were over?

The controversy over the 2000 presidential election, which concluded with a Supreme Court decision that placed George W. Bush in the White House, featured numerous complaints of civil rights abuses on the part of the Florida state government. With the presidency riding on a breathtakingly close finish in Florida, a huge number of African American Floridians argued either that their votes for Bush's opponent Al Gore had been improperly excluded from the state's official totals—or that they had been denied the opportunity to vote in the first place.

Many pundits and activists noted the irony of the final Supreme Court decision, which relied heavily on the Fourteenth Amendment to the United States Constitution in its legal reasoning. That amendment was passed to ensure, among other things, equal access to the ballot by African Americans.

According to U.S. Congresswoman Cynthia McKinney, one of the important (but overlooked) figures in the Florida election fiasco was the Choicepoint Company. "Using lists of misdemeanor offenders in Texas," McKinney argued, "Choicepoint 'padded' the Florida list of ineligible voters to include more ineligible voters than there actually were in Florida. This resulted in thousands of African Americans not being allowed to vote in the presidential election. This, joined with the high number of thrown-out ballots and a Supreme Court decision that stopped the ballot counting, resulted in a Bush victory in Florida."

McKinney's anger was shared by many who viewed the 2000 election outcome as the latest in a series of cynical efforts to minimize or eliminate the impact of African

American voters. After the election, there was impressive talk of reform in Florida. There has, of course, been impressive talk of reform at other points in American history following electoral abuses that put African Americans at a disadvantage.

Voices from the 2000 Presidential Fiasco in Florida

Black voters in Florida came out in record numbers on November 7th to exercise their constitutional rights to vote. It is shameful that qualified voters were prevented from voting or from having their vote count because they were purged from registration rolls or because they used voting machines that did not accurately record a vote. These measures have become the literacy tests of the new millennium. These and other practices unlawfully suppressed the black vote. We need to ensure that in our democracy this unfair disenfranchisement never happens again.

—Barbara Arnwine, Executive Director of the Lawyers' Committee for Civil Rights Under Law

Perhaps the most dramatic undercount in this election was the nonexistent ballots of the countless unknown eligible voters, who were wrongfully purged from the voter registration rolls, turned away from the polls, and by various other means prevented from exercising the franchise. While statistical data, reinforced by credible anecdotal evidence, point to widespread disenfranchisement and denial of voting rights, it is impossible to determine the extent of the disenfranchisement or to provide an adequate remedy to the persons whose voices were silenced in this historic election by a pattern and practice of injustice, ineptitude and inefficiency …. The Commission on Civil Rights did not find conclusive evidence that the highest officials of the state conspired to produce the disenfranchisement of voters. Instead, the Commission found that the governor and the secretary of state, in particular, chose to simply ignore the mounting evidence that many counties were experiencing rising voter registration rates in communities with out-dated voting technology. Furthermore, they ignored the pleas of some supervisors of elections for guidance and help …. The State's highest officials responsible for assuring effective uniformity coordination and application of the election were grossly derelict in fulfilling their responsibilities and unwilling to accept accountability.

—Excerpts of executive summary points from the Commission on Civil Rights report on the 2000 Florida general election

The Reparations Movement

The possibility of seeking reparations for abuses and exploitation suffered under slavery has become an important and controversial question in the African American community in recent years.

Should African Americans be compensated for the damages suffered by their ancestors? Opponents to this idea argued that any large-scale reparations campaign would inevitably be murky, would deepen racial fault lines, dredge up a bygone past best left buried, and risk obscuring the economic and social gains African Americans have made. Proponents of such a campaign argued that African Americans had served as uncompensated, unwilling slaves for generations. They had their lives, families, property, and land systematically taken from them, and their labor exploited by plantation owners and industrialists for large profits. If groups such as the interned Japanese Americans of World War II and the many Native American groups in the United States had been compensated, many wondered, why not African Americans?

As this book goes to press, several high-profile legal suits are pending against contemporary companies that existed before the Civil War and benefited economically from the institution of slavery. It will be interesting to see what becomes of them.

FAQ

Do African Americans support a campaign to seek reparations for slavery? An unscientific poll conducted by the website Black Voices (www.blackvoices.com) posed the following question to its visitors: "In the past, the United States has paid reparations to other minority groups, such as Japanese Americans. With this in mind, do you think the country should pay reparations to African Americans?" Over 75 percent of respondents answered "Yes."

A Wave of Scam Artists

Recently, the Internal Revenue Service (IRS) reported a wave of confidence schemes designed to manipulate African Americans supporting the Reparations Movement. As an IRS bulletin explained, "The Internal Revenue Service issued a nationwide warning for taxpayers not to be misled into filing slavery reparation claims. The IRS has recently seen a significant surge in these false filings, and the agency urged taxpayers not to fall victim to this tax refund scam."

The advisory continued: "There is no provision in the tax law that allows African Americans to get tax credits or refunds related to slavery reparations. Unscrupulous promoters are deceiving people into paying money for advice on how to file these false (tax) claims, in which they generally seek $40,000 to $80,000."

For more information on the Reparations Movement, consider visiting the following websites.

- **The Economic Predicate for Black Reparations**

  What it is: Carefully argued case in favor of the Reparations Movement by Robert Westley.

  Potent quote: "Structures of white supremacy have asserted hegemony over numerous aspects of social, political and personal life in the United States. This is the reality that lies behind the statistics. Racism, as the practice of white supremacy, cannot be circumscribed by the petty injustices that individuals commit against individuals. Racism is a group practice."

  URL: www.udayton.edu/~race/02rights/repara02b.htm

- **We Won't Pay**

  What it is: Site for those opposed to the Reparations Movement.

  Potent quote: "The reparations debate within black America is not the slam-dunk you might believe. There's a little rebellion that's taking root."

  —Niger Innis, spokesman for the Congress of Racial Equality, quoted in an Associated Press article by Deborah Kong, "Calls for Reparations Brew Revolt of Blacks."

  URL: www.wewontpay.com

- Black Reparations

  What it is: Site promoting discussion of the reparations issue.

  Potent quote: "Read up on the question, make your opinion heard, and discover what your peers think."

  URL: www.blackreparations.com

At Century's End

As the old century gave way to the new, it was hard to say whether African Americans as a group were in a better or a worse situation than they had been a half-century earlier.

The civil rights movement had won integrated schools and transportation, voting rights, better job opportunities, and real political power. Consider the following benchmark statistic: When Congress passed the Voting Rights Act in 1965, fewer than 100 African Americans held elective office in the United States; by 1990 there were more than 7,000.

On the other hand, despite these gains, there was a steadily enlarging sense of crisis and alienation in the urban areas where many African Americans lived, a crisis that carried with it the kind of shocking statistics that reflected over a century of inequity in America's cities.

◆ In 1995, an incredible 70.4 percent of African American babies were born out of wedlock; 35 years earlier, the figure had been 30 percent.

◆ As of this writing, it is reliably estimated that 33 percent of all African American males over the age of 20 are in prison or possess criminal records.

◆ African American infants are roughly twice as likely to die from sudden infant death syndrome as other infants.

◆ African Americans are ludicrously over-represented in the ranks of the American homeless.

◆ The suicide rate for African American teens is not only rising, but rising significantly faster than the rate for white teens.

Given these alarming social signals, it is not surprising that there is still a sense that much remains undone in the African American community.

African American Contributions

1992: Mae Jemison becomes the first female African American astronaut.

1993: Quincy Jones publishes the first issue of *Vibe* magazine.

1996: *Forbes* magazine names Oprah Winfrey the highest-earning celebrity of the year. Her 1995–1996 earnings are estimated at $171 million.

1997: Michael Jordan guides the Chicago Bulls to their fifth consecutive NBA championship.

2001: Colin Powell is confirmed as secretary of state.

The Least You Need to Know

◆ The Million Man March appealed to African American men in a unique and powerful way, but it was not reported objectively by the mainstream media.

◆ Julian Bond has spoken out eloquently against institutionalized racial prejudice in recent years.

◆ The election fiasco in Florida in the year 2000 demonstrated that the days of excluding blacks from the polls were far from over.

◆ The Reparations Movement has emerged as an important topic in the African American community.

Part

Power on the Inside: Spirit and Soul

Throughout its four-century odyssey, the African American community has developed institutions and traditions to support itself and sustain its vision. In this part of the book, you find out about some of those cultural foundations: faith, entrepreneurship, celebration, and the proud history of inspired, powerful African American women.

Chapter 13

Faith

In This Chapter

◆ The African American religious experience

◆ Diversity in faith expressions

◆ Seven pioneers

In this chapter, you find out about some of the elements of the rich heritage of African American religious experience. The spotlight in this chapter is on six representative stories of faith and commitment within the African American community.

Early African American Religious Experience

It took a while for African American believers to secure African American preachers.

Heavily influenced by the long-standing "invisible institution" of spontaneous religious practice among Africans held in captivity, the first African American houses of worship with African American pastors were Baptist churches in the South. These were founded during the pre-Revolutionary period. There were, of course, many African American Christian communities at that time with (often self-serving) *white* leadership.

Although many whites believed that it was a mistake to allow slaves to convert to Christianity—fearing that exposure to religion could lead to open opposition to slavery—others argued that faith could be a "civilizing" influence. As a practical matter, whites in the South attempted to use Christianity—whatever the color of the leading officiant—as a justification for the institution of slavery, and as a strategy for social control.

In the short run, the strategy fulfilled its purpose. In the long run, however, it backfired.

The Drive for Self-Determination and Religious Expression

Inevitably, African American religious practice became a powerful force for self-determination and education. It eventually carried major implications in social organization, political awareness, and community development.

FAQ

Why is the religious tradition so important in African American history? For one thing, members of the clergy have historically assumed a special role in the leadership of African American communities. Religious leaders like Gabriel Prosser, Denmark Vesey, and Nat Turner headed slave revolts; African American clergy were instrumental in organizing abolitionist campaigns and, later, in the struggle for civil rights.

The six stories that follow will give you some sense of the struggles, the triumphs, and the deep faith commitments of a few remarkable people. Each made significant contributions to the larger African American community through their religious practices and beliefs.

A Side Note

Because the African American religious experience has historically centered on Christianity, that's the tradition I'll be exploring most closely here. A number of other dynamic traditions emerged in the twentieth century, of course. I'll offer a summary of some of the most influential non-Christian movements within the African American community later in the chapter.

Richard Allen

Born into slavery in 1760, Richard Allen underwent a powerful conversion to Christianity when he was 20. He purchased his own freedom and that of his brother in 1783.

In 1787, Allen and a number of fellow African American Christians were told that they were not welcome with the white worshippers at Philadelphia's St. George Methodist Episcopal Church. Allen led a tactful departure from the church and subsequently launched a religious movement that eventually became the African Methodist Episcopal Church.

Allen was a persuasive, intuitive preacher of his faith, and he was comfortable spreading the gospel to people of all colors and religious backgrounds. He placed a special

ry to people of African descent, believing their salva-
he social organization that would allow them to
s, in fact, the first in a long line of African American
blended his message of salvation with a message of
sm, and community action. In his footsteps would
end Martin Luther King Jr.

en became known as the moral leader of a huge num-
mericans in the early nineteenth century, or that he
despite the fact that he was never elected to any public
years, the only above-board social institution (outside
African Americans. As a result, the social agenda merged
distinctive way that continues to this day. Allen, the orig-
omination, was also an important pioneer in his coun-
onal organizer, spokesman for, and moral leader of a
community of otherwise unrepresented Americans.

On the March

For many African Americans in the eighteenth and nineteenth centuries, participation in religious services at established white churches came at a steep cost: segregation and white control of all ceremonies and missions. The rise of the African Methodist Episcopal Church and the African Methodist Episcopal Zion Church are early examples of African American parishioners deciding to take control of their own religious institutions by founding entirely new denominations.

Peter Williams Sr.

Peter Williams was the most important early figure in the New York–based movement that eventually became the African Methodist Episcopal Zion Church (not to be confused with the similarly named African Methodist Episcopal Church). Williams was a sexton at a traditional Methodist church when the Loyalist who claimed him as a slave made his way to England in 1783, following the victory of American forces in the war for independence. The trustees of the church Williams served raised the necessary funds to purchase Williams's freedom.

It was a sign of their respect for Williams's great faith. Yet the trustees, like so many other white Christians of the day, did not want to worship in proximity with people of color; they left in place the segregated worship arrangements that relegated African American believers to pews at the rear of the church. This state of affairs did not sit well with Williams, who finally led a group of African American believers to form an independent church where they would be able to pursue their religious beliefs without cowering in the rear of the building. The movement included outspoken proponents of "spiritual, social, and economic emancipation" such as James Varick, Abraham Thompson, and William Miller; it was ultimately chartered as the African Methodist Episcopal Zion Church, and was the first African American church in New York.

On the March

The African Methodist Episcopal Zion Church was the first Christian denomination—of any color, anywhere in the world—to extend clerical ordination and full voting rights on church matters to women. It did so in 1898.

The organization Williams helped to found came to be known as the Freedom Church, and was a key institution in the abolitionist movement of the nineteenth century. AME Zion facilities were used as havens for escaped slaves using the Underground Railroad, and the church claimed as members such extraordinary figures as Frederick Douglass, Sojourner Truth, and Harriet Tubman.

Today, the church boasts 3,000 churches on five continents and claims a million and a half active members.

Hiram Revels

Neither Richard Allen nor Peter Williams Sr. ever ran for or won an election for public office. Hiram Revels, on the other hand, was the pioneer of the preacher/politician tradition that emerged in the Reconstruction period (1865–1877). Revels, a minister with a gift for oratory and organization, recruited for the Union during the Civil War and served as a chaplain for an African American Mississippi regiment. After the war, Revels relocated to Mississippi and founded new congregations there. He also took the newly amended Constitution at its word and turned African American believers into voters.

The Mississippi preacher became, in succession, alderman of Natchez, Mississippi, then a state senator, and then the first African American senator. In an irony that did not escape notice at the time, the charismatic Mississippi preacher was elected to complete the vacated term of former senator (and disgraced Confederate president) Jefferson Davis. Revels served out the balance of Davis's term, a little more than a year, then took up the presidency of Alcorn College, Mississippi's first institution of higher learning for African Americans. He continued his duties as a minister until he died in 1901.

On the March

Revels's dual career as a minister and a politician is, today, a little-known episode in American history. It is, however, one of the most important breakthroughs in American social and political history. Revels provided the career template for a wave of later African American preacher/politicians such as Adam Clayton Powell Jr., William Gray, and John Lewis—to say nothing of the 1984 and 1988 campaigns for the presidency led by the Reverend Jesse Jackson. Revels is also a reminder that, although African Americans were systematically deprived of civil rights in the South following the 1877 back-room deal that concluded the Reconstruction period, they continued to vote in their own churches. They elected men and women committed to fulfilling the spiritual, social, and educational aspirations of their parishioners.

William J. Seymour

In 1906, William J. Seymour led the Azusa Street Revival in Los Angeles—and helped bring about an explosion of interest from people of all races in a form of ecstatic worship that eventually developed into *Pentecostalism*—a powerful, ecstatic strain of Christianity that had people (according to the *Los Angeles Times*) "breathing strange utterances and mouthing a creed which it would seem no sane mortal could understand."

At the time of Seymour's landmark California event, there were under a thousand practitioners. Today, the movement boasts over seven million members. That makes the sect Seymour helped to develop the fastest-growing strain of Christianity of the past century.

Seymour made much of the fact that his exuberant form of worship—which sought direct connection to the Holy Spirit through sustained, unscripted vocalization, prolonged swaying, and the "gift of tongues"—was a global phenomenon that transcended race. "People of all nations came and got their cup full," he said of his gatherings at Azusa Street. "Some came from Africa, some came from India, China, Japan, and England."

What's the Word?

Pentecostalism is a global twentieth-century Christian movement that highlights the importance of direct experience of the Holy Spirit. This often takes the form of speaking in tongues, which is often regarded as tangible evidence of a believer's baptism in the Holy Spirit. In the book of Acts, early Christians are reported as receiving the "gift of tongues" on the Pentecost, or Feast of Weeks, which takes place on the fiftieth day following Passover. Pentecostalism emerged from the Holiness Movement of the late nineteenth and early twentieth century.

The mode of worship that Seymour made popular was quickly taken up by one of the participants at the Azusa Street sessions, Charles Harrison Mason, an African American preacher from Tennessee who brought his followers into the Pentecostal movement.

As it happened, Mason initiated the largest African American denomination of the sect, the Church of God in Christ. Today, it boasts more than five million members.

Thomas A. Dorsey

Not the white jazz star of similar name, but the legendary "Georgia Tom" widely regarded as the father of modern gospel music. Thomas Dorsey was born in rural Georgia in 1899. The son of a Baptist preacher, he lived a rough-and-tumble life as a young man; he spent time playing piano in a speakeasy owned by the gangster Al Capone and headed up the band that backed up the legendary singer Ma Rainey. In the late 1920s, Dorsey began a collaboration with a guitarist with the colorful name of Hudson Tampa Red Whittaker. The result was a blues hit, "Tight Like That."

Dorsey soon tired of the lifestyle he had set up for himself, however, and experienced a powerful religious conversion. His musical output continued in a new vein, and he began writing religiously themed songs. Recalling his own experiences of white exploitation of African American artists, he founded the Dorsey House in 1932, thereby becoming the first independent publisher of African American gospel music. Dorsey was also the founder—and the first president—of the National Convention of Gospel Choirs and Choruses.

A vitally important figure in both contemporary religion and contemporary music, Dorsey is widely credited with bringing an unapologetic blues influence to twentieth-century African American religious observance. Of the many gospel classics he wrote, Dorsey is most famous for "Precious Lord," composed in 1932 following his first wife's death during childbirth. It was recorded by countless performers—including Mahalia Jackson and Elvis Presley—and was a special favorite of Dr. Martin Luther King Jr.

Dorsey was the first African American elected to the Nashville Songwriters International Hall of Fame.

Howard Thurman and Sue Bailey Thurman

Howard and Sue Bailey Thurman were instrumental in founding the groundbreaking Church for the Fellowship of All Peoples, the first American church founded explicitly on ideas of racial tolerance and nondenominational inclusion. The two also played a key role in disseminating Mahatma Gandhi's ideas of passive resistance and nonviolence in a Christian context—ideas that would later be put to practical application by Dr. Martin Luther King Jr. and others within the modern civil rights movement.

The influence was direct, not theoretical—because Sue Bailey Thurman had been, for a time, an important adviser to Gandhi. She was also the first editor of the influential *Afro-American Women's Journal.*

Her husband Howard was an extraordinarily influential theologian who won praise for his work as pastor of the Church for the Fellowship of All Peoples, and later for his promotion to the post of Dean of Marsh Chapel and Professor of Spiritual Resources and Disciplines at Boston University. In winning the post, Thurman became the first African American to hold a top ministry position at a prominent white institution of higher learning.

On the March

During a conversation with Mahatma Gandhi in India, Howard Thurman asked the great spiritual and political leader what he, Thurman, should try to communicate to Americans when he returned. Gandhi responded by telling Thurman of his disappointment at not having done a better job of making nonviolent philosophy a global, rather than an Indian, movement. He asked Thurman to see what he could do about spreading the word to African American activists in the United States. As a result of that conversation, Thurman became committed to popularizing Gandhi's ideas among American civil rights leaders. One of them was Dr. Martin Luther King Jr.

Other African American Faith Traditions

Over the past century, a number of non-Christian faith traditions have taken root in the African American community. Here's a brief overview of some of the most influential movements.

Nation of Islam

The Nation of Islam is probably the most visible African American expression of the Islamic tradition.

Emphasizing austerity, devotion to Allah, a distinct cultural identity, and tangible support for the African American community, this faith combines elements of traditional Islamic practice and ideas adapted from a variety of other belief systems. The Nation of Islam has often been outspoken in its rhetoric, but its pronouncements on race relations in the United States may be best understood as an inevitable cultural reaction to the centuries-long legacy of white brutality and hatred toward African Americans.

In recent years, Islamic practice in the United States has been enriched and broadened by exposure to other forms and structures of this international religion. In particular, the 1964 visit to Mecca by Malcolm X, and his much-analyzed spiritual development after being exposed to Muslims of many nations, has taken on great symbolic importance for many African Americans attracted to the tenets of Islam.

> **On the March**
>
> The Nation of Islam, also known as the Lost-Found Nation of Islam, was founded in 1930 in Detroit by Wallace Fard, a salesman who described receiving a vision from Allah intended specifically for African Americans. Fard was succeeded by the Honorable Elijah Muhammad (born Elijah Poole), who led the faith from 1934 onward and was regarded by his followers as the "messenger from Allah."

Rastafarianism

This Jamaican tradition fuses an ecstatic version of that island's Christianity with the Pan-African ideology made popular by Marcus Garvey. It is heavily influenced by Garvey's reading of the Old Testament and places sacramental emphasis on marijuana and the communal power of reggae music.

This tradition, popular in many corners of the United States, has a strong "back-to-Africa" element that is also a sign of Garvey's influence on the faith. Rastafarianism emphasizes Africa's role as the birthplace of humanity and promotes autonomy and self-reliance among people of African descent. Rastas are well known for their celebration of ecstatic music and their use of marijuana in health and religious settings; what has received less attention is the tradition's insistence on wholesome, chemical-free food and its tradition of pacifism.

Santeria

This intriguing, fast-growing tradition combines certain elements of Christianity and a variety of African-based nature religions. It is popular in immigrant Afro-Cuban communities, and has been the subject of a great deal of scholarly research and popular investigation in recent years.

The Least You Need to Know

- ◆ African American religious practice became a powerful force for self-determination and education.

- ◆ Important figures in the development of African American religious traditions include Richard Allen, Peter Williams Sr., Hiram Revels, William J. Seymour, Thomas A. Dorsey, and the husband-and-wife team of Howard Thurman and Sue Bailey Thurman.

- ◆ Christianity has been the dominant faith tradition within the African American community.

- ◆ In the twentieth century, alternate faith traditions have gained popularity among African Americans, among them the Nation of Islam, Rastafarianism, and Santeria.

Festivities

In This Chapter

- The meaning of Kwanzaa
- Celebrating Martin Luther King day
- Black History month

Here, you'll learn about three modern African American observances, all of which came to prominence in the twentieth century, and all of which are now widely celebrated. Each offers a different window on the experience, spirit, and endurance of the African American community.

Kwanzaa

The weeklong holiday ceremonies collectively known as Kwanzaa make up a distinctly African American tradition. That tradition derives from both African terminology and symbolism—and from a conscious attempt to develop a set of ceremonies reinforcing ties to the long-standing cultural heritage of African Americans.

Kwanzaa is celebrated yearly from December 26 to January 1. It is thus an African American counterpart to seasonal celebrations like Christmas and

What's the Word?

The word **Kwanzaa** comes from the Swahili phrase for "first fruits," *matunda ya kwanzaa.*

Hanukkah. Kwanzaa has now been celebrated for nearly four decades; it was first observed in 1966 and has become increasingly popular in the years following.

The holiday, which is celebrated by Africans and African Americans of many religious traditions, centers on the themes of traditional harvest rituals common to a number of African peoples. It emphasizes principles and symbols that support and enhance harmonious community life.

The Primary Symbols of Kwanzaa

Mkeka *(muh-KAY-kuh)*	A straw mat, symbolizing tradition, on which other objects related to the holiday are placed.
Kinara *(kih-NAR-ah)*	A candle-holder, symbolizing the common and continuing source of all life.
Mshuna *(mee-SHOO-ma)*	The candles that represent the Nguzo Saba (Seven Principles) that support and sustain the community: unity, self-determination, collective work and responsibility, cooperative economics, purpose, creativity, and faith.
Muhindi *(mu-HEEN-dee)*	Ears of corn (one for each child in the family) symbolizing the continuity of the family unit and the community.
Kikombe Cha Umoja *(kee-KOAM-beh cha oo-MOE-jah)*	A Unity Cup that celebrates the wisdom and courage of the family's ancestors.
Zawadi *(za-WAH-dee)*	Gifts meant to emphasize both the labor of the parents and the rewards earned by the family's children.
Karamu *(kah-RAH-moo)*	A feast held to commemorate the events of the year past and in gratitude to the Creator. The high-spirited feast is celebrated on the evening of December 31.

Kwanzaa is a distinctively African American holiday, the purpose of which is to reinforce traditional African principles and heritage in a modern setting. It is celebrated by millions of people of African descent in North America, as well as in other parts of the world.

On the March

In 1997, the U.S. Postal Service issued a first-class Kwanzaa stamp. At the ceremonies announcing the release of the stamp, Dr. Maulana Karenga, the creator of Kwanzaa, said, "[Kwanzaa] speaks to the best of what it means to be both African and human in its stress on the dignity of the human person, the well-being of family and community, the integrity of the environment and our kinship with it, and the rich resource and meaning of a people's culture."

The U.S. Postal Service's 1997 Kwanzaa stamp.

(Judith Burros)

The Father of Kwanzaa

Kwanzaa, as we have seen, first arose in the 1960s. It was developed by Dr. Maulana (Ron) Karenga against the backdrop of the turbulent social changes—and, occasionally, bitter power struggles—that accompanied the civil rights and Black Power movements. The new holiday expressed the emerging desire of African Americans to define themselves and emphasize their own traditional values and identity. That desire has grown only stronger with the passage of the years, and Kwanzaa has won acceptance as a mainstream holiday.

Today, Dr. Karenga chairs the Department of Black Studies at California State University, Long Beach. He is also the director of the Kawaida Institute of Pan-African Studies, Los Angeles, and the president of The Organization Us, an organization devoted to cultural and social change that emphasizes "the communitarian focus of the organization and its philosophy, Kawaida, which is an ongoing synthesis of the best of African thought and practice."

Karenga himself has seen his fair share of controversy over the years; today, he is known primarily as an academic and as the originator of Kwanzaa. The holiday he developed has taken on a life of its own. It is a cultural phenomenon that continues to gain momentum with each holiday season.

The websites below offer online resources for those who are interested in learning more about Kwanzaa. Check them out!

The Official Kwanzaa Website

www.officialkwanzaawebsite.org

Dr. Karenga's overview of the holiday he created. Informative, detailed, and well designed, it also offers an interesting profile on Karenga himself.

The Kwanzaa Information Center

www.melanet.com/kwanzaa

An in-depth summary of the history of the holiday and its rituals that also offers such features as an online discussion group.

Kwanzaa

www.swagga.com/kwanzaa.htm

Image-rich discussion of the various elements of the holiday; part of the larger "Afrocentric Experience" site.

Everything About Kwanzaa

www.tike.com/celeb-kw.htm

A concise review of the most important points related to the holiday and its celebration; an excellent resource if you only have time for a short overview.

Martin Luther King Day

Every year, federal facilities, schools, and banks across the country observe the third Monday in January as a holiday in memory of the life and works of Dr. Martin Luther King Jr. It took 15 years, millions upon millions of signatures, and the committed efforts of many dedicated people to turn King's birthday into a national holiday.

Along the way, those who sought a formal national observance of Dr. King's contribution to American life were told that what they sought was unprecedented, impossible, too costly, or too radical. In hindsight, it is tempting to conclude that simple racial bias was one of the major reasons some American lawmakers waited a decade and a half to set aside a day of remembrance for the greatest civil rights leader of them all.

Resistance

Among the reasons that were cited in opposition to the national observance of Martin Luther King day were the following:

♦ The campaign for the holiday (which began almost immediately after King's death) was too close to contemporary events, and would not withstand the test of time.

♦ The campaign for the holiday (which had continued steadily through the Johnson, Nixon, Ford, Carter, and Reagan administrations) was built around events that were far in the past, and was not necessary given the changes in America that had taken place since King's death.

♦ The country had set aside holidays for specific individuals only twice in its history (for George Washington and Christopher Columbus); those in opposition to the new holiday implied that honoring Dr. King could somehow begin a trend toward honoring figures with only narrow, sectarian appeal. In response to this criticism, the comedian Richard Pryor, appearing on the *Tonight* show, pointed out that African Americans weren't seeking a day to honor Wilt Chamberlain, but the man who had delivered the "I have a dream" speech at the Lincoln Memorial.

♦ The holiday was too expensive, given the overtime and paid-time-off expenses associated with any national holiday. To those who made this objection, Senator Robert Dole of Kansas said, "I suggest they hurry back to their pocket calculators and estimate the cost of 300 years of slavery, followed by a century or more of economic, political, and social exclusion and discrimination."

♦ The holiday was somehow meant exclusively for African American people. Those who voiced (or subtly implied) this objection had obviously missed the philosophy of inclusion and participation that guided Dr. King's mission. The notion that the Fourteenth Amendment to the Constitution applies equally to all people and that the Constitution itself is color-blind are not African American ideas. They are American ideas. The principle that we should each be judged according to the content of our characters and that we should have the opportunity to move toward the highest aspirations we select without facing discrimination or bias are not African American ideals. They are American ideals.

The Adoption of the King Holiday—a Timeline

April 4, 1968	Reverend Martin Luther King Jr. is assassinated in Memphis, Tennessee.
April 8, 1968	Rep. John Conyers of Michigan proposes legislation to make King's birthday a national holiday. The sitting Congress ignores the bill.
January 1969	Over a thousand auto workers at a Tarrytown, New York, plant take a day off from work to celebrate King's birthday. Suspensions greet 60 of the workers; management threatens many other workers with formal reprisals.
March 1970	Six million signatures in support of a national King holiday arrive in Washington. Representative Conyers and Representative Shirley Chisholm, Democrat of New York, begin the process of conducting Congressional hearings.
January 1981	Seattle dockworkers are fired shortly after passing out literature in support of a formal King holiday.
1982 and 1983	Major marches in support of voting rights and the King legacy continue to place pressure on Congress. Petition drives continue.
August 1983	The House of Representatives passes a bill honoring Dr. King's birthday.
October 1983	Despite persistent efforts by North Carolina Senator Jesse Helms, the Senate passes the King holiday bill.
November 1983	President Reagan signs the measure into law.
January 20, 1986	Dr. King's birthday is observed as a federal holiday for the first time.

Community Service

In recent years, the focus of the King holiday has broadened to include an emphasis on service to the community. This turn of events would certainly have met with agreement from the man whose memory the day celebrates; as King was fond of saying, "Everybody can be great, because everybody can serve."

This increasingly popular theme for the day is captured in the slogan, "Remember! Celebrate! Act! A day *on*, not a day *off!*"

The following websites offer online resources for those who are interested in learning more about Martin Luther King day. Check them out!

The Holiday Zone: Martin Luther King Day Activities

www.geocities.com/Athens/Troy/9087/mlk

Features activities for children, a bulletin board, discussion topics, and other material relevant to the holiday.

Martin Luther King Day on the Net

www.holidays.net/mlk/holiday.htm

Offers a brief history of the holiday and links to related sites.

Martin Luther King Jr. Day of Service

www.mlkday.org

Emphasizes Dr. King's own tradition of service to local communities, and offers an online toolkit "to help you develop a service project of your own." Also offers links to social service groups in need of volunteers.

Infoplease: Martin Luther King Jr. Day

www.infoplease.com/spot/mlkjrday1.html

Offers an intelligent overview of the holiday and its history, a summary of Dr. King's life and works, and a series of well-written articles on civil rights and affirmative action.

The Martin Luther King Jr. Papers Project at Stanford University

www.stanford.edu/group/King

Provides just about everything you'd need for an in-depth assessment of the man and his mission. Includes an archive of published documents, a detailed biography, recommended reading, and much more.

Black History Month

Not a holiday, as such, but an established national tradition nonetheless, Black History month is the result of one man's determination to rectify 300 years of official neglect of the story of African Americans.

The Father of Black History

Dr. Carter G. Woodson, the son of former slaves, worked his way out of the coal-mines of Kentucky to receive a Ph.D. from Harvard University. He was troubled by the virtual absence of any meaningful historical work on the American saga as it reflected (as the term he coined went) Negro history.

Woodson was a pioneer in a field that hardly even existed. Virtually every historical account of the United States omitted, minimized, misstated, distorted, or lied out-right about the nature of the struggles and triumphs of African Americans. What Woodson set about was not so much setting the record straight as establishing the record in the first place.

? FAQ

What was Carter G. Woodson's most celebrated work? His textbook *The Negro In Our History* is probably the best candidate for the honor; the book was an extremely popular selection in many high schools and colleges in the first half of the twentieth century.

 On the March

Thanks in part to the research and promotional campaigns of the Association for the Study of Afro-American Life and History, Negro History week became more and more popular. It evolved into Black History month during a period that was practically devoted to popular history: America's bicentennial year, 1976.

In 1915, Woodson founded the Association for the Study of Negro Life and History. (Today, it operates under a different name, the Association for the Study of Afro-American Life and History.) A year later, he started what would become a highly influential historical publication, the *Journal of Negro History*.

By 1926, Woodson was on something of a crusade. The scholar had an inspiration: a national week devoted entirely to telling the African American story, from the point of view of African Americans. He called it Negro History week. It began as a nationwide campaign to shine a spotlight on the achievements, trials, and self-determination of African Americans. Today, the focus is on an entire month of discovery.

Black History month is celebrated in February; Woodson originally selected February for Negro History week because of its resonance with a number of historical events affecting African Americans, including the birthdays of Fredrick Douglass and Abraham Lincoln.

Woodson died in Washington, D.C., in 1950 at the age of 74. His work has been the subject of increasing interest and attention since the mid-1970s.

By the dawn of the twenty-first century, Woodson's work had paid off. Whereas black history was once a scandalously under-researched area of scholarly inquiry, it is today a vibrant and important feature of the American cultural landscape. A recent query on a popular search engine turned up over 1,400,000 World Wide Web references to the term "black history month"; the latest edition of Microsoft's popular Encarta encyclopedia features the Encarta Africana, a section devoted exclusively to black history and culture.

The websites below offer online resources for those interested in learning more about Black History month. Check them out!

Stamp on Black History

library.thinkquest.org/10320/stamps.htm#anchor305420

Offers well-written profiles of the many African Americans who have been honored on commemorative stamps by the U.S. Postal Service.

The Encyclopedia Britannica Guide to Black History

blackhistory.eb.com

Superb multimedia site offering biographical profiles, audio and video excerpts, and much more.

The Internet African American History

www.brightmoments.com/blackhistory/

Use the online tests to see how much you know! An excellent teaching resource.

Black History Month

www.black-history.biz

Intriguing site featuring articles on popular myths concerning black history, as well as a number of biographies of key figures.

The Least You Need to Know

◆ Kwanzaa is a distinctively African American holiday celebrated from December 26 to January 1.

◆ Kwanzaa was created in 1966 by Dr. Maulana Karenga; it has grown in popularity in recent years.

◆ After years of lobbying and millions of signatures on petitions, the federal government finally authorized a holiday celebrating the birthday of Dr. Martin Luther King Jr. in 1983.

◆ The King holiday was first celebrated in 1986.

◆ Dr. Carter G. Woodson, the "father of black history," launched Negro History week in 1926.

◆ By 1976, Negro History week had become Black History month; it is observed throughout the month of February.

15

Fortune: African American Entrepreneurship

In This Chapter

♦ African American entrepreneurs from American history

♦ Adversity and triumph

♦ Today's challenges and opportunities

In this chapter, you get an overview of the long and rich African American entrepreneurial tradition. This is a story that is being written and rewritten every day, a story that constantly yields new distinctions affecting community, autonomy, decision, and empowerment.

Building Prosperity, Building the Community

Contrary to the impression one is likely to receive from any number of mass media sources, the African American entrepreneur is not a recent phenomenon. There is a long history of African American business development extending long before the Civil War.

A Selected Timeline: African American Entrepreneurship

(A few of the high points from the history of African American business.)

1770: African-born slave Amos Fortune buys his own freedom and establishes a thriving tannery business with clients in Massachusetts and New Hampshire.

1779: Jean Baptiste Point du Sable sets up a trading post on the site that will later be known as the city of Chicago. His operation encompasses a bakery, a mill, a meat-smoking facility, a dairy, and a lumberyard.

1817: African American shipping magnate Paul Cuffe, based in New Bedford, Massachusetts, dies, leaving a substantial estate.

Circa 1840: William Johnson is a thriving Mississippi businessman. Born into slavery in Mississippi, he raised sufficient money to purchase his own freedom and later conducted business as a successful money broker, barber, real estate lessor, retailer, and farmer, among many other enterprises.

1860: Robert Gordan posts annual earnings of $60,000 in his coal and real estate operations; he had been born into slavery, but purchased his own freedom.

1868: Dressmaker Elizabeth Keckley, a former slave who had purchased her own freedom with a loan from one of her customers, becomes one of Washington D.C.'s top creators of dresses.

1896: Minister Richard H. Boyd launches the National Baptist Publishing House in Nashville, which targets African American religious congregations as its market. By 1920, it is one of the most successful African American-owned companies in the nation.

1905: Alonzo Franklin Herndon founds the Atlanta Life Insurance Company with funds raised from his chain of upscale barbershops; Atlanta Life is a major success.

1907: African American business districts are thriving in New York; Chicago; and Durham, North Carolina.

1923: Harry Herbert Pace sells his successful Black Swan Record Company—the first African American-owned record firm—to Paramount.

1929: The stock market crash hits many businesses hard, including the African American-owned C. H. James & Company, a food processing and distribution firm founded in 1881. The company emerges from bankruptcy under the leadership of Edward Lawrence James Sr. in the 1930s, who bought a truck on credit and started from scratch. Today the firm operates as C. H. James & Son (Holdings) and is the oldest African American-owned company in the United States; C. H. James III, the fourth generation of James leadership, heads up the company, which in 1993 acquired a 51 percent interest in food processing giant North American Produce.

1959: Berry Gordy founds Motown Records. The company goes on to produce some of the most successful recordings of the 1960s and 1970s, and to launch the careers of many of the biggest recording acts in American history.

1970: Earl Graves launches the magazine *Black Enterprise*.

1992: TLC Beatrice International Holdings Inc. posts sales of just under $1.6 billion. For years the nation's largest African American-owned business, the firm faced later challenges after the death of its visionary chief, Reginald Lewis.

African American Business in Early America

Although there were successful African American innkeepers, landholders, and tradesmen in America from the seventeenth century onwards, the African American entrepreneurial spirit began to blossom in earnest in the period from the 1790s to the years before the Civil War. During this era, African Americans started businesses in many fields, but focused strongly on enterprises related to crafts production and personal services. In part, this was because as an enslaved people they had most access to those trades that profited the slaveowner. (Skilled slaves—blacksmiths, dressmakers, and the like—were often "leased" by their owners for additional income.) These fields also required less in the way of startup capital.

Then as now, African Americans often found it difficult to secure credit for new businesses. Additionally, access to business and clerical trades were stymied by systemic and institutionalized prohibitions to formal education.

By the late 1850s and early 1860s, it is estimated, there were at least 21 African American business owners worth more than $100,000—quite a substantial figure for the period. The wealthiest was probably Stephen Smith, a former slave who built a lumber and coal operation, founded a bank, and invested in stocks and real estate. In 1865, his wealth was listed at an impressive half-million dollars. Financial records for the period are not as complete as one would wish, but it seems fair to assume that there must have been a large base of business people operating at a smaller level during the same period.

In Chicago in the years following the turn of the century, a profusion of African Americans launched successful businesses that specifically targeted African American consumers. One was the "Perfect Eat" Shop, run by one Ernest Morris. The restaurant was located on 47th Street (now King Drive), a buzzing center of African American business and cultural activity.

Where It All Happened

Oh, 47th Street was where it all happened. 47th Street, you'd stand on the corner of 47th Street and South Park and … if you stayed there long enough almost anybody you knew in Chicago would come past there sometime during the day. It was the hub. It was the center of our community. And almost—we had a department store; we had entertainment up and down the street; we had places to eat, nice restaurants; we had places to—there was just lots and lots of things going on on 47th Street.

—Historian Timuel Black on one of the most vibrant sections of Chicago's South Side, quoted on the Palm Tavern website (http://palmtavern.bizland.com/palmtavern/id16.html)

In California, a wave of African American entrepreneurial achievement accompanied the Gold Rush of 1849 and continued for three decades or so thereafter. During this period, when demand for economic output severely outstripped supply, African Americans successfully targeted white customers and thrived in a number of areas. After about 1880, however, as the white majority settled in, and the demand for goods and services came to match supply, African American business owners found their opportunities severely limited. White business operators orchestrated a campaign to limit opportunities available to African American entrepreneurs, and white consumers fell into line.

A pattern of both formal and informal denial of access to the most lucrative markets was firmly in place by the turn of century—and it persisted for the next sixty years. In the Golden State, as elsewhere in the country, African American business owners opted to target consumers in their own communities. In Los Angeles, Dr. J. A. Summerville opened a hotel for African Americans and named it after himself.

African American Entrepreneurialism at the Dawn of the Twentieth Century

In the early part of the twentieth century, most African American entrepreneurs started small and were limited to mainly local services. Among these were neighborhood dry cleaning stores, beauty shops, barber shops, nightclubs, and bars. Their clientele was also almost exclusively African American, unless the services offered were of the most menial sort, like boot-blacking and garbage-hauling.

There were notable exceptions to this pattern, however. Some African American entrepreneurs managed to extend ingenuity beyond the narrow limits envisioned for them by white society. As the century progressed, African American entrepreneurs offered more advanced services, and on a larger scale. Their customer base expanded racially as well. Firms like the North Carolina Mutual Life Insurance Company, headquartered in Durham, launched in 1898 by African Americans John Merrick and Aaron McDuffie, prospered over time. By 2001, North Carolina Mutual Life Insurance Company's assets totaled $200 million.

Madam C. J. Walker

One notable entrepreneur targeting the African American community was Madam C. J. Walker (1867–1919) of St. Louis. Born Sarah Breedlove, she worked for a time as a sales representative for the Poro Company, a cosmetics firm founded by another African American female entrepreneur, Annie M. Turnbo-Malone.

Walker launched her own company in 1905, developing an entire line of products for African American women out of the beauty school she opened. She offered shampoos, pomades, hair-growers, hair-straighteners, and a method for hot-comb hair straightening. Her "Walker system" was an extraordinary success across the country.

Madam Walker predated Mary Kay and Avon by a long distance, becoming a nationally known name in cosmetics and introducing several lasting marketing innovations.

Walker was the first marketer to use similarly dressed sales employees to make house calls. They were all women, and they were known as Walker Agents. She was also one of the first American self-employed female millionaires—of any race.

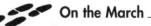 **On the March**

I had to make my own opportunity ... Don't sit down and wait for the opportunities to come; you have to get up and make them.

—Madam C. J. Walker

On the March

On January 28, 1998, the U.S. Postal Service issued a commemorative stamp honoring entrepreneur Madam C. J. Walker. The photograph on the stamp was produced by Scurlock Studio around the year 1914; it was used extensively in Walker's promotional campaigns of that era. The stamp was designed by Richard Sheaff as part of the U.S. Postal Service's Black Heritage series; 45 million were produced. The New York-based Madam C. J. Walker Foundation helped in promoting the commemorative stamp.

Madam Walker's own ascent from washerwoman to the highest levels of business success was nothing less than extraordinary, and she is remembered today for bringing financial independence to a vast number of African American women who might otherwise never have known it. Committed to the education and development of the African American community, she left a rich legacy of entrepreneurial achievement and philanthropy that has inspired men and women from all walks of life.

At its height, Walker's company employed over 5,000 agents, and compensated them by means of a carefully designed incentive program. Her business model was a landmark in the development of the cosmetics industry. Her story is today one of the most prominent and celebrated African American life accounts of the early twentieth century. A book about her by her great-great-granddaughter A'Lelia Bundles, *On Her Own Ground* (Scribner, 2001) made the *Washington Post* and *Los Angeles Times* bestseller lists.

Madam C .J. Walker.

(Judith Burros)

Walker served as the inspiration for the Madam C. J. Walker Foundation, a charitable organization with the mission of supporting African American entrepreneurs. To learn how to support the Foundation and its work in encouraging business development in the African American community, contact the Duncan Group at 212-697-3737.

Move Over, Thomas Edison

A number of other individual African Americans made particularly important entrepreneurial contributions, often on a national or international scale.

Beard's Breakthroughs

Andrew Jackson Beard (1849–c.1921) invented and patented a rotary engine in 1892. A former slave, he also developed new kinds of plows for farmers. He received another patent for his most famous invention, the Automatic Railroad Coupler, known as the Jenny Coupler. This allowed cars to be connected by simply being bumped together. Previously, a worker had to position himself between the two cars, and then drop a pin through two holes at just the right moment. The procedure was the cause of many accidents, often fatal. Beard himself lost a leg as the result of such an accident. The Jenny Coupler revolutionized railroad practice.

The Real McCoy

Another self-taught African American engineer became the inspiration for a phrase that entered the English language. Born in Canada, Elijah McCoy (1844-1929) became a railroad fireman in the United States. He invented the lubricator cup, which, although little remarked by the general public, allowed machines to be oiled in use. It was a major contribution to the Industrial Revolution. When imitations came on the market, they were dismissed as not "the real McCoy," or genuine article.

A Scientist Steps Up for Southern Agriculture

One remarkable man straddled the worlds of business and science in a way that few Americans have and deserves notice for achievements in both areas.

George Washington Carver (1864–1943) won worldwide fame, in part because he offered an irresistible media angle. Carver, among the most acclaimed scientists of his era, was a former slave whose scientific advances revolutionized a southern farming economy that was in deep trouble in the 1890s and the years following.

? FAQ

How prominent was George Washington Carver? As one of the most renowned scientists of his era, Carver was in demand as a researcher (and, let's face it, public relations icon). Among the people who offered him jobs—and won publicity for doing so—were Thomas Edison and Joseph Stalin. He turned them both down.

Teaching and researching at the Tuskegee Institute, Carver developed a number of vegetables from limited roles as home-table foods to large-scale crops. Two that became mainstays of the southern economy were the peanut (from which he developed 325 products) and the sweet potato (108). He invented Carver's Hybrid cotton, a more resilient strain of the original plant. Holder of three patents, he introduced over 100 industrial uses for various agricultural entities.

In 1896, when Carver began the most momentous phase of his career, peanut production was so low that its production was not even formally measured. By 1940, it was the South's second-largest cash crop.

Carver's patient, methodical work and commitment to research that benefited others set a high scientific—and human—standard. "Anything will give up its secrets," he once observed, "if you love it enough. Not only have I found that when I talk to the little flower or to the little peanut they will give up their secrets, but I have found that when I silently commune with people."

A George Washington Carver Timeline

1864: Born in Diamond, Missouri.

1877: Attends school in Neosho, Missouri.

1890: Enrolls at Simpson College in Iowa; later transfers to Iowa State College of Agricultural and Mechanical Arts.

1894: Receives bachelor's of agriculture degree; becomes member of faculty at Iowa State.

1896: Begins focusing on research projects designed to help southern agriculture, which had exhausted many of its best farmlands with years of over-reliance on cotton. Encourages desperate southern farmers to plant soybeans, sweet potatoes, and peanuts; later, sets out to develop commercial applications based on derivatives from these crops. Derivative products he helped to develop included flour, vinegar, molasses, ink, synthetic rubber, glue, cheese, milk, coffee, flour, ink, dyes, plastics, wood stains, soap, linoleum, medicinal oils, and a wide array of cosmetics.

1916: Having more or less single-handedly rejuvenated southern agriculture, Carver emerged as an international celebrity and was elected to Britain's Royal Society for the Encouragement of Arts, Manufactures and Commerce.

1923: Received the Spingarn Medal in acknowledgment of his scientific and agricultural accomplishments.

1940: Donates life savings to Carver Research Foundation at Tuskegee. Later, begins work to develop substitutes for textile dyes available only from war-torn Europe; ultimately develops new dyes in 500 shades.

1943: Dies in Tuskegee, Alabama.

Beyond the Color Line

After World War II, many middle- and upper-class African American men and women benefited from new educational opportunities, attending business and law schools in larger and larger numbers. When they graduated, they built companies located outside African American neighborhoods that sought customers across and beyond racial lines. They worked to establish themselves in state, national, and international markets, not just their local city or town.

African American–owned construction firms also began to take on large-scale commercial projects, as the result of state and federal affirmative action policies. Despite some resistance from entrenched white competitors, these building firms are now a part of the urban and suburban landscapes.

The Modern Era

Many African American entrepreneurs have had to go it alone, and have struggled in the process. The modern era has seen a rise in organized support for African American entrepreneurs from within the African American community itself. Chapters of the *National Black MBA Association* now routinely sponsor conferences and workshops directly aimed at helping young African American entrepreneurs develop their ideas, find the venture capitalists to fund them, and cultivate contacts with major corporations and their executives. Recent gatherings in Boston and Chicago brought together

African American graduates of many different business schools to learn from each other, network, and, literally, capitalize on their graduate educations.

What's the Word?

Founded in 1970, the **National Black MBA Association** is "dedicated to creating partnerships that result in creating intellectual and economic wealth in the black community." It offers partnerships with over 400 business groups, advice on obtaining venture capital, and much more. To find out more, visit www.nbmbaa.org or call the national headquarters in Chicago at 312-236-2622.

In 1996, three African Americans founded the Harlem Venture Group expressly to provide financing and support for area entrepreneurs. This organization offers startup assistance through its eight-week Be Your Own Boss workshops for developing detailed, workable business plans, and helps existing businesses grow and expand through its contact-building series of breakfast forums.

Since the 1980s, the Internet has opened another new door. African American Roosevelt Gist was a car salesman in Virginia. He often had white customers bypass him for a white salesman. When he started an online car sales service, this problem vanished. With 40,000 visitors a month, he now books nearly $200,000 in ad revenue annually. On the Net no one knows Gist's color, so he loses no business to prejudice.

Another Internet-related advance is Minority.net, created with grants and support from the Urban League and the Commerce Department. The site connects 75 minority-owned firms with major corporations, making it easy for the latter to buy goods and services from the former.

However, despite these and other advances for African American entrepreneurs, significant obstacles and inequities still exist. Sociologist Timothy Bates of New York's New School of Social Research found that African American entrepreneurs still receive close to 40 percent less in financing for their ventures, compared to their white counterparts.

Nonetheless, the concept of African American entrepreneurship on a sophisticated scale is clearly here to stay. As the dawn of the twentieth century saw the establishment of many neighborhood, locally focused African American businesses, the early years of the twenty-first century may well see a similar slow, steady growth—only this time of companies offering advanced services in a host of locations.

Growth and Challenge

Today, blacks still suffer from low rates of business formation because credit and access to capital remains problematic for black businessmen (and women). Overall, black businesses are still characterized by [their] apparent dominance in human service and retail trade, which represents no more than a 1% share of sales receipts of all businesses. However, according to the US Department of Commerce, the number of all black businesses grew 46% between 1987 and 1992 … Meanwhile, the Small Business Administration (SBA) is looking to play a larger role in facilitating African-American entrepreneurship by assembling an aggressive plan to double the volume of business it does with African-American entrepreneurs.

—from "Exploring 100 Years of Black Business," Charles Brooks (available at http://www.imdiversity.com/villages/african/Article_Detail.asp?Article_ID=385)

The Least You Need to Know

- ◆ Notable African American entrepreneurs from the pre–Civil War era include Stephan Smith and Robert Gordan.

- ◆ Madam C. J. Walker was among the first female millionaires—of any race.

- ◆ George Washington Carver straddled the worlds of business and science—and developed new product and new markets for them that rejuvenated southern agriculture.

- ◆ Often denied access to the most lucrative markets, many African American entrepreneurs targeted African American consumers.

- ◆ Significant obstacles and inequities—particularly with regard to access to capital and credit—still remain for today's African American entrepreneurs.

Chapter 16

Femininity: African American Women

In This Chapter

◆ Remarkable African American women from the world of business

◆ Remarkable African American women from the world of politics and activism

◆ Remarkable African American women from the world of arts and literature

◆ … and others worthy of remembrance and discussion

Many extraordinary African American women have helped to move the nation and the world forward. You'll meet 14 of them in this chapter. Some people may ask why African American women deserve "special attention," or why we should make a point of focusing on the merits of these 14. Here is one answer.

Too often, the stories of African American women receive far less attention than they deserve. This is a fairly reliable historical principle, and it has been a dream of mine to help rectify the problem by bringing the stories of some of the most amazing African American women to a wider audience—and showing people how to learn more about each. These are certainly not the only 14 stories that deserve to be told about African American femininity, but they are a starting point.

In these pages, we follow the wise instruction of the gifted writer Alice Walker, who urged women to "summon up courage to fulfill dormant dreams."

Here, in (roughly) reverse chronological order, are introductions to 14 women who took dormant dreams and fulfilled them.

Barbara Jordan

Barbara Jordan won election to the Texas State Senate in 1966, thus becoming the first African American senator in the state since 1883. She won election to the U.S. Congress in 1972; her 1974 speech during hearings considering the impeachment of Richard Nixon catapulted her to national prominence. Her electrifying keynote speech before the 1976 Democratic National Convention left many wondering whether they were looking at a major new force in national politics. Jordan cut her political career short, however, retiring from the House of Representatives in 1979 to focus on teaching. (The decision was motivated in part by the debilitating nerve disorder that eventually required her to use a wheelchair.)

Jordan received the Presidential Medal of Freedom in 1994; she died in Austin, Texas, in 1996. Shortly after her death, in its January 17, 1996, edition, the Houston *Chronicle* described her as a woman who had risen "from a poor preacher's family in Houston's Fifth Ward to build a career in government that some believe could have carried her to the White House." The *Chronicle* went on to note that Jordan had a "will of iron and a voice of gold," and was "one of the few black women to make a name in U.S. politics."

Potent Quotes

In the extraordinary speech she made during the hearings considering the impeachment of President Nixon, Jordan said: "If the impeachment provision of the Constitution of the United States will not reach the offenses charged here, then perhaps that eighteenth-century Constitution should be abandoned to a twentieth-century paper shredder."

Jordan's two-sentence summary of her vision of democracy is as pertinent today as the day she uttered it in 1977: "What the people want is very simple. They want an America as good as its promise."

On diversity, she asked, "How do we create a harmonious society out of so many different kinds of people?" Her answer: "The key is tolerance—the one value that is indispensable in creating community."

To Learn More About Barbara Jordan ...

Visit www.elf.net/bjordan/ for a wealth of Jordan-related links—including full texts of her 1974 speech on Richard Nixon's impeachment and her 1976 keynote address to the Democratic National Convention, courtesy of Elf Systems Corporation.

Oprah Winfrey

A one-woman cultural phenomenon, Oprah Winfrey has steadily enlarged her media influence beyond the daytime talk-show format she conquered and has dominated since the mid-1980s.

She is notable for her unique bond with American women, her extraordinary business instincts, and her ability to appeal consistently to a mass audience without ever compromising her own intelligence or personal standards. As these words are written, she remains a global icon and the most indomitable current hero of the American rags-to-riches story.

Winfrey has won numerous accolades for her broadcasting, publishing, and philanthropic work, and today oversees a multimedia empire as head of Harpo, Inc.; Harpo Productions, Inc.; Harpo Studios, Inc.; Harpo Films, Inc.; Harpo Print, LLC; and Harpo Video, Inc. Her show has received, at last count, 35 Emmy awards.

FAQ

Where did Oprah get her start? At the age of 19, Oprah was anchoring a local news broadcast in Tennessee. She was the station's youngest anchor ever and the first African American to hold the top news job there.

In 2001, *Newsweek* magazine named Winfrey the "Woman of the Century." Considering the extraordinary events of her life (especially the humble origins and social obstacles this modern-day media titan faced as a child in rural Mississippi), it was an inspired choice.

Potent Quotes

Winfrey's outlook on life and business radiates an optimism and energy that is an important part of her appeal. "I don't believe in failure," she has said. "It is not failure if you enjoyed the process."

She has managed to keep her perspective on her own enormous success: "Everyone wants to ride with you in the limo … but what you need is someone who will take the bus with you when the limo breaks down."

To Learn More About Oprah Winfrey …

Visit www.oprah.com/about/about_landing.jhtml for detailed info on Oprah's life story, achievements, and current projects, courtesy of Oprah Winfrey's official website.

Rita Dove

In 1985, Rita Dove won the Pulitzer prize for *Thomas and Beulah* (Carnegie Mellon University Press, 1986), a volume of poems that drew on the lives of her grandparents. Eight years later, she was named poet laureate of the United States—the first African American to hold the honor. She remained poet laureate until 1995.

Dove's poetry output includes the volume *On the Bus with Rosa Parks* (W. W. Norton, 1999). She is also a playwright; her drama *The Darker Face of the Earth* had its premier at Oregon Shakespeare Festival in 1996 and was later produced at a number of theaters around the country.

Rita Dove's career has been marked by many accolades. She has received a Mellon Foundation grant, an NAACP Great American Artist award, and fellowships from the Fulbright and Guggenheim foundations, as well as support from the National Endowment for the Arts and the National Endowment from the Humanities. As one critic, quoted on the Voices from the Gaps website (see following section "To Learn More About Rita Dove …") noted, "[S]he speaks with a directness and a dramatic intensity that commands attention… [Rita Dove] fashions imaginative constructs that strike the reader as much by their 'rightness' as their originality."

 On the March

In 1970, Rita Dove was named one of the one hundred top high school students in the United States. She was honored as a Presidential Scholar and made a trip to the White House.

Potent Quote

Asked about her early experiences with literature, Dove recalled, "My childhood library was small enough not to be intimidating. And yet I felt the whole world was contained in those two rooms. I could walk any aisle and smell wisdom."

To Learn More About Rita Dove ...

Visit the Voices from the Gaps website at voices.cla.umn.edu/authors/RitaDove.html—it features excerpts from her work and a detailed biography.

Angela Davis

Political activist, left-of-center academic, and world-class political lightning rod, Angela Davis's articles, addresses, and brushes with the law riveted America during the late 1960s and early 1970s. She was, and remains, a divisive and brilliant intellectual figure.

A protégé of Herbert Marcuse, Davis was a dazzling and opinionated professor. Denied reappointment as a lecturer in philosophy by the California Board of Regents in 1970, apparently because of her political beliefs, Davis became an influential social critic of racial injustice. She was pursued on charges related to a deadly kidnapping and prisoner escape plan in Marin County, California, in 1970, and appeared for a time on the FBI's "Most Wanted" List. (A gun legally registered in her name had been used in the crime.) Apprehended later that year, Davis was acquitted by an all-white jury.

Her writings include a popular autobiography and the books *Women, Race, and Class* (Random House, 1983) and *Blues Legacies and Black Feminism* (Random House, 1999). She currently teaches in California, and has been described as a "soft-spoken" instructor with a talent for eliciting insights from her students.

Potent Quotes

Davis's enduring skepticism about government and social institutions is evident in one of her most popular remarks: "What this country needs is more unemployed politicians."

She also shed new light on a word frequently applied to her own life when she observed that "radical simply means 'grasping things at the root.'"

To Learn More About Angela Davis ...

Visit voices.cla.umn.edu/authors/AngelaDavis.html for an intriguing summary of her writings and tumultuous life, courtesy of the Voices from the Gaps: Women Writers of Color site.

Shirley Chisholm

After being elected into the U.S. House of Representatives in 1968, Shirley Chisholm, the outspoken congresswoman from New York's Bedford-Stuyvesant area, drew stares of disbelief when she announced in 1972 that she was running for President of the United States. Her campaign was notable not for victory—which was hardly likely in a country that had, in the most recent election, accorded segregationist George Wallace a significant chunk of its electoral votes—but for Chisolm's emergence as a national political figure.

Chisholm won 152 delegates at the 1972 Democratic National Convention, placing well behind Hubert Humphrey and the eventual nominee, George McGovern.

Shirley Chisholm's 1972 campaign for president drew national attention.

(Library of Congress)

Her unflinching style and uncompromising remarks on integration, drug abuse, social justice, and the war in Vietnam won attention, headlines, and (perhaps most important) mainstream acceptance for a new kind of American politician—brash, honest, and unafraid to bring up issues previously considered too extreme for prime time. Later media-savvy African American social and political figures owe this trailblazer a significant debt. Chisholm also founded the National Women's Political Caucus.

Her never-boring career in Congress, which lasted from 1969 to 1983, was marked by support for a range of women's-rights issues and enthusiastic advocacy for full-employment and education initiatives.

On the March

Chisholm's 1970 address in support of the Equal Rights Amendment was named as one of the top 100 American speeches of the twentieth century by a group of 137 scholars polled by the University of Wisconsin, Madison, and Texas A & M University. The speech is accessible on the Internet via the Women's Internet Information Network at www.undelete.org/ library/library0102.html.

Potent Quotes

Chisholm put a spotlight on the special challenges facing African American women when she observed, famously, that "Of my two 'handicaps,' being female put more obstacles in my path than being black."

As a member of the House Select Committee on Crime, Chisholm challenged easy assumptions about drug abuse with words that are as worthy of note today as they were in the late 1960s. "It is not heroin or cocaine," she noted, "that makes one an addict; it is the need to escape from a harsh reality. There are more television addicts, more baseball and football addicts, more movie addicts, and certainly more alcohol addicts in this country than there are narcotics addicts."

And in a deft analysis of her own career, Chisholm noted that "[t]here is little place in the political scheme of things for an independent, creative personality, for a fighter. Anyone who takes that role must pay a price."

To Learn More About Shirley Chisholm ...

Visit search.eb.com/blackhistory/micro/721/78.html for an informative overview of her life and career, courtesy of the *Encyclopedia Britannica Guide to Black History*.

Fannie Lou Hamer

Fannie Lou Hamer's most widely celebrated moment was her stinging rebuke of the 1964 Democratic National Convention's Credentials Committee.

The committee ultimately denied her upstart Mississippi delegation the right to be seated at the convention, but she won the media war when network news shows aired her remarks. President Lyndon Johnson, uneasy about losing political support in the South, decided not to support Hamer's competing Mississippi slate of delegates. He acquiesced in the seating of an all-white delegation from Mississippi and scheduled a news conference at the same time Hamer was taking the Credentials Committee to task.

The maneuver kept Hamer off live television—but she nevertheless won a huge audience when the nightly news broadcasts showed videotape of her appearance. All of America heard her press her case that the "official" Mississippi delegation was a sham, since the vast majority of African Americans in the state had been deprived of the right to vote.

A founder of the Mississippi Freedom Democratic Party and a ceaseless agitator for civil rights, Hamer was one of the most important and effective activists of the 1960s and 1970s.

Potent Quotes

Hamer's now-famous address to the 1964 Democratic Convention's Credentials Committee included the following passage: "Is this America, the land of the free and the home of the brave, where we are threatened daily because we want to live as decent human beings? … I question America."

Recalling a civil rights protest from the 1960s, she said, "I do remember, one time, a man came to me after the students began to work in Mississippi, and he said the white people were getting tired and they were getting tense and anything might happen. Well, I asked him how long he [thought] we had been getting tired? … All my life I've been sick and tired. Now I'm sick and tired of being sick and tired."

To Learn More About Fannie Lou Hamer ...

Visit www.beejae.com/hamer.htm for an in-depth autobiography, provided by Minerva Computer Services.

Rosa Parks

The courageous refusal of Rosa Parks to yield her seat on a Birmingham bus sparked the historic bus boycott in that city. (See Chapter 8.)

In a March 1999, article, *Ebony* magazine named her one of the 100 most important African American women of the twentieth century, and joined the large group of those considering her momentous act of civil disobedience one of the pivotal events in American history.

Parks is frequently referred to as the "Mother of the Civil Rights Movement."

Potent Quote

On the larger meaning of her act of civil disobedience, Parks had this to say: "No matter how much a person or law may try to tell you what to do and/or deny you of your liberty, do not give up your seat on the bus of life. Don't give up your freedom and integrity. Stand for something or you'll fall for anything. Today's mighty oak is yesterday's nut that held its ground."

Rosa Parks's arrest led to the Montgomery bus boycott.

(Judith Burros)

To Learn More About Rosa Parks ...

Visit www.time.com/time/time100/heroes/profile/parks01.html for a very detailed biography, composed by Rita Dove and published in *Time* magazine.

Dorothy Dandridge

The first African American woman nominated for an Academy award for best actress, Dorothy Dandridge presented Hollywood with a problem it wasn't prepared to solve: How do you build a career for a African American leading lady?

Dandridge was an important and tragic figure in American cultural history. Her career foundered after her nominated performance in *Carmen Jones* (whose cast was entirely African American); Hollywood's powers-that-were failed to find a suitable follow-up vehicle for her.

Dandridge's personal life was complex, and she struggled with financial and substance-abuse problems. She is remembered today as a vibrant, sensual, and trailblazing performer—someone who helped make later mainstream success possible for the next generation of African American actors. One can only wonder what heights she would have attained had she been born 20 years later. She died in 1965 as the result of a barbiturate overdose.

Potent Quote

Dorothy Dandridge on racial prejudice, a topic with which she was familiar: "It makes you … half alive. It gives you nothing. It takes away."

To Learn More About Dorothy Dandridge ...

Visit home.hiwaay.net/~oliver/dandridge.html for a filmography, biography, and links.

Ella Fitzgerald

One of the most acclaimed artists in the history of jazz, Ella Fitzgerald evolved as dramatically as the music itself did and enjoyed a career of extraordinary versatility and longevity. Her *scat* improvisations won adulation from a worldwide legion of fans, and her interpretations of what has come to be known as the Great American Songbook remain definitive.

What's the Word?

Scat is a form of improvisational jazz singing, in which the human voice is used to deliver melodies rather than lyrics. Ella Fitzgerald was the supreme practitioner of this form.

Fitzgerald was a true innovator whose career spanned six decades. She served as one of the great ambassadors of jazz music. Fitzgerald managed to maintain her own artistic vision at the same time that she commanded the attention, audiences, and cultural influence of an upper-tier mainstream pop music star. To say that this is rare among prominent jazz artists would probably be the musical understatement of the century.

When she died in 1996 at the age of 79, an unprecedented wave of an emotion hard to describe—part grief, part love, part joy—swept music lovers around the world.

Potent Quote

Among the most prolific and enduring musicians of the twentieth century, Fitzgerald was always focused on the next goal: "It isn't where you came from," she advised. "It's where you're going that counts."

To Learn More About Ella Fitzgerald ...

Visit museum.media.org/ella/index.html for detailed bio of Ella, a discography, and information on her historic performances at Carnegie Hall.

Mary McLeod Bethune

Born to former slaves, Mary McLeod Bethune devoted her life to providing educational opportunities to African American children.

The life of this dedicated educator and reformer was built on an extraordinary faith in God and a corresponding commitment to service. She taught in Georgia, South Carolina, Florida, and Illinois; she also made a habit of visiting jails, frequently singing to the inmates there.

She spent a great deal of time working with the homeless. In 1904, she opened the Daytona Normal and Industrial Institute for Negro Girls. The institution, which later accepted boys as well, charged 50 cents per week in tuition, but its founder made sure that no child was denied access because of family financial problems. Later, she opened a high school and a hospital for African Americans. In 1923, she oversaw a merger as the Daytona Normal and Industrial Institute for Negro Girls became Bethune-Cookman College.

> **On the March**
>
> In 1940, Bethune was named vice president of the NAACP; many other appointments and honors followed. By the time she died in 1955, she had worked with deep commitment on child welfare, housing, employment, and education issues from the time of the Theodore Roosevelt administration all the way through to the Eisenhower era.

The list of Mary McLeod Bethune's life achievements parallels America's slow awakening to the educational and social inequities built into its social institutions. (For example, she agitated, successfully, for integration of the Red Cross.) In 1917, she became head of the Florida Federation of Colored Women; in 1924, she was named to lead the National Association of Colored Women. In 1935, she formed the National Council of Negro Women, and the following year she served as Director of the National Youth Administration of Negro Affairs. Also in 1936, she was named Director of the Division of Negro Affairs, making her the first African American to head a federal agency.

Potent Quotes

Bethune was big on personal accountability in the face of injustice. "If we accept and acquiesce in the face of discrimination," she once advised, "we accept the responsibility ourselves. We should, therefore, protest openly everything … that smacks of discrimination or slander." She also warned that "If our people are to fight their way up out of bondage, we must arm them with the sword and the shield and the buckler of pride."

To Learn More About Mary McLeod Bethune …

Visit www.nahc.org/NAHC/Val/Columns/SC10-6.html for detailed biographical overview developed by Homecare Online.

Ida Wells-Barnett

A titanic figure in American social and journalistic history, Ida Wells-Barnett was a tireless opponent of lynching and one of the premier investigative reporters of her day. She was editor of the *Memphis Free Speech*, a paper whose outspoken anti-racist articles so enraged local white supremacists that they destroyed its offices.

They did not, however destroy Wells-Barnett's fighting spirit; she continued to speak and write forcefully against racism and lynching and continued a largely successful campaign to "tell the world the facts" about mob violence and discrimination against African Americans.

Potent Quote

From her days on the beat in Memphis: "The city of Memphis has demonstrated that neither character nor standing avails the Negro if he dares to protect himself against the white man or become his rival. There is nothing we can do about the lynching now, as we are out-numbered and without arms. The white mob could help itself to ammunition without pay, but the order is rigidly enforced against the selling of guns to Negroes. There is therefore only one thing left to do; save our money and leave a town which will neither protect our lives and property, nor give us a fair trial in the courts, but takes us out and murders us in cold blood when accused by white persons."

To Learn More About Ida Wells-Barnett ...

Visit www.lkwdpl.org/wihohio/barn-ida.htm for an in-depth biography courtesy of the Women In History project.

Madam C. J. Walker

In 1905, Madam C. J. Walker sold her first bottle of hair straightening conditioner. Before her death in 1919, she became the first female millionaire in American history. She built her fortune on a popular line of hair-care products and used her wealth and social influence to promote progressive causes and advocated social progress for African Americans.

You'll find more on Madam Walker's extraordinary story in Chapter 15.

Potent Quote

Walker captured the American entrepreneurial spirit in two pithy sentences when she famously advised business owners to take the initiatives in their lives and careers: "Don't sit down and wait for the opportunities to come. You have to get up and make them."

To Learn More About Madam C. J. Walker ...

Visit www.princeton.edu/~mcbrown/display/walker.html for a biography and bibliography, courtesy of Princeton University.

Harriet Tubman

Harriet Tubman now ranks as one of the nation's authentic heroes as a result of her heroic work in the rescue effort known as the *Underground Railroad*. She was hailed by many as the Moses of the middle nineteenth century.

By risking her life to shepherd others to freedom, Tubman helped to lay the nation's moral cornerstone.

What's the Word?

The **Underground Railroad** was a secret network of people, African American and white, who opposed slavery and risked their lives to help fugitive slaves to safety and freedom in the North. The phrase is strongly associated with Harriet Tubman, who made 19 trips into the South to liberate over 300 slaves. There were similar operations in place long before Tubman escaped from slavery in 1849; Quakers from Pennsylvania and New Jersey were particularly active in helping fugitive slaves get the assistance and protection they needed.

Potent Quotes

In later life, Tubman recalled that she prayed for her physically abusive master using the following words: "Oh, dear Lord, change that man's heart and make him a Christian."

When she received word that the master planned to send her to a chain gang, she amended her prayer slightly: "Lord, if you ain't never going to change that man's heart, kill him, Lord, and take him out of the way, so he won't do no more mischief."

Shortly after she made this appeal to God, the master did in fact die suddenly. Tubman was sick with grief for some time after this episode, but eventually consoled herself, concluding, as she recalled the event, that "I couldn't pray for him no more."

To Learn More About Harriet Tubman ...

Visit www.nyhistory.com/harriettubman/life.htm for a detailed biography.

Sojourner Truth

A nineteenth-century preacher, abolitionist, and advocate of *women's suffrage*, Sojourner Truth was one of the most spellbinding orators of her era.

What's the Word?

The **women's suffrage** movement was the name applied to the long-running effort to win women the right to vote in the United States. The campaign took shape in the mid-nineteenth century; in 1920, a constitutional amendment gave women the right to vote. White women, however, often found it considerably easier to do so than African American women.

She worked ceaselessly to raise food and clothing donations for African American regiments during the Civil War and was received by President Lincoln in 1864. She is perhaps best known for the "Ain't I A Woman?" address, which still carries a visceral impact a century and a half after it is said to have electrified attendees of an Ohio women's rights conference in 1851.

Potent Quote

Whatever the circumstances of its composition or delivery (the details are murky, and some scholars have questioned the speech's authenticity), the following, attributed to Sojourner Truth, is one of the most celebrated speeches in American history:

> Well, children, where there is so much racket there must be something out of kilter. I think that 'twixt the negroes of the South and the women at the North, all talking about rights, the white men will be in a fix pretty soon. But what's all this here talking about?

> That man over there says that women need to be helped into carriages, and lifted over ditches, and to have the best place everywhere. Nobody ever helps me into carriages, or over mud-puddles, or gives me any best place! And ain't I a woman? Look at me! Look at my arm! I have ploughed and planted, and gathered into barns, and no man could head me! And ain't I a woman? I could work as much and eat as much as a man—when I could get it—and bear the lash as well! And ain't I a woman? I have borne thirteen children, and seen most all sold off to slavery, and when I cried out with my mother's grief, none but Jesus heard me! And ain't I a woman?

> Then that little man in black there, he says women can't have as much rights as men, 'cause Christ wasn't a woman! Where did your Christ come from? Where did your Christ come from? From God and a woman! Man had nothing to do with Him.

> If the first woman God ever made was strong enough to turn the world upside down all alone, these women together ought to be able to turn it back, and get it right side up again! And now they is asking to do it, the men better let them.

> Obliged to you for hearing me, and now old Sojourner ain't got nothing more to say.

To Learn More About Sojourner Truth ...

Visit www.sojournertruth.org/History/Biography/Default.htm for a detailed biography, courtesy of the official Sojourner Truth website.

The Least You Need to Know

- ◆ Inspiring stories of African American women from the world of business include that of Madam C. J. Walker.

- ◆ Inspiring stories of African American women from the world of politics and activism have included those of Barbara Jordan, Shirley Chisholm, and Fannie Lou Hamer.

- ◆ Inspiring stories of African American women from the world of arts and literature have included those of Rita Dove and Ella Fitzgerald.

- ◆ All these women had a knack for (as Alice Walker put it) "summon[ing] up courage to fulfill dormant dreams."

- ◆ There are many more like them, and their stories are ready to be told, too.

Part 4

Power on the Outside: Contributions to American Culture

The more closely you look at "African American history," the more you realize how densely interwoven it is with "American history." Here are examples of great cultural contributions, not to a narrowly defined racial group, but to the American experience as a whole.

Chapter 17

Five Giants

In This Chapter

- ◆ The uneasy road of Martin Luther King Jr.
- ◆ The evolving vision of Malcolm X
- ◆ The enduring commitment of Asa Philip Randolph
- ◆ The cautious pragmatism of Roy Wilkins
- ◆ The genius of Ralph Bunche

Here, you learn about five remarkable twentieth-century civil rights figures who, in different ways, dragged the United States of America into a new era.

All five are now gone; two of them met violent deaths as a result of their personal beliefs and principles. All five had the kind of commitment to freedom and equal rights that accepted the possibility of death for the cause. It is, in large measure, because of the work of such giants that we now live in a society in which huge numbers of people have no direct experience of what it meant to live in a racially segregated country. The debt we all owe them is hard to calculate.

Dr. Martin Luther King Jr.

Often labeled the "American Gandhi," King freely credited Indian leader Mahatma Gandhi's strategies of personal commitment, nonviolence, and passive resistance for the effectiveness of his own campaigns in areas such as integration and voting rights.

Like Gandhi, King put himself on the line. In response to death threats, King's aides sometimes attempted to convince the reverend not to march prominently at the front of protest gatherings. King ignored their pleas, leaving his aides to improvise security measures to the best of their ability. (Once, they put as many men with a similar build to King's as they could find at the front of the march, and equipped them with suits that matched his.)

A powerful and compelling orator, King contributed something unique and enduring to the entire American family when he delivered his "I Have a Dream" speech during the 1963 March on Washington. Of greater long-term impact than his eloquence, though, was his example of personal courage in the face of constant intimidation and covert operations from individual racists, paramilitary organizations, state governments, and a hostile FBI. (Those who are inclined to think of the Kennedy Administration as an unyielding ally of civil rights should consider its willingness to place wiretaps on Dr. King's phone lines.)

?

FAQ

What was Dr. King's philosophy in dealing with the federal government? It evolved over time. From the middle of the 1950s until the fateful 1965 voter-registration drive in Selma, Alabama, King, a shrewd tactician, carefully avoided antagonizing or defying the federal courts or their representatives, which had been key allies of the civil rights movement since the *Brown* v. *Board of Education* decision. (He routinely ignored racist *state* court decrees and police orders.) In the later years of his life, however, King's public pronouncements grew more openly critical of federal policies, especially in the areas of economic inequality and the war in Vietnam.

The Significance of Selma

On March 7, 1965, 600 demonstrators attempted to hold a voter-registration march that was to begin in Selma, Alabama, and conclude 54 miles later in Montgomery. The marchers, whose sense of political theater had to be admired, intended to march down route 80—otherwise known as the Jefferson Davis Highway—and across the Edmund Pettus Bridge.

Shock troops under the command of local law enforcement and the governor of Alabama were waiting for them. After the demonstrators ignored an order to disperse, state troopers and local lawmen tore into the group, assaulting them with clubs and whips. They turned back the protestors—but network news cameras captured the violence, and the image of the beatings provoked outrage around the country (and the world).

Dr. King, who had been in Atlanta at the time of the attack in Selma, quickly made his way to Alabama and announced plans for a second march on the bridge. Legions of supporters appeared, and were ready to join him in another attempt to cross the bridge. But there were complications.

A federal judge had just ordered the demonstrators *not* to march; he needed time to study the case. This put Dr. King in an exquisitely difficult position. To call off the march entirely would have alienated countless supporters, many of whom had traveled to Selma for the express purpose of joining King in a march across the bridge. But to cross the bridge in defiance of a federal—rather than a state—court order would probably be a significant tactical error, given the larger goal of maintaining the support of the federal judiciary in the struggle for civil rights.

Today, with hindsight and with knowledge of his later death by assassination, we may be tempted to think of Dr. King as an eternally inspired, even saintly figure. It's important to acknowledge, though, that he was a leader of men during a fateful and often chaotic time, and that he was consistently forced to make difficult choices. Selma was one of those choices. Rather than defy a federal judge, King chose to mount a symbolic effort—a march halfway across the bridge.

King Alienates the Political Left

The younger demonstrators on the scene were furious. They accused King of selling out, of being an Uncle Tom, of letting the white man turn him around. It was an early indication of a fault line between the "freedom now" wing of the growing movement and what would come to be known as the *Black Power* wing.

King's "split-the-difference" approach led to an extremely awkward moment on the bridge, and it produced outrage from many of his followers, but it was soon overshadowed by events. On March 15, President Lyndon Johnson addressed

What's the Word?

The **Black Power** movement of the 1960s and early 1970s celebrated African American autonomy and emphasized exclusive roles for African Americans in civil rights agitation. The movement was generally more radical in outlook, and less media-friendly, than Dr. Martin Luther King Jr.'s inclusive campaign of passive resistance.

What's the Word? _____

The **Voting Rights Act of 1965**, signed into law by Lyndon Johnson in the same room where Abraham Lincoln had signed the Emancipation Proclamation, explicitly prohibited state disenfranchisement of African American voters. It was a triumph for Dr. King and the entire civil rights movement, probably the most influential and effective piece of civil rights legislation in the nation's history.

a joint session of Congress, and used the assault in Selma to underline Congress's moral duty to pass sweeping voting rights legislation. (It did—and the eventual result was the *Voting Rights Act of 1965*.)

We Shall Overcome

On March 15, 1965, in the aftermath of the violence of Selma, President Lyndon Johnson addressed a joint session of Congress in support of voting rights legislation. The high point of the speech adopted the language of the anthem of the civil rights movement: "It is not just Negroes but all of us who must overcome the crippling legacy of bigotry and injustice. And we shall overcome."

On March 17, the federal judge authorized the march from Selma to Montgomery; George Wallace, the governor of Alabama, had declared that he could not guarantee the safety of the protesters, thus clearing the way for an overwhelming display of federal force in support of the march. Demonstrators crossed the bridge in triumph, with King leading the way.

It was a victory like no other.

Malcolm X

While Martin Luther King frequently received glowing press coverage and appealed successfully to the conscience of white America, the charismatic militant leader Malcolm X won little but negative attention from the mainstream media during his lifetime—and he terrified most white people.

On the March _____

Our religion (Islam) teaches us to be intelligent. Be peaceful, be courteous, obey the law, respect everyone; but if someone puts his hand on you, send him to the cemetery.

—Malcolm X, "Message to the Grass Roots" speech, 1963

Malcolm briskly rejected talk of nonviolence, pointing out (accurately) that the white supremacists of the day had no commitment to it, and he urged African Americans to defend themselves energetically when confronted by those who would deny them their rights.

He was born Malcolm Little on May 19, 1925, in Omaha, Nebraska. His parents were followers of the black nationalist Marcus Garvey, publisher of the influential *Negro World* and advocate of the "back to

Africa movement." The Littles' activism appears to have drawn the attention of white supremacists. When Malcolm was four years old, two white men set the family's home ablaze and burned it to the ground. Then, in 1931, Malcolm's father Earl Little was found dead on the Lansing, Michigan, trolley tracks; rumors would circulate for years that the death was no accident. Malcolm's mother Louise suffered a mental breakdown six years later, and the family was separated. Malcolm drifted into a life of crime, and was arrested in 1946 for running a burglary ring.

Malcolm X was one of the most controversial figures of the 1960s.

(Library of Congress)

While in prison, he converted to the Nation of Islam. In 1953, having served his time, he became an assistant minister at the Detroit temple. Charismatic, committed, and eloquent, Malcolm quickly rose through the ranks and established himself as an important figure within the Nation of Islam. His message to African Americans was stark and bitter: You are enslaved, whether you realize it or not, and only you can take action to change that state of affairs.

A fierce advocate for his people's autonomy and self-awareness, Malcolm lived the message he preached. He had turned his own life around, made the transformation from penny-ante crook to disciplined, eloquent, austere, and pious spokesman for the Nation of Islam. He himself embodied the kind of radical change that he proposed to his audiences. He was a one-man advertisement for an utterly unafraid model of African American life, a model of life that sought, not reconciliation with whites, but separation from them—and swift retaliation, not passive resistance, in the event of trouble. "We are nonviolent," he was fond of saying, "with people who are nonviolent with us."

In 1964, after a dispute with Nation of Islam leadership, Malcolm left the church and began a mosque of his own. He changed his name to El-Hajj Malik El-Shabazz.

A New Vision

In 1964, the former Malcolm X returned from a pilgrimage to Mecca convinced that his earlier pronouncements that whites were inherently evil had to be revised. The following month, he founded the Organization of Afro-American Unity, which rigidly advanced the cause of African American nationalism—but also left the door open to the goal of interracial harmony.

In February 1965, he was assassinated in New York City; three African Americans were tried and convicted for the crime, and received life sentences.

What's In a Name?

Malcolm Little. Detroit Red (his "hustling" name). Malcolm X. El-Hajj Malik El-Shabazz. The succession of names is revealing, if only because it demonstrated that their owner was—and understood he was—a work in progress. He changed and grew with time, as he learned more and experienced more in life.

Four decades ago, his rhetoric—which has been described as the kind of language meant to open wounds—won attention and sparked controversy, exactly as it was designed to do. Today, the words are still compelling, and they still inspire, but they can now be seen more clearly as means to an end: freedom.

FAQ

Why did Malcolm Little change his name to Malcolm X? The rejection of the last name "Little," in favor of the place-holder "X", emphasized Malcolm's intent to sever his connection with his "slave name." (While slavery ruled, white masters gave their own last names to those they held in subjugation.)

The contemporary portrait of Malcolm X as a fire-breathing apostle of racial hatred may have made arresting copy in the white mainstream media in the 1960s, but it was at odds with those who actually knew the man. After his death, when the papers were full of predictable moralizing about the violent ends reserved for proponents of violence, people who had actually listened to Malcolm's evolving message reminded the world of his compassion, his personal commitment, his commitment to his faith, and his enduring sense of decency. His integrity and his commitment to his cause are what have endured in the years since his passing.

One incident in particular captures his mission and his personality. After delivering a characteristically powerful and frank speech at a noontime mass in Selma, Alabama, in February 1965, Malcolm took his place on the platform, which was near where Coretta Scott King, wife of Dr. Martin Luther King Jr. was sitting. (At that time, Dr. King was in jail.) Some on the platform were concerned about the tone of Malcolm's remarks, which did not seem in keeping with the spirit of a nonviolent movement.

Malcolm leaned over to Mrs. King and apologized that his schedule did not permit him to visit Dr. King in jail, as he had planned to do. Then he told the wife of the civil rights leader, "I want [Dr. King] to know that I didn't come here to make his job more difficult; I thought that if the white people understood what the alternative was, that they would be willing to listen to Dr. King."

Asa Philip Randolph

Randolph founded the Brotherhood of Sleeping Car Porters in 1925. Twelve years later, despite intense opposition from the Pullman Company, at that point one of the largest and most influential businesses in America, he finally won a contract. It was the first time in American history that a company had entered into a formal agreement with an African American union.

Randolph was the union's president for the first 43 years of its existence. He was also one of the leading figures of the civil rights movement in the 1940s and 1950s, and an outspoken critic of discrimination in the union movement and segregation in the armed forces. (He ceaselessly lobbied President Harry Truman on the latter issue, finally securing a desegregation order in 1948 while Truman, conducting a long-shot campaign to retain the White House, counted potential African American votes in the North.)

Randolph was passionately committed to civil rights, and is today best remembered for his role in two mass marches on Washington—one of which did not occur and the other of which did. The march that did not occur would have taken place on July 4, 1941. In order to avoid it, President Franklin D. Roosevelt agreed to issue a proclamation mandating equal hiring practices and banning discrimination in defense-industry operations.

The March on Washington

Twenty-two years later, Randolph chose to ignore the misgivings of a sitting president. John F. Kennedy was just as unenthusiastic as FDR had been about the possibility of a huge civil rights march on Washington, but when it became obvious that

Randolph's March on Washington for Jobs and Freedom was to take place anyway, Kennedy positioned himself as a supporter of the undertaking.

Asa Philip Randolph lobbied a series of American presidents to take action on civil rights issues.

(Library of Congress)

Randolph's prestige and experience—not to mention his ability to build bridges between various factions of the civil rights movement—were what made the 1963 March on Washington possible. Martin Luther King's "I Have a Dream" speech may have been the most memorable single moment from that remarkable event—but the dream might never have entered our national vocabulary without Randolph's unflagging efforts.

The march was the pinnacle of one man's extraordinary half-century career of organization and agitation on behalf of civil and economic rights for African Americans.

Roy Wilkins

From 1955 to 1977, the cautious and inherently optimistic Roy Wilkins served as head of the NAACP. That's 22 years reckoned by the calendar, but it's also a distance that can't really be measured accurately by units of time.

In 1955, African Americans in the Deep South were still routinely terrorized and murdered for attempting to exercise their civil rights, and segregation was still a national disgrace. In 1977, segregation was dead; an African American (Thurgood Marshall, former lead lawyer for the NAACP) sat on the United States Supreme Court; an African American woman (Patricia Roberts Harris) served in the cabinet of the president; and Andrew Young was ambassador to the United Nations. Wilkins had served as head of the nation's most important civil rights organization during a period of unparalleled change, crisis, and progress in American racial relations, and he himself was one of the reasons for the progress that did occur.

Wilkins, an eloquent advocate, superb organizer, and gifted writer, worked steadily and relentlessly for 46 years as an NAACP executive in order to, as he put it, "work for Negroes." He worked for equality by appealing to constitutional rights that were, for millions of African Americans in the mid-1950s, not yet tangible realities. He spoke out against both white supremacist movements and the black separatist ideal; his goal was nothing less than the attainment, by constitutional and democratic means, of full social and political equality for African Americans. Wilkins, who met frequently with presidents and congressional leaders, is regarded today as the driving force behind many of the civil rights movement's most enduring achievements in the areas of school desegregation and civil rights legislation.

He was criticized by many younger and more radical activists for his measured, pragmatic approach to civil rights issues. From the late 1970s onward, however, most African Americans recognized the immensity of his contribution and the importance of his life's work.

Wilkins died in 1981 in New York City. A measure of his enduring influence was President Ronald Reagan's order that American flags at government buildings and installations be flown at half-staff in his honor. Reagan, of course, was no civil rights activist, but not even the president was in a position to deny Wilkins's lifetime of achievement or his status as a great American.

Ralph Bunche

The great African American intellectual Ralph Bunche lived a life so crammed with incident and achievement that its summary reads, implausibly, like the life story of at least three men, each of them a genius. He achieved distinction as one of the nation's premier diplomats, as an academic, and as a prominent civil rights leader. He was also one of the rare African American celebrities of his day whose prominence was based on his extraordinary intellectual vision.

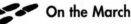 **On the March**

Bunche was awarded the Nobel Peace Prize in 1950 for his work in the Arab-Israeli peace talks that began in September 1948 and concluded in a formal armistice.

Despite the troubling fact that much of his thinking on racial matters never reached the large number of people who admired him, Bunche retains his status as one of the truly great minds of his era.

A brilliant student who graduated valedictorian from his high school, Bunche received summa cum laude honors from UCLA, and joined the faculty of Howard University at the tender age of 24. He was the first African American to receive a Ph.D. in political science from a U.S. institution of higher learning. (He received the degree from Harvard in 1934.)

In 1936, he founded the National Negro Congress, an umbrella organization that brought together over 500 separate organizations. (Asa Randolph was chosen as the Congress's first president.) In 1938, Bunche helped the Carnegie Corporation to conduct an influential in-depth assessment of the status of African Americans. Two years later, he published his book *Ideologies, Tactics, and Achievements of Negro Betterment and Interracial Organizations.*

His primary emphasis, however, was on world affairs. He was one of America's most accomplished diplomats, the first African American to serve as a division head in the State Department, and a member of the American delegation at the founding of the United Nations in 1945. In an era when African American presence at the highest levels of public life was all but unheard of, Bunche won the Nobel Peace Prize for his work in arranging an armistice following the Arab-Israeli conflict of 1948. (He was principal secretary of the UN's Palestine Commission.)

In 1955, he was named undersecretary of the United Nations; in that role, he coordinated UN peacekeeping efforts in the Suez region and in the Congo. In 1963, Bunche received the Medal of Freedom—the highest civilian honor in the United States—from President Kennedy.

During his life, Bunche was effectively "mainstreamed"—meaning that his image was often manipulated for the benefit of white audiences in ways he neither intended or approved. Major media outlets often presented his life story as "proof" that racial prejudice had been overcome in the United States; many African Americans came to resent his prominence in American life and saw it as evidence of tokenism. Only in recent years has a reassessment of his extraordinary work and achievements taken place.

Walking the Path

In 1965's triumphant civil-rights procession from Selma to Montgomery, Bunche walked at the head of the march, next to Dr. Martin Luther King Jr. Together, facing down the obscenities and insults of the racists they passed, two of the greatest Americans of their era, or any era, resolutely walked their own chosen path ... and led the procession to its rightful destination.

And Let's Not Forget ...

Besides the five remarkable men profiled in this chapter, this section highlights other significant African American leaders of the twentieth century.

James Farmer was instrumental in founding the Congress of Racial Equality, or CORE, in 1947. CORE was on the front lines of the civil rights movement from the late forties onward, winning public awareness of unconstitutional segregation practices in the South through campaigns of nonviolent civil disobedience.

Bayard Rustin's organizational prowess and deep personal commitment to equal rights brought him to the forefront of the civil rights movement in the early 1940s. Rustin was part of a group of CORE activists who received sentences in 1947 for violating North Carolina's Jim Crow laws integrating public transport.

Whitney Young helped to expand the scope of the National Urban League; his demand for a "domestic Marshall Plan" was an important influence on Lyndon Johnson's social policy.

John Lewis chaired the Student Nonviolent Coordinating Committee (SNCC), a student-led organization emphasizing nonviolent direct action in opposition to racist practices. Both CORE and SNCC took part in such landmark events as the Freedom Rides of 1961 and the Freedom Summer campaign to combat the disenfranchisement of African Americans in the south. (Lewis later served in Congress.)

Jesse Jackson, the former aide to Martin Luther King Jr., led two presidential campaigns that inspired so many; his Operation PUSH and Rainbow Coalition movements emphasized progressive ideals. Jackson's powerful and idealistic oratory—exemplified by his stirring "I am somebody" call-and-response sermons—empowered and enriched African American life over the past three decades.

The Least You Need to Know

- ◆ Martin Luther King Jr. was a pragmatic, inspiring leader committed to nonviolence whose greatness arose despite disunity within the civil rights movement.

- ◆ Malcolm X offered a different vision that rejected nonviolence in the face of white violence.

- ◆ Asa Philip Randolph made remarkable contributions over half a century as a labor leader and one of the nation's leading civil rights activists.

- Roy Wilkins led the NAACP during a time of unparalleled turmoil and change in American race relations.

- Ralph Bunche was an American Renaissance man whose massive achievements in diplomacy, academia, and civil rights activism remain unique.

Chapter 18

African American Writing

In This Chapter

- ◆ Early traditions and achievements
- ◆ The Harlem Renaissance
- ◆ Today's masters

Rich and varied, African American writing developed from a strong oral tradition. Setting aside the famous orators of the last two centuries—Frederick Douglass, Harriet Tubman, Martin Luther King Jr., Coretta Scott King, Barbara Jordan, and others—we are still left with an incredible richness, all the more astonishing because of the relatively short time in which it developed. This chapter offers a glimpse at some of the highlights of African American writing in America.

From the start, it was a woman's, as well as a man's, realm.

Beginnings

One Phillis Wheatley of Boston appears to have been the very first published African American writer.

A poet who learned English from her owners' daughter, she was also the first African American person to publish a book. However, because of racism, she was able to find a publisher only in England, not in the United States. Her 1773 book *Poems on Various Subjects, Religious and Moral* made her an instant celebrity overseas. Unfortunately, this attention was not reciprocated at home.

Born in Africa in 1752, and sold into slavery at the age of 8, Wheatley died in abject poverty in Boston at 32 without publishing another book.

Our Sable Race

Religious faith, and a certain informed cynicism about race relations in the United States, emerged as powerful themes in Phyllis Wheatley's work. Consider the following from her 1773 volume *On Being Brought from Africa to America:*

> Some view our sable race with scornful eye,
> "Their color is a diabolical dye."
> Remember, Christians, Negroes, black as Cain,
> May be refined, and join the angelic train.

Slave Narratives

The oral tradition that captives brought with them from Africa persisted in their communities in the American colonies. Stories and song generally revolved around African themes and subjects. However, the mid-to-late eighteenth century saw the birth of a new genre, the slave narrative.

Briton Hammon's 1760 autobiography was the first. With it, attention shifted to what would become, and remain, a central theme in African American writing: the social condition of the African American people.

The 20-year period between 1840 and 1860 saw the publication of the narratives of William W. Brown, *A Fugitive Slave*; Henry Bibb, *An American Slave*; Solomon Northtrup, *Twelve Years a Slave*; Austin Steward, *Twenty-Two Years a Slave*; and two individuals who would become household names, Frederick Douglass and Sojourner Truth.

Frederick Douglass's narrative appeared in 1845 with a preface by New England abolitionist William Lloyd Garrison, editor of *The Liberator*. Garrison had noticed the escaped slave, who had managed to make his way to an anti-slavery meeting in New Bedford, Massachusetts. Garrison spotted the young man's verbal gifts early on and recruited him as a speaker for the cause.

On the March

Frederick Douglass's writings emphasized autonomy, self-sufficiency, and education, and his writings show a firm moral sense that is unafraid to challenge social conventions. He once wrote of his time as a slave, "I prayed for twenty years, but received no answer until I prayed with my legs."

To learn more about Frederick Douglass, visit the website "American Visionaries: Frederick Douglass," maintained by the Museum Management Program and the Frederick Douglass National Historic Site: www.cr.nps.gov/museum/exhibits/douglass/.

Douglass went on to become a stirring orator, an important leader in the abolitionist movement, an adviser to presidents, and one of the great figures in American letters. After the Civil War, he focused his efforts on the struggle for equal opportunity and education for African Americans.

Frederick Douglass was, for most of his public life, a prominent and outspoken supporter of women's rights. He attended the historic Women's Rights Convention in Seneca Falls, New York, in 1848.

Immeasurable Distance

I am not included within the pale of this glorious anniversary! Your high independence only reveals the immeasurable distance between us. The blessings in which you, this day, rejoice, are not enjoyed in common. The rich inheritance of justice, liberty, prosperity and independence, bequeathed by your fathers, is shared by you, not by me. The sunlight that brought life and healing to you, has brought stripes and death to me. This Fourth [of] July is yours, not mine. You may rejoice, I must mourn. To drag a man in fetters into the grand illuminated temple of liberty, and call upon him to join you in joyous anthems, were inhuman mockery and sacrilegious irony. Do you mean, citizens, to mock me, by asking me to speak today? If so, there is a parallel to your conduct. And let me warn you that it is dangerous to copy the example of a nation whose crimes, lowering up to heaven, were thrown down by the breath of the Almighty, burying that nation in irrecoverable ruin!

—Frederick Douglass's 1852 Independence Day address, "What to a Slave Is the Fourth of July?"

Sojourner Truth's *Narrative* appeared five years after Douglass's print debut. Her volume was "as told to" abolitionist Olive Gilbert. The detailed story told how Truth, born Isabella Baumfree, survived and escaped slavery to become a New England preacher, and, later, an abolitionist. (For more on Sojourner Truth, see Chapter 16.)

To learn more about slave narratives, visit "American Slavery: A Composite Autobiography" at www.slavenarratives.com—the excellent site sponsored by Greenwood Publishing Group.

Regionalist Stories

In the years immediately following the Civil War, regionalist literature grew in popularity. Readers sought to recapture the local sense of place that the struggle for nationhood had displaced. The South and the West were centers of this movement. While African American authors were not contributors, many white writers used them as their subjects.

To learn more about African American folk tales, visit the "Afro-American Almanac" website—point your browser toward www.toptags.com/aama and check out the many traditional stories recorded there.

Novels

African American writers have long made the novel their province. The list is long and rich, but it was in the twentieth century that the most notable works in this category were completed beginning with Jean Toomer's *Cane*, published in 1923. Arna Bontemps's *Black Thunder* was published in 1936. This piece of historical fiction described an 1880 slave revolt that ultimately failed.

Richard Wright published *Native Son* in 1940 and *Black Boy* in 1945. These two novels, autobiographical in places, have become international classics not only because of the realistic way in which they depict the lives of African Americans, but also because of the convincing human emotions with which Wright invests his characters.

In 1952 Ralph Ellison raised the bar with his long, intense *Invisible Man*. In telling the story of a young man's growth and radicalization, he also showed how unnoticed the life of an African American could be in American society. Saul Bellow's review of the landmark novel said in part, "[W]hat a great thing it is when a brilliant individual victory occurs, like Mr. Ellison's, proving that a truly heroic quality can exist among our contemporaries."

The latter part of the twentieth century only built on these successes. James Baldwin explored Harlem, homosexuality, and racism, respectively, in *Go Tell It on the Mountain* (1953), *Giovanni's Room* (1956), and *Another Country* (1962).

Claude Brown described the underbelly of inner-city life in *Manchild in the Promised Land* (1965), while Maya Angelou surfaced the particular concerns of African American women in her sexually explicit *I Know Why the Caged Bird Sings* (1970).

Nonfiction

There have also been serious contributions by African Americans in nonfiction writing. The most important early offering was W. E. B. DuBois' *Suppression of the African Slave Trade*, which appeared in 1896. This was his doctoral dissertation for Harvard, from which he received his Ph.D. the same year. His seminal work, *Black Reconstruction in America*, was published in 1934.

Booker T. Washington's 1901 *Up From Slavery*, his life story, was the testament of another highly educated young African American. Washington graduated from Hampton Institute and went on to found Tuskegee Institute in 1881. His relentless campaign for economic independence and improvement in educational standards for African Americans drew a great deal of attention over the years; so did his often-controversial ideas about racial equality. He was a compelling and influential writer whose other works included a biography of Frederick Douglass and 10 years after *Up From Slavery*, a survey of his own intellectual development called *My Larger Education*.

The Dignified and the Beautiful

Many seem to think that industrial education is meant to make the Negro work as he worked in the days of slavery. This is far from my conception of industrial education. If this training is worth anything to the Negro, it consists in teaching him how not to work, but how to make the forces of nature—air, steam, water, horse-power and electricity—work for him. If it has any value it is in lifting labor up out of toil and drudgery into the plane of the dignified and the beautiful. The Negro in the South works and works hard; but too often his ignorance and lack of skill causes him to do his work in the most costly and shiftless manner, and this keeps him near the bottom of the ladder in the economic world.

—From Booker T. Washington's landmark essay "Industrial Education for the Negro," the first chapter of *The Negro Problem*, an anthology of articles by African American writers (James Pott and Company, 1903)

In the 1960s four African American writers expressed new depths of anger and frustration. The year 1963 saw the appearance of both James Baldwin's *The Fire Next Time* and Martin Luther King Jr.'s *Why We Can't Wait*. Written in the heat of the Civil Rights movement, they put America on notice with a prescience that went sadly unheeded.

The 1965 *Autobiography of Malcolm X*, as told to Alex Haley, became another instant classic, as it chronicled the evolution of a young criminal into a highly-effective political and religious leader. (In 1976, Haley's *Roots*, inspired by the multi-generational story of his own African ancestors, became an international phenomenon that resulted in the sale of over a million copies in one year and a record-setting television miniseries.)

Eldridge Cleaver's 1968 *Soul on Ice*, a voice from jail, showed that for many young African American males, prison had become almost a rite of passage.

Poetry

African American poetry developed in a straight, if sometimes discontinuous, line from Phillis Wheatley. In 1855 Lucy Terry became the second African American poet when her "Bars Fight" appeared in Holland's *History of Western Massachusetts*. However, her poetry was very different from Wheatley's heroic couplets:

> Eunice Allen see the Indians coming
> And hoped to save herself by running
> And had not her petticoats stopped her
> The awful creatures had not cotched her
> And tommy-hawked her on the head
> And left her on the ground for dead.

Paul Laurence Dunbar's *Lyrics of Lowly Life*, which appeared in 1896 with an introduction by the novelist William Dean Howells, paved the way for the attention which the writers of the *Harlem Renaissance* would garner. Dunbar was celebrated not only in the United States, but also in England. The transplanted Jamaican sonneteer Claude McKay's 1919 "If We Must Die" struck a new note of defiance:

> If we must die—let it not be like hogs
> Hunted and penned in an inglorious spot,
> While round us bark the mad and hungry dogs…
> If we must die—oh, let us nobly die….

This Renaissance, which occurred in the period roughly between 1920 and 1945, saw an explosion of writing, particularly poetry, by African American men and women based in New York City.

Gwendolyn Brooks' second book of poetry, *Annie Allen*, was published in 1949, earning her the Pulitzer Prize in Poetry in 1950. It marked the first time an African American had won the award.

What's the Word? _____

The **Harlem Renaissance** was a remarkable outpouring of creativity in many branches of African American art, and particularly poetry and prose, that occurred between the early 1920s and the middle 1940s in and around New York City. Major figures of the Harlem Renaissance included the critic Alain LeRoy Locke; social activist Marcus Garvey; magazine editor W. E. B. DuBois; the poets Langston Hughes, Counteé Cullen, and Angelina W. Grimke; fiction writers Zora Neale Hurston and Nella Larson; and painters William H. Johnson and Palmer Hayden, among many others. For a great introduction to the Harlem Renaissance, visit Jill Diesman's site devoted to the topic at www.nku.edu/~diesmanj/harlem_intro.html.

Poet Jean Toomer published his collection *Cane* in 1923. Counteé Cullen followed with his own collection, *Color*, in 1925. Langston Hughes brought out *The Weary Blues* in 1926, in which he tried to capture the rhythms of African American speech and jazz. Gwendolyn Brooks published *A Street in Bronzeville*, with characters such as "Satin Legs" Smith, in 1945.

Langston Hughes asked what befell "a dream deferred," asking whether it dried "like a raisin in the sun" … or exploded.

(Library of Congress)

The energy generated by the Renaissance continued in the latter part of the twentieth century, if more diversely expressed. LeRoi Jones, playwright, poet, and author of the 1961 *Preface to a 20 Volume Suicide Note*, changed his name to Imamu Amiri Baraka. (*Imamu* is a title of respect, as in teacher or leader.) Nikki Giovanni's *Black Feeling, Black Talk* (1968) revealed the inner life of the contemporary, professional African American woman. Maya Angelou, author of *Just Give Me a Cool Drink of Water Before I Die* (1971) and other collections of poetry, read at the inauguration of President Bill Clinton in 1993.

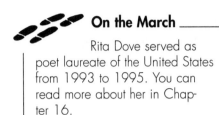

On the March

Rita Dove served as poet laureate of the United States from 1993 to 1995. You can read more about her in Chapter 16.

Theatre

African American writers for the stage to the fore in the mid-twentieth century.

Lorraine Hansberry's 1959 *A Raisin in the Sun*, titled after an image in a Langston Hughes poem, showed the frustration of young African Americans, caught between the "go-slow" advice of the older generation and the beckoning opportunities of a capitalist economy. Her play won the New York Drama Critics' Circle Award.

FAQ

Who's the most recent African American playwright to win a Pulitzer for drama? As of this writing, it's Suzan-Lori Parks, for her haunting *Topdog/ Underdog* in 2002.

Lonnie Elder III's 1965 *Ceremonies in Dark Old Men*, set in a Harlem barbershop, examined the life choices of young African Americans. Amiri Baraka's *The Dutchman*, which won the Obie Award for Best Off-Broadway Play in 1964, was an "in your face" assertion of African American pride.

August Wilson: The Theatrical Champ

In recent years, the leading African American playwright—and the leading American playwright, period—has been easy to identify. He is August Wilson, probably the most celebrated American dramatist to come of age since World War II.

Wilson's ongoing cycle of plays chronicling the African American experience—one for each decade of the twentieth century—has emerged as one of the major theatrical achievements of our time. His mastery of speech rhythms (often reflecting blues idiom), the long monologue, and head-on conflict have made him a force in the American theater.

Wilson's focus on the African American family, and the struggles and challenges it faced in the twentieth century, have been particularly rewarding for theatre audiences. Among his many gifts as a writer is his ability to focus on generational patterns and histories within families.

In an interview with *Black World Today* (April 2000), Wilson showed a writer's ability to identify the human essentials of a story, and his own preference for beginning with the African American experience. "I remember my daughter calling me from college," he recalled, "and telling me she had joined some Black Action Society and they were studying about Timbuktu. I told her that was nice, but asked why didn't she start with her grandmother and then work your way back to Timbuktu. It didn't make any sense to me for her to know all about Timbuktu and know nothing about her grandmother."

Wilson's success as a playwright on Broadway (and elsewhere) is without recent parallel. (See the following timeline.)

Timeline: August Wilson

1945: Born Fredrick August Kittel in Pittsburgh, Pennsylvania. His father was a red-haired German immigrant, Fredrik Kittel; his mother, an African American woman from North Carolina, Daisy Wilson.

1959: Endures abuse as the only African American student at a local Catholic school.

1960: Drops out of high school.

1962: Serves a year in the Army, and then works at a variety of jobs, with no clear career path emerging.

1965: Changes his name to August Wilson shortly after the death of his father.

1968: Establishes Black Horizons Theatre in St. Paul, Minnesota.

1978: Gets work writing for a science museum.

1982: Wilson's *Ma Rainey's Black Bottom* is workshopped at National Playwrights Conference; connects with NPC head Lloyd Richards, who will direct many of his later productions.

1984: *Ma Rainey* hits Broadway; it later wins a New York Drama Critics Circle award.

1987: Wilson's *Fences* is a Broadway smash; it wins the Pulitzer Prize and sets a then-box-office record for a non-musical, grossing $11 million.

continues

---

continued

1988: Wilson's *Joe Turner's Come and Gone* hits Broadway.

1990: Wilson's *The Piano Lesson* hits Broadway; it wins Wilson his second Pulitzer Prize.

1992: Wilson's *Two Trains Running* hits Broadway.

1996: Wilson's *Seven Guitars* hits Broadway.

1997: Engages in prominent debate with American Repertory Theatre director Robert Brustein on race and theatrical casting.

1999: Wilson's *King Hedley II* opens on Broadway.

Walking a Long Road

Looking to the future, it seems clear that the world can count on the richness and variety of African American writing to continue. However, where Wright, Baldwin, and Baraka once held sway, now writers like Terry McMillan (*Waiting to Exhale)*, Walter Mosley (*Bad Boy Brawley* Brown), and E. Lynne Harris (*Any Way the Wind Blows*) hold center court, while Colson Whitehead (*The Intuitionist*), Stephen Carter (*The Emperor of Ocean Park*), Gayle Jones (*Mosquito*), and Percival Everett (*Erasure*) are the vanguard.

The Least You Need to Know

♦ Slave narratives—such as those by Sojourner Truth and Fredrick Douglass— were an important early expression of the African American experience.

♦ Important African American novelists include Arna Bontemps, Richard Wright, James Baldwin, and Ralph Ellison.

♦ Important African American nonfiction writers include W. E. B. DuBois, Booker T. Washington, and Alex Haley.

♦ Important African American poets include Langston Hughes, Counteé Cullen, and Angelina W. Grimke, all of whom were associated with the Harlem Renaissance (roughly 1920-1945). Later, poets like Rita Dove, Amiri Baraka, and Maya Angelou made significant contributions.

♦ Important African American dramatists include Lorraine Hansberry, Amiri Baraka, and August Wilson. Wilson is the most celebrated and successful American playwright of his generation.

Chapter 19

In the Groove: African American Rhythm

In This Chapter

◆ The rich African American music tradition

◆ The anonymous contributors

◆ Some of the great innovators

There is an erratic but unbroken line rising from the centuries-old songs of African American churchgoers, field workers, and steel drivers … and extending all the way to the heart-attack scratch of the latest hip-hop dance track. Along that line you'll find the beating, restless heart of American music, and in that music you'll find pretty much everything that's distinctive about America: tragedy, power, and emotion in the blues; devotion and transcendent spirit in gospel; genius and diversity in jazz; irreverence and honesty in rock and roll. The best of it has the ultimate power, the power to transform someone's emotional state in a heartbeat. And none of it would have come about without African Americans.

In an unguarded moment circa 1964, John Lennon once told an interviewer, "It's all a big rip-off, you know."

Lennon meant that the Beatles' success arose from a desire to imitate African American artists such as Chuck Berry, Little Richard, and Smokey Robinson; in that imitation, his band had found a way of making the music it loved accessible to a mass global audience. Bing Crosby, an icon of an earlier generation, made basically the same point about the same endlessly repeated process when he said, of Louis Armstrong: "I'm proud to acknowledge my debt to the 'Reverend Satchelmouth' … He is the beginning and the end of music in America." And the entire career of the "King of Rock and Roll," Elvis Presley, stands as an example of the repackaging of African American traditions and sensibilities for a white audience. (One of Presley's breakthrough hits, "Hound Dog," was, for example, an earnest but ultimately inferior reworking of a Big Mama Thornton blues number.)

In this chapter, you learn about some of the most important pioneers of American music. These are African American innovators who made extraordinary things possible—as well as one "pioneer" thrown in for good measure, someone whose name you definitely don't know. I'll begin there, with the first of the great African American musical innovators … Anonymous.

The Anonymous Tradition

From ageless gospel tunes to work-songs punctuated with the swings of hammers, and from the musical celebration of the steel-driver John Henry to the dawn of the blues, great anonymous music has driven the African American tradition. Even the people we celebrate today as musical virtuosos owe important debts to musical "ancestors" whose names they never knew, and we will never know.

On the March

To find out more about the great African American folk music tradition, visit the Smithsonian Folkways Recordings website at www.folkways.si.edu/folk-col.htm—and learn how to track down recordings such as *The Smithsonian Folkways American Roots Collection* and *Wade in the Water: African American Sacred Music Traditions*.

African American folk music, like all folk music, was handed down from generation to generation, and the line between "songwriter" and "performer" was often so blurry as to be meaningless. The music was revised, extended, and kept alive by direct transmission from one person to the next. The result was often something vital, something honest, something far away from power chords or gold records or world tours or awards ceremonies—but something that somehow laid the foundation for all those things.

One can only imagine the reactions of the countless anonymous "singer/songwriters" if they could somehow have seen the eventual global impact (and, eventually, the immense financial rewards) of music that would eventually become known by labels like rock and roll, blues, jazz, gospel, and hip-hop. At the time, however, these great composers were not interested in putting labels on kinds of music. They were too busy living—working, caring for children, grieving, worshipping—in ways that simply could not be separated from musical expression.

James Carter, Where Art Thou?

In 1959, James Carter, an inmate at Mississippi's Parchman Penitentiary, was working on a field crew chopping wood. He led his fellow convicts in a work song about a lethal conflict between a "high sheriff" and a man named Lazarus who swears he's done no wrong. The song was a traditional bluesy lament whose author remains unknown; its slow, stately rhythm allowed the prisoners to swing their axes in time and complete the task at hand. ("When you sing those songs, you can do a lot of work," Carter would say later.)

Unknown to Carter, the legendary musicologist Alan Lomax was on the scene, recording the performance for posterity. Forty-three years later, after "Po Lazarus" had been licensed to Lost Highway Records for what would become the blockbuster soundtrack album to the movie *O Brother, Where Art Thou*, representatives of the Lomax Archive finally tracked down Carter—who was 70 and living in Chicago. Lomax had tried for decades to locate Carter (and many of the others whose music he had preserved over the years); his organization presented Carter with a check for back royalties and a plaque commemorating the sale of the two millionth copy of the *O Brother, Where Art Thou?* recording. Without ever meaning to, James Carter had become a multi-platinum pop star.

 On the March

James Carter's story is an inspiring exception to a much more common pattern in the music industry: undercompensated (or entirely uncompensated) African American talent providing the impetus for someone else's large-scale commercial success.

Robert Johnson

A perfect example of undercompensated African American talent can be found in the career of a bluesman who inspired countless superstar musicians ... but who spent most of his brief and troubled life on the road, playing obscure roadhouse gigs for low pay. He chose a wandering musician's lifestyle, with all its difficulties, because he believed it was better than picking cotton or submitting to the exploitation of sharecropping— the only other career alternatives he could see in 1930s Mississippi. He was Robert Johnson.

Robert Johnson, the "King of the Delta Blues."

(Illustration: Judith Burros.)

In November of 1936, this gangly, huge-handed guitarist walked into a San Antonio recording studio and laid the foundations of the music we know today as the Delta blues. Robert Johnson's surrealistically uncompromising lyrics meshed with his incomparable guitar work in a way that won him a regional following in countless juke-joints throughout the Mississippi Delta. No one had heard anything like his music in the 1930s; no one has heard anything like it since.

After a lot more playing and a little more recording, Johnson died in 1938, the victim of strychnine poisoning. He had, apparently, seduced one married woman too many; a jealous husband was said to have been behind Johnson's last, fatal, drink.

On the March

To learn more about Robert Johnson, visit the Robert Johnson Notebooks website at xroads.virginia.edu/~music/rjhome.html and check out *Robert Johnson: The Complete Recordings* (Sony).

At the time of his death, Johnson did not know that he was tantalizingly close to being offered a slot in a New York City concert that could have brought him to national prominence. Instead of a massive estate, Johnson left behind a string of dysfunctional relationships, a rumor that he'd sold his soul to the devil for his mind-boggling guitar skills, and a handful of scratchy blues recordings.

Those 29 tracks go so far beyond the borders of the term "influential" that one is constantly tempted to coin a new word to describe Johnson's mammoth impact. He has been called the "King of the Delta Blues." Whether any one individual can lay claim to such a title is open to debate; Johnson certainly had his own influences.

What is certain is that Johnson's work inspired such artists as Muddy Waters, Eric Clapton, Elvis Presley, Jimi Hendrix (profiled later), the Rolling Stones, Bob Dylan, the Red Hot Chili Peppers, and countless others. In fact, Robert Johnson's tiny catalog may well be the most imitated in the history of American popular music.

Johnson is one of those rare artists whose impact was incomparable, and whose entire recorded output can be listened to in an afternoon. If you haven't heard what all the fuss is about, you're in for a treat—and for a great many repeat performances.

Louis Armstrong

Now acknowledged as one of the foremost musicians of the twentieth century, Armstrong was a ridiculously gifted trumpeter whose innovations shaped an emerging, distinctly American musical form: jazz.

Just as important as his towering technical and improvisational skills on the trumpet, however (and more often overlooked), was his influence as a singer. Armstrong's unique vocal delivery had a huge impact on the development of American popular music: Anyone who ever improvised within the structure of a song, putting a unique personal impression on the material, is, in essence, following Louis Armstrong's lead. That puts figures as diverse as Frank Sinatra, Ella Fitzgerald, Bobby McFerrin, and Erykah Badu in the debt of the man called Satchmo.

A tireless performer and a gifted comic actor, Armstrong maintained his extraordinary popularity over five decades. Over that time, he won the kind of accolades from critics and fellow musicians that only true masters ever earn.

Shortly before he died, Armstrong dismissed the plea of a doctor that he cancel an upcoming concert with the following words: "What we play is life, my whole life, my whole soul. My whole spirit is to blow that horn."

He played the gig.

> **On the March**
>
> To learn more about Louis Armstrong, visit the "Louis Armstrong: 1901-1971" website at www.redhotjazz.com/louie.html, and check out the boxed set *The Hot Fives and Sevens* (JSP Records).

"Duke" Ellington

Widely regarded as the greatest American composer of them all, Edward Kennedy "Duke" Ellington came up with an ingenious solution to the problem of getting his band through towns whose hotels and restaurants denied service to African Americans. Ellington simply equipped his private train with sleeping and dining facilities and held parties on the train.

Ellington's contribution to American music was so immense that it could only be contained within *two* extraordinary and long-lasting careers. The first began with his big band's rise to prominence at Harlem's Cotton Club in the late twenties, and continued through the swing era, when Ellington's music was consistently at the top of the national charts. The second career came around in the mid-1950s, years after the nation's appetite for swing had diminished, and Ellington launched a comeback with a legendary appearance at the 1956 Newport Jazz Festival. (The band's extraordinary set very nearly unleashed a riot from appreciative fans). Throughout both careers, Ellington balanced his unerring gifts for melody and appealing rhythms with his desire to experiment musically. A superb pianist, he composed many of his most timeless pieces in collaboration with the gifted Billy Strayhorn.

> **On the March**
>
> To learn more about "Duke" Ellington, visit www.dukeellington.com and check out *The Blanton-Webster Band* (RCA Records).

In 1965, at the age of 66, Ellington was considered for, but inexplicably lost, the Pulitzer Prize for music. The never-fazed Ellington took the news in typical, jaunty form: "Fate is being kind to me. Fate doesn't want me to be too famous too young."

Ella Fitzgerald

She was called "The First Lady of Song," and over a six-decade period she more than earned the title. Fitzgerald is today regarded as the premier female jazz singer of the twentieth century, and while adherents of Billie Holliday or Sarah Vaughan might quibble, there can be little doubt that Fitzgerald earned a special place in the hearts of music fans around the world. She had a three-octave range, a passion for exquisite vocal improvisation, and a habit of delivering definitive renditions of compositions from the great American Songbook. (For more about Fitzgerald, see Chapter 16.)

> **On the March**
>
> To learn more about Ella Fitzgerald, visit the Ella Fitzgerald Pages at http://jump.to/ella, and check out *Pure Ella: The Very Best of Ella Fitzgerald* (Polygram Records).

Fitzgerald received numerous awards during her long and eventful career, including 13 Grammy awards, honorary degrees from Yale and Dartmouth, and a Kennedy Center Award. She remained an active performer from 1934 to 1992; her motto throughout her career was, "It isn't where you came from, it's where you're going that counts."

Miles Davis

Known by many as "The Picasso of Jazz," Davis, a composer and trumpeter, consistently revised and expanded his own approach, style, and image. He was the creation of no public relations department; he made himself.

Davis is famous both for the extraordinary range and diversity of his work (the official Columbia Records website requires no less than five different time periods to summarize him) and for a single breathtaking achievement: 1959's *Kind of Blue*, often cited as the greatest jazz recording of all time. The album is one of the few twentieth-century American achievements in music—perhaps the only one—that has won, and held on to, virtually unanimous popular and critical agreement on its greatness. *Kind of Blue* is, perhaps, the easiest jazz album of all time to fall in love with.

Having begun his professional career accompanying the incomparable saxophonist Charlie Parker, Davis embarked on a solo career in the late 1940s. Despite winning recognition from fellow musicians for his immense talent, Davis didn't hit his stride until 1954, when he overcame a heroin addiction.

From that point forward, he occupied himself with a campaign of relentless musical experimentation and self-invention that won attention and commercial success that most jazz players could only dream of. Uneasy about labels, Davis would spend most of his career attempting to transcend them; for nearly half a century, he pursued an elegant, innovative approach to playing and composing that was both highly influential and accessible to those not familiar with the intricacies of jazz. He managed, in other words, to be both a pacesetter and (by jazz standards, anyway) a populist.

On the March

To learn more about Miles Davis, visit www.milesdavis.com, and check out *Kind of Blue* (Columbia).

In 1959, the year of *Kind of Blue*, Davis was relaxing between sets outside the most celebrated jazz venue in the world: New York City's Birdland. A passing policeman, apparently uneasy at the sight of a black man standing his own ground, began to harass him. Davis, a fiercely proud man, talked back—and received a beating at the hands of New York's finest. Davis's attempts to bring legal proceedings came to nothing, and the already hard-bitten musician became even more cynical than he had been about race relations in America. On tour in Europe, by contrast, Davis consistently found that he was treated as what he was: one of the great geniuses of the century.

Chuck Berry

A composer of rock anthems that now seem somehow to have always existed. A riveting performer. A shrewd promoter. A rock and roll pioneer. A canny combiner of blues and country. Chuck Berry has been all of these things at one point or another during his long career; he is also remembered more and more, however, for pulling the music industry's equivalent of the Jackie Robinson breakthrough in baseball.

At a time when African American pop artists often weren't even allowed to appear on the covers of nationally distributed LPs, and were often relegated to segregated "regional" status, Berry managed to become one of the hottest acts in the country and built a passionate following of white teenagers. He wrote songs that blurred racial barriers and mirrored the lives and concerns of young people. He did all this at a time when America was not, supposedly, "ready" for an African American man to sing of love, desire, and automobiles to an audience consisting largely of white adolescent girls. The songs he wrote and played, however, were so obviously, danceably, and joyously relevant to the American experience that they carried the day on sheer wisecracking adrenaline.

On the March

To learn more about Chuck Berry, visit www.chuckberry.com, and check out *Chuck Berry: The Anthology* (MCA Records).

An immensely influential musician, songwriter, and performer, Berry navigated a career with both ups and downs. He has been imitated—and openly acknowledged—by such superstar acts as the Beatles, the Rolling Stones, and the Beach Boys. He was, appropriately, included in the inaugural group of musicians inducted into the Rock and Roll Hall of Fame in 1986, and a brief excerpt from his song "Johnny B. Goode" was selected for inclusion on the Voyager I space probe as a prime example of American culture.

Berry was, and remains, an American original.

Jimi Hendrix

An astonishing innovator who pushed the technical boundaries of his instrument while incorporating a dizzying range of blues, jazz, and rock influences, the great guitarist Jimi Hendrix had a brief but incandescent solo career that oddly recalls that of Robert Johnson. Thirty-five years after his death, Hendrix's work has yet to be fully assimilated; in many ways, rock and roll is still trying to catch up with him.

Hendrix has been called the greatest and most flamboyant lead guitarist who ever lived, but he began his career as a backup player for bands like the Isley Brothers and the Impressions. His big break came when the former Animals bassist Chas Chandler saw him play at a New York venue called café Wha?

Chandler signed on as Hendrix's manager, got him to change the spelling of his name from "Jimmy" to "Jimi," and brought him to England. There, Hendrix became the leader of a high-powered rock trio built specifically around his virtuoso guitar skills. The band, known as the Jimi Hendrix Experience, exploded onto the London scene late in 1966; Hendrix's performance at the Monterey Pop Festival in June of 1967 won him a passionate following in the United States as well.

Attempting to describe the essence of Hendrix's sound is a little like attempting to describe the essence of a tornado or some other force of nature. It is worth noting, though, that, three and a half decades after his passing, Hendrix's legion of imitators over the years have not yet come close to capturing the incendiary fury and technical sophistication of his solos. He was, by all accounts, obsessed with the act of playing a guitar as no one else had ever played it.

Drug abuse, overwork, a lack of personal discipline, and the pressures of stardom conspired against Hendrix. He died in his sleep in 1970 after releasing three extraordinary studio albums and setting a new standard for rock concert performance. A relentless perfectionist, he had recorded so much unused material that a steady stream of "new" Hendrix product—officially released and otherwise—has come out in the years following his death.

On the March

To learn more about Jimi Hendrix, visit www.jimihendrix.com, and check out "Are You Experienced?" (MCA Records).

FAQ

What was the high point in Jimi Hendrix's career? His 1969 rendition of "The Star Spangled Banner" at the epic Woodstock concert—complete with guitar effects evoking jet planes, falling bombs, and the screams of Vietnamese peasants—remains one of the most stunning performances in rock history.

The List Goes On

These are just a few of the great African American innovators in music. There are many more in our past—and an even greater number to be discovered in our future.

The Least You Need to Know

◆ The African American music tradition has profoundly enriched American cultural life.

◆ Its many anonymous contributors emphasize a chain of folk music that extends far into the past.

◆ Some of the most influential African American musical innovators include Robert Johnson, Louis Armstrong, Duke Ellington, Ella Fitzgerald, Miles Davis, Chuck Berry, and Jimi Hendrix.

◆ There are many more great African American musical innovators in the past … and many more waiting in the wings to make their mark.

Chapter 20

Big Screen, Small Screen: African Americans and Modern Media

In This Chapter

◆ Media pioneers

◆ Race and commerce in the American media

◆ Moving beyond the stereotypes

In this chapter, you learn about a few of the important African American pioneers in American films and television.

These performers and creators—some well known, some hardly remembered—frequently fought against personal and professional barriers to reach their audience. They all made important contributions to their fields.

Today, pioneer African American figures in the media are the subject of increasing interest, celebration, respect, and attention. They are seen, increasingly, as influential vitally important figures in the modern, multiracial, media-driven society in which we live. This may be because their professional struggles and triumphs took place in a time that people born after about 1970 often can't envision: the seemingly endless period when blacks were either depicted through words and images that reinforced notions or cultural inferiority ... or (more commonly) not depicted at all.

African American Film Pioneers

In 1963, the gifted Bahamian-born actor Sidney Poitier won the Academy Award for Best Actor for his performance in *Lilies of the Field*. It was a breakthrough moment in American media: Hollywood bestowing its highest honor on an actor of African descent who embodied intelligence, decency, honor, and personal initiative.

In the five decades before that breakthrough, however, racist stereotypes abounded in mainstream American media, with portrayals of servants, maids, and other subservient types prevailing, and with broad, unflattering generalizations about the sexuality, intelligence, and work ethic of African Americans as a whole quite common.

There was, however, one media channel in which a less abusive portrayal of African Americans often carried the day, however: the so-called "race movies," features created by and intended specifically for African Americans.

 Obstacles and Opportunities

"Race movies" were films by, about, and for African Americans that were exhibited in segregated theatres, churches, public halls, and other venues. The films were popular in the South and in Northern urban areas from the late 'teens to the late twenties, although some African American filmmakers hung on until the early forties. The shift away from African American-produced films occurred because Hollywood realized there was money to be made in the genre, and started releasing bigger-budget "all-black" films of its own.

Here's a look a two remarkable figures from the (now largely forgotten) period of the "race movie." Two of them went on to achieve recognition in other media; the third is now almost entirely overlooked, although there is every reason to regard him as one of the most important independent voices in the early history of American cinema. The name of this trailblazing filmmaker: Oscar Micheaux.

Hollywood's First "Oscar" Challenges and Stereotypes

Submissive African American characters were the order of the day mainstream Hollywood films between 1920 and 1950. An early *Little Rascals* short, for instance, made a point of finding a flimsy reason for Buckwheat to absent himself from the group before the rest of the gang confronted a white bully; no African American child could be shown challenging a white male. Members of a popular jazz orchestra once had to use black makeup in order to be granted a screen appearance in a Hollywood feature; they were light-skinned, and studio executives feared that audiences would mistake them for an integrated band.

There was, to all appearances, a complete absence of screenplays addressing racial issues from a African American point of view during the American cinema's so-called "Golden Age." You'd be forgiven, then, for assuming that there were no American films during this period that were built around strong African American protagonists, or that dealt frankly with themes like lynching, white sexual predators, or white-dominated political systems. But you'd be wrong.

Cinema pioneer Oscar Micheaux dealt freely and frankly with such themes between the late 'teens and the late 1940s, releasing over 30 films, most intended exclusively for African American audiences. Micheaux—originally a novelist, but eventually a screenwriter, director, and producer—headed up one of the most successful African American studios of the day. His operation produced films that drew attention, debate, and (most important of all) substantial audiences in African American communities from the silent era to the postwar period. Among his productions were the following:

- ◆ *The Homesteader*   This 1919 silent feature, based on Micheaux's novel of the same name, was based largely on the author's own experiences as a settler on a patch of South Dakota land to which he had obtained a claim in the early 1900s. Micheaux subsidized the film by securing investments from the region's farmers.

- ◆ *Within Our Gates*   Another silent release from 1919, this film told the story of a sharecropper falsely accused of killing a white man. Set firmly within the context of melodrama, *Within Our Gates* pushed every social button it could, and openly challenged prevailing notions of white supremacy.

FAQ

What kind of reactions did Oscar Micheaux's films provoke? If the trailblazing filmmaker set out to attract controversy, he often succeeded; religious leaders in Chicago, for instance, attempted to cancel showings of *Within Our Gates* in 1920. Many feared that the film would stir up racial violence of the kind the city had endured during the riots of 1919.

On the March

To learn more about Oscar Micheaux, see the profile and related materials at http://shorock.com/micheaux.

◆ ***Body and Soul*** The great actor and singer Paul Robeson made his screen debut in this 1925 exploration of religious hypocrisy. Robeson played both a manipulative preacher and his well-intentioned brother.

Micheaux's films made a point of placing African Americans in positions of influence, authority, and accountability, thus ensuring that a positive message and inspiring role models would reach the African American community.

With the entrance of the big studios into the market in the late 1920s and early 1930s, many African American studios fell by the wayside. Micheaux managed to keep his operation up and running until the late 1940s. When he died in 1951, his passing was barely noted; even today, his contributions to the medium and his steadfast refusal to accept the limiting stereotypes of the day are not widely celebrated, which is a shame.

Spencer Williams

Best known for his portrayal of Andy in the controversial network television version of the stereotype-riddled radio comedy *Amos 'n' Andy*, Williams should be better noted for a remarkable career as an actor, producer, director, composer, and screenwriter in African American films. For a long period before he won his starring role in the 1951 television show, Williams was the creative force behind dozens of movies popular within the African American community, including *Tenderfeet* (1928), *Framing of the Shrew* (1929), *Harlem on the Prairie* (1938), and *Juke Joint* (1947).

When network television beckoned, Williams's big break appeared to have come at last. The *Amos 'n' Andy* broadcasts proved divisive, however, and the coarse, dialect-driven comedy—which ultimately drew the condemnation of the NAACP—served as a kind of shorthand for his entire career. The broad and demeaning images of a long-cancelled television show, however, should not overshadow Williams's work as an entrepreneur and filmmaker, which was impressive.

 **On the March**

To learn more about pioneering African American filmmaker Spencer Williams, see the *Concordia Sentinel* profile at www.geocities.com/Hollywood/2587/ConcordiaSentinel.htm.

Williams was a multitalented man whose energy and unfailing good humor were, by all accounts, extraordinary. He was, like Micheaux, a pioneering success in a medium that was built to exclude his participation in it, and for that he deserves to be remembered.

Spencer Williams died in Los Angeles, California, in 1969.

Other Early African American Film Pioneers

Other pioneering African Americans in the cinema included …

♦ The brothers Noble and George Johnson, who, in 1916, formed the first African American–owned film production company, the Lincoln Motion Picture Company.

♦ Jeni LeGon, the first African American woman to win an extended contract from a major Hollywood studio. She worked for MGM in the thirties, and, though underutilized, danced up a storm as "Hollywood's Chocolate Princess" in a number of mainstream releases.

♦ Ethel Waters, an accomplished performer (and influential early jazz singer) who crafted a successful, long-lasting career. Her early accomplishments featured screen appearances in such releases as *On With the Show* (1929) and *Check and Double Check* (1930). Her later success as a singer and actress has led many to overlook her early work in the talkies.

 FAQ

Where can I learn more about African American contributions to Hollywood? To find out more about African American cinema pioneers, contact the Black Hollywood Education and Resource Center by calling 323-957-4747, or visiting www.bherc.org.

A New Era

A new medium took America by storm in the late forties and early fifties: television. It threatened Hollywood's monopoly on America's eyes and ears … and offered a new mirror on the country's racial attitudes.

To understand how very far the new medium had to come in its depictions of African Americans, it's probably a good idea to get a sense of where it started. And that means looking at the controversy surrounding the *Amos 'n' Andy* television show.

Amos 'n' Andy Revisited

In June 1951, U.S. television viewers got their first look at *Amos 'n' Andy*, and many in the African American community weren't at all pleased with what they saw. Based on a phenomenally popular radio show created by two white actors, Freeman Gosden and Charles Correll, the TV series (recast, with great fanfare, with African American actors) drew huge audiences. It also drew bitter criticism, however, from the NAACP and other civil rights organizations.

CBS's *Amos 'n' Andy*, premiering on television at a time when African Americans were increasingly impatient for social change, marked a turning-point in American culture. Its (usually white) defenders made much of the fact that the show featured the first "all-black" cast in television, and that some of its characters had professional jobs. Its detractors pointed out that the show's humor derived from outdated stereotypes that derived from the minstrel period, that it presented no positive images of African Americans, and that its jokes tended to rely on the assumption that African Americans were stupid and lazy.

Just a few years earlier, the radio show's one-dimensional depiction of the fast-buck schemes of Kingfish and his perpetually gullible dupe Andy had won the show's characters status as national icons. Now, with the plots transferred to television, and with a different feeling about race relations in the air, *Amos 'n' Andy*'s high ratings had to contend with something new: organized protest.

The show ran for two years, and then went into reruns, but the calls to end its broadcast altogether continued, as did condemnations of the program's crude racial caricatures and its depictions of African Americans as essentially scheming, lazy, and unintelligent. CBS continued to sell the show to local stations, however, and it was aired extensively for thirteen years after its network run had concluded.

 On the March

Today, videotapes of the original shows are available on the Internet for people who can't get enough of lines like, "Holy mackerel, Andy—we's all got to stick together in dis heah thing—remember, we is brothers in that great fraternity, the Mystic Knights of the Sea."

Finally, in 1966—with the nation in turmoil over civil rights issues—executives at CBS finally decided that continuing to sell the show represented a major corporate-image problem. It withdrew *Amos 'n' Andy* from the airwaves, and the show has stayed off to this day.

A National Disgrace: The Failure of *The Nat "King" Cole Show*

In 1956, while CBS was still raking in profits from *Amos 'n' Andy* reruns, the network was failing to follow through on a contract with entertainer Nat "King" Cole to produce a variety show with Cole as host. Rival network NBC decided to give the show a chance in a prominent national time slot, CBS dropped its contract, and *The Nat "King" Cole Show* was born.

Cole, the velvet-toned singer responsible for such chart hits as "Mona Lisa," "Nature Boy," and "Too Young," was one of the most popular entertainers in the country. His skin color, however, would prove an impossible barrier to national television success.

Obstacles and Opportunities

Performers such as Pearl Bailey, Sammy Davis Jr., and Mel Torme—headliners all—appeared at union minimum wage levels in order to perform on *The Nat "King" Cole Show* during its 13-month run on NBC. They gave up huge performing fees they could have secured in other bookings in order to support Cole's attempt to launch the first variety show hosted by an African American. Cole himself estimated that he had missed out on half a million dollars in performing income as a result of his commitment to the show.

Having set out to become (as he put it) "the Jackie Robinson of television," Cole stuck with the project while NBC searched for a national sponsor. None was forthcoming.

Advertisers were terrified of the show, which—unlike the comfortably condescending *Amos 'n' Andy*—threatened the very ideology of segregation by placing a talented African American on an equal social footing with his white guest performers.

Fearing southern boycotts of their products, potential national backers stayed away in droves. (There were a number of local advertisers, but NBC and Cole both wanted the prestige and revenue of a single national sponsor.) NBC stood behind the program for 13 months, essentially subsidizing *The Nat "King" Cole Show*. Despite Cole's steadily rising ratings, and top-tier guests such as Mel Torme, Ella Fitzgerald, Tony Bennett, and Harry Belafonte, national advertising agencies simply wouldn't recommend the show to their clients.

The ride came to an end in 1957, when Cole politely declined a request from NBC to demote the show by placing it in a less appealing time slot. He ended his variety-show experiment, and spoke out bitterly to the media about the cowardice of the industry. Cole had no complaint with NBC; his anger was reserved for craven potential sponsors and advertising agencies. As he put it, "I was the pioneer, the test case, the Negro first ... On my show rode the hopes and tears and dreams of millions of people .... I turned down $500,000 in dates in order to be on the scene ... [and] the men who dictate what Americans see and hear didn't want to play ball."

The truth is that the men who dictated what Americans saw and heard in the mid-fifties were deeply afraid of Southern boycotts that might be launched against products advertised on *The Nat "King" Cole Show*. Those fears may well have been justified; during this period, African Americans and whites were not even permitted to touch each other on network television for fear of offending white sensibilities. The show's failure is probably more of an indictment against the racially divided society in which it operated than against the skittish advertising agencies that so infuriated Cole.

In any event, *The Nat "King" Cole Show* was the last U.S. network attempt at a African American-hosted variety show until 1970s *The Flip Wilson Show* (also on NBC).

Invisible Men and Women ... Become Visible

Throughout the 1950s and the first half of the 1960s, African Americans were poorly served by, and very nearly invisible on, network television. A handful of major African American stars showed up from time to time on the big variety shows. One could wait a very long time indeed, though, for a televised drama or comedy episode to place an African American actor in a leading, or even supporting, role that did not reek of the stereotypes associated with Hollywood. Even roles lacking in significance were fairly rare, for the simple reason that sponsors, as Cole's experience had demonstrated, were not eager to offend Southern viewers.

The surrealistic absence of African American faces on the nation's television screens began to change—slowly—as the most impossible-to-ignore advances of the national civil rights movement won heavy coverage in the 1960s.

As African Americans became more and more prominent on national news broadcasts, they gradually became more visible in the nation's comedies, dramas, and entertainment programming as well. At the same time the United States began the long-overdue process of coming to terms with racial problems that had been ignored for far too long, television served as a kind of barometer of the nation's emotional willingness to address the possibility of openly embracing a racially diverse society.

Here are some of the landmark moments in television's—and America's—ongoing internal discussion on race in America.

Some High Points: African Americans on U.S. Television

1965	Bill Cosby wins a costarring role (with Robert Culp) in *I Spy*, the first weekly network drama built around an African American actor.
1967	The first interracial kiss on network television shows up on *Star Trek* between Captain Kirk (William Shatner) and Lt. Uhura (Nichelle Nichols). Nervous network executives ordered that two versions of the episode in question, "Plato's Stepchildren," be filmed, one with the kiss and one without. Shatner deliberately spoiled the take for the "no-kiss" version by staring at the camera and crossing his eyes, leaving only one version for the network to air.
1968	Diahann Carroll takes the lead role in *Julia*, a trailblazing drama about a widowed African American nurse with a son to raise. Carroll had the spotlight all to herself, which meant both adulation (from the show's admirers) and hate mail and death threats (from racists).

1974	Cicely Tyson wins acclaim for her performance in *The Autobiography of Miss Jane Pittman*.
1977	ABC airs the miniseries adaptation of Alex Haley's novel *Roots*. The show sets new ratings records and initiates a national dialogue on race and the legacy of slavery.
1984	Bill Cosby sets the pace again, this time with the runaway hit *The Cosby Show*. Heathcliff Huxtable and company offer a new and positive image of the African American family: intelligent, professional, well educated, and comfortable. It was about as far from *Amos 'n' Andy* as you could get. Although there are still many obstacles to overcome in the mass media's portrayal of African Americans, *The Cosby Show* proves that this particular job can, on occasion, be done right.
1999–2002	HBO sets new standards in television by launching award-winning African American programming (*The Corner*, *Soul Food*).

The Least You Need to Know

◆ In the early part of the century, "race movies" produced by and for African Americans, provided some filmmakers with the opportunity to create cinema from a minority perspective.

◆ Early pioneers in African American filmmaking included Oscar Micheaux and Spencer Williams.

◆ It took 15 years of protests from the NAACP and other civil rights groups to get CBS to stop perpetuating the racist stereotypes of its *Amos 'n' Andy* television show.

◆ Nat "King" Cole was one of the most popular and beloved entertainers in the country in the mid-fifties … but his popularity was not enough to assuage the fears of potential sponsors, who feared white southern boycotts of products advertised on the show.

◆ Although many obstacles remain in America's mass-media depiction of African Americans, there have been significant advances and at least one memorable high point: *The Cosby Show*.

Chapter 21

Fighting Anyway: Heroism in a Segregated Military

In This Chapter

◆ America's forgotten defenders

◆ Unpaid debts to those who paid the ultimate sacrifice

◆ Fighting despite discrimination and abuse

In this chapter, you learn about the extraordinary sacrifices and profound heroism of Africans in the American armed services in the long era of military segregation—and also about some of the social issues brought to the forefront of American society by African American service in the armed forces.

For many years, history ignored the recurring story of the African American's willingness to stand, fight, and die for the United States. All too often, African American soldiers fell in the defense of principles of liberty and autonomy that were rarely if ever put into actual practice in their own lives. For most of the nation's history, African Americans fought for ideals of "democracy" and "equality" in a segregated military and social system that offered them neither. Their deeds deserve to be remembered.

The Revolutionary War

This was, of course, the military conflict by which the 13 British colonies in North America became a new and (initially) very loosely confederated nation, the United States of America.

The date we usually associate with the founding of the nation is July 4, 1776, the date celebrated as that of the signing of the Declaration of Independence. The conflict between British imperial power and American colonists had, however, been unfolding for some years before that.

One of the most important early flashpoints was the Boston Massacre (1770), which many regard as one of the two galvanizing events that made revolution possible (the other being the publication of Thomas Paine's *Common Sense* in 1776). It is worth noting that blood was shed in only one of these nation-sparking events. The blood was that of Crispus Attucks, a colored man who was probably either an escaped or a freed slave who came to be regarded as the first American martyr, and ten other colonists. A total of five people died in the event that came to be known as the Massacre, a conflict that is best understood as an example of poor crowd control by the British—and superior propagandizing by the colonists.

Little is known of Attucks's life or his precise role in the chaotic events that took place in front of the custom-house in Boston, then a British-occupied city, on March 5, 1770. An advertisement offering a reward for the return of a slave named "Crispus" appeared in a Massachusetts newspaper in 1750; this has led to speculation that he escaped from captivity and eventually came to work in the port of Boston.

Relegation to Outer Darkness

After each war—of 1776, of 1812, of 1861—history repeats itself in the absolute effacement of remembrance of the gallant deeds done for the country by its brave black defenders and in their relegation to outer darkness. History further repeats itself in the fact that in every war so far known to this country, the first blood, and, in some cases, the last also, has been shed by the faithful Negro, and this in spite of all the years of bondage and oppression, and wrongs unspeakable.

—Christian Fleetwood, nineteenth-century essayist

Attucks appears to have been one of a group of wharf-workers who resented British tax initiatives (and the fact that British soldiers had recently appropriated their jobs). The disgruntled colonists pelted a single British soldier with snowballs; the captain on duty decided that the situation warranted an escalation of force. The crowd evidently came to the same conclusion, and the snowballs were quickly replaced by rocks. The British opened fire.

Contemporary reports suggest that Attucks was the first of the five people killed in the attack. In the weeks and months following the shootings, all five of those who died in the Boston Massacre were hailed as martyrs in sympathetic, and highly influential, colonial newspaper coverage. As the years passed, however, Attucks came more and more to the forefront. Despite his essential ambiguity, Attucks is today the only figure who has assumed heroic—and even legendary—status as the result of the bloody events in Boston.

FAQ

What happened to the British soldiers who fired on Crispus Attucks and other colonists during the Boston Massacre? Six were acquitted; two were punished and discharged from the British army. The defense lawyer for the soldiers was none other than John Adams, a future president of the United States.

Thanks to growing discontent with the high-handed military and tax policies of the British (and the feverish propagandizing of the anti-British press), something like ten thousand people participated in the funeral services for Attucks and the other victims of the Boston Massacre. To get an understanding of the impact of that number, understand that in the year 1770, the population of Boston, Massachusetts was 16,000!

In the face of such overwhelming displays of grief, anger, and focused political opposition, the British decided to withdraw from Boston for a time. If their aim was to wait out a brief surge of popular outrage, however, that hope was to be frustrated.

(Slaveholding) Founding Fathers

Without George Washington, there would have been no United States of America. Yet those accustomed to thinking of Washington exclusively as a benevolent, egalitarian, liberty-loving Founding Father tend to ignore the fact that he was the wealthiest man in America, and that his livelihood (like that of Thomas Jefferson, another revolutionary and future president) was built on slave labor. Both of these white slaveholding revolutionaries won enduring fame for struggling successfully against the British, and for setting out noble aims for the new republic. The conflicts between their best-known, and long-enduring, ideals and the realities of their domestic lives, however, has, for many African Americans, tarnished their legacy.

It is easy, even today, for white Americans to forget that the Declaration of Independence's promises of life, liberty, and happiness were initially intended to be applied only to white males, and that the Constitution quietly sanctioned the institution of slavery.

Washington Rebuffs the Slaves

Slaves made up one-quarter of the populations of the new nation. A large number of them appealed to General Washington to join the army—and thereby secure their freedom. Washington chose not to grant freedom in exchange for military service.

The result of the British overture to American slaves was quite alarming to whites accustomed to seeing African Americans in an entirely menial and servile position. As one Maryland newspaper reported:

> The insolence of the Negroes in this county is come to such a height, that we are under a necessity of disarming them, which we affected on Saturday last. … The malicious and imprudent speeches of some among our lower classes of whites have induced them to believe that their freedom depended on the success of the King's troops. We cannot therefore be too vigilant nor too rigorous with those who promote and encourage this disposition in our slaves.

For a time, enslaved Africans were prohibited from serving in the American army, but in 1778, with the revolutionary cause facing grave challenges, Rhode Island broke ranks and permitted slaves to enlist. Within two years, slaves were fighting and dying on the front lines. So it was that, despite white skittishness, large numbers of African Americans took to arms in defense of the new nation. These troops showed a deep attachment to the American homeland, an attachment that few whites bothered to try to comprehend.

On the March

Many colonial African Americans took up the British offer of freedom in exchange for service to the Crown, with the result that African Americans served on both sides of the conflict as fighters, workers, trail guides, messengers, and haulers of cargo. On the colonial side, many African Americans saw service as foot soldiers replacing whites.

African American forces fought side by side with whites at Lexington and Concord, at the seizure of Fort Ticonderoga, and at the Battle of Bunker Hill and Breed's Hill; slaves and free African Americans served with distinction in most of the major battles of the war.

The War of 1812

This war played out between the United States and Great Britain between 1812 and 1815. Among its several causes were these:

♦ American demands for neutrality on the high seas for shipping vessels during a period of war between the French and the British.

♦ British seizure of American ships and impressment of American sailors.

♦ Conflicts in the Western United States between roving American settlers and British forces (allied with Native Americans) claiming territorial rights there.

♦ American ambitions for expansion in North America.

African American fighters made up two battalions serving under Andrew Jackson when he defeated the British at the Battle of New Orleans. Jackson delivered a soaring address in praise of his African American troops.

The Land of Your Nativity

TO THE MEN OF COLOR—Soldiers! From the shores of Mobile I collected you to arms; I invited you to share in the perils and to divide the glory of your white countrymen. I expected much from you, for I was not uninformed of those qualities which must render you so formidable to an invading foe. I knew that you could endure hunger and thirst and all the hardships of war. I knew that you loved the land of your nativity, and that like ourselves, you had to defend all that is most dear to you. But you surpass my hopes. I have found in you, united to these qualities, that noble enthusiasm which impels to great deeds.

—Andrew Jackson's address to African American troops, December 18, 1814

The conflict, which unfolded primarily on American waterways, was waged with the aid of approximately 2,500 African Americans. Squadrons on Lake Champlain, Lake Ontario, and Lake Erie are known to have employed African American fighting forces—proving early on in the nation's history that an integrated fighting force was viable as a practical reality (if not as a formal governmental policy).

Formal Segregation in the Armed Forces

Racial segregation in the American armed forces was firmly entrenched as official policy early in the nineteenth century.

In the years to come, politicians, both northern and southern, would deflect talk of reform with a combination of two responses: emphasis on the current pressing national security and military challenges faced by the nation, and appeals to existing precedent. In this way, the precedent of segregation was extended from war to war.

What's the Word?

Segregation is the establishment of separate facilities and institutions for separate races. **Racial segregation** in the U.S. military was the official policy of the United States government for most of this country's history.

For instance, in responding to an (unsuccessful) lawsuit seeking to establish the unconstitutionality of racial segregation in the armed forces in the 1940s, Franklin D. Roosevelt said, of racially separate force deployment, "What's wrong with it? We've always done that." As the war progressed, Roosevelt frequently told civil rights leaders that he agreed with their aims—but was unable to make progress on civil rights (in the military or elsewhere) a major priority because of the demands of waging the war.

What would have been closer to the truth would have been for Roosevelt to acknowledge that he was a nationally successful politician … and that, like successful politicians for a century and a half before him, he had refined to high art the act of sidestepping civil rights questions.

The Civil War

It is easy to forget that the momentous conflict between North and South was not formally "about" freeing slaves until Abraham Lincoln issued the Emancipation Proclamation. Equally easy to overlook are Lincoln's own policy pronouncements on race, which today carry more than a whiff of the white supremacist:

> I will say, then, that I am not, nor ever have been, in favor of bringing about in any way the social and political equality of the white and black races… [Audience applauds] … that I am not, nor ever have been, in favor of making voters or jurors of Negroes, nor of qualifying them to hold office, nor to intermarry with white people … And inasmuch as they cannot so live, while they do remain together there must be the position of superior and inferior, and I as much as any other man am in favor of having the superior position assigned to the white race.

> —From Lincoln's 1858 Senate campaign speech in Charleston, Illinois

Words like these must be taken in the context of the (white) political climate of the times, but they must also be remembered in any sober contemporary assessment of the realities of Lincoln as "the Great Emancipator" and of the Civil War as a whole. Not always consciously, Lincoln and the nation struggled to come to terms with the vast and agonizing implications of the institution of American slavery—an institution that abolitionist John Brown had declared to entail a sin so grave that it "would never be purged away but with blood." He was right, of course. Much of the blood, as it turned out, came from the veins of African American soldiers.

In the North

Roughly 185,000 African Americans served in the Union army; roughly 29,000 served in the Union navy. (The North also employed approximately 200,000 African Americans in various service and support roles.) African American troops took part in 449 battles during the war, of which 39 were significant engagements.

African Americans received significantly less pay than their white counterparts in the Union army, and typically had to make do with substandard equipment and facilities.

On the March

A number of African American Union soldiers received the Congressional Medal of Honor for their service during the Civil War. The first was Sgt. William H. Carney of the 54th Massachusetts Volunteers, the regiment that would later be immortalized in the film *Glory*. Lieutenant Stephen A. Swails, also of the 54th, was the first African American to be commissioned as an officer in the American Civil War.

In the South

The Confederacy realized early on that African American labor was an essential component of the war effort, and quickly established a program of military-related forced labor projects. These projects—repairing railroads, constructing fortifications, and mining, for instance—enabling the largest possible number of eligible whites to serve in the Confederate Army.

Southern troops committed what would today be considered brutal crimes of war against African American Union soldiers. On September 18, 1864, for instance, Confederate forces murdered all the African American Union soldiers they had captured in a battle at Poison Spring, Arkansas.

The Buffalo Soldiers

The Buffalo Soldiers were African American troops of the Ninth and Tenth U.S. Cavalry who served on the American frontier and had frequent engagements with Native American tribes after the Civil War. Their name arose from Native Americans, who found the soldiers' hair reminiscent of the fur of buffalo.

In addition to Native Americans, the Buffalo Soldiers did battle with bandits, cattle rustlers, thieves, trespassers, and (in a different kind of battle) the United States Army itself, which consistently saw fit to supply the men with substandard horses, housing, and equipment. Despite these adversities, the men of the Ninth and Tenth Cavalry compiled an honorable record, and eventually won 16 Congressional Medals of Honor.

The Spanish-American War

The Spanish-American War, which took place in 1898, saw the United States weigh in on the side of Cuban rebels who sought independence from Spain. The Spanish were routed and Cuba won an American-dominated variety of independence.

The African American Tenth Cavalry took part in several important engagements during the war, at one point relieving Theodore Roosevelt's famed Rough Riders at El Caney. In all, 16 African American regiments were inducted for the war.

Having served with valor and distinction in the conflict with Spain, African Americans returned to the United States to find, not honor, but intensified racial hatred and violence. Some of the worst abuses took place in Florida, where many African Americans were stationed. A gang of inebriated whites in Tampa saw fit to use an African American child for shooting practice. African American soldiers fought back, and a bloody race riot erupted. An African American chaplain, reacting to the violence, posed some stark questions in a letter to the *Cleveland Gazette*:

> Is America any better than Spain? Has she not subjects in her very midst who are murdered daily without a trial of judge or jury? Has she not subjects in her own borders whose children are half-fed and half-clothed, because their father's skin is black...?

The questions went unanswered.

World War I

In April of 1917, the United States entered World War I, a complex and carnage-strewn conflict that pitted the Allies (France, Britain, Russia, and eventually the United States) against the Central powers (Austria-Hungary, Germany, and Turkey). Nationalism and German expansionism were among the causes of this horrific war; U.S. President Woodrow Wilson hailed the conflict as a chance to make the world "safe for democracy."

African Americans flocked to enlist in the armed forces to fight in World War I, but many of those who sought combat roles were frustrated. White military officials often simply refused to train African American units properly; many African American servicemen who did receive training were shipped off, for some unfathomable reason, to the American West. The services of African American women hoping to make front-line contributions as nurses were ignored or formally rejected.

 FAQ

Who was the first American to win the French War Cross (also known as the Croix de Guerre)? That would be Sgt. Henry Johnson, of the Harlem Hellfighters. During World War I, Johnson and Private Needham Roberts combined to fight off a brutal assault from a group of over 30 German raiders.

There were exceptions to the trend. An African American National Guard unit that came to be known as the "Harlem Hellfighters" (formally called the 369th Infantry Regiment) became the initial American force, of any color, to reach the fighting in France. The Hellfighters won recognition for being the first Americans to cross the Rhine in the assault on Germany, and for the duration of their time in combat: 191 straight days, the longest of any U.S. unit serving in the war.

Roughly 370,000 African American soldiers served in the bitterly fought conflict, which concluded in victory for the Allies in 1918.

World War II

The global conflict between the Axis and the Allies was the costliest—in terms of both life and money—the world had ever seen. By the time it was formally concluded on September 2, 1945, over a million African Americans had served in the U.S. military in the struggle against Germany, Japan, and Italy.

A number of African American units were honored with Distinguished Unit Citations for their service during the war, including the 614th Tank Destroyer Battalion and the 969th Field Artillery Battalion.

The Tuskegee Airmen

Pressure from the NAACP and the African American press caused the War Department to form the African American 99th Pursuit Squadron. On July 19, 1941, the U.S. Army opened its first flight training facility for African Americans at the Tuskegee (Alabama) Army Air Field.

The following March, the first of the Tuskegee Airmen graduated. In all, Tuskegee trained 992 pilots, of whom 450 flew missions in North Africa. The Airmen destroyed 261 enemy aircraft, and won over 850 medals.

FDR Cuts a Deal

Under heavy pressure from African American civil rights leaders threatening a march on Washington, President Franklin D. Roosevelt issued Executive Order 8802 in June of 1941. The order barred discrimination on racial or religious grounds in government programs and industrial programs. FDR's action did not end racial segregation in the military or anywhere else ... but it did make possible the first African American Marine Corps unit the following year.

As a result of the executive order, roughly 19,000 African Americans served in World War II as Marines. They were trained at Camp Montford Point in Lejeune, North Carolina, and came to be known as the Montford Point Marines. Many were honored for bravery in combat.

A White Missourian Desegregates the Armed Forces

Senator Harry S. Truman of Missouri won the wartime Vice Presidential nomination as a compromise candidate who would help maintain vital (white) Southern support for the Democratic ticket. As everyone predicted, President Roosevelt and his new running mate swept to victory in November 1944. Within a year of the Democratic Convention whose back-room maneuverings elevated Truman to the Vice Presidency, however, Franklin Roosevelt was dead, and Truman himself was president.

When the time came for Truman to seek election in his own right, in 1948, something strange happened. The man who had been selected, in part, because of his ability to mollify white racists took two steps that stunned the white South. In February of 1948, Truman (having been lobbied energetically by Asa Philip Randolph for some time) urged Congress to take action on a civil rights program, and spoke out forcefully against poll taxes and lynchings. Then, in July, Truman issued Executive Order 9981, which officially desegregated the armed forces of the United States.

Truman was no civil rights activist, although he did have firm beliefs about equality of opportunity. He took the steps he did in 1948 as part of an inspired (and desperate) election-year gambit. The president, far behind in the polls, was praying that the white South would remain Democratic in the upcoming election *despite* his actions on civil rights—because support for either the Republican Thomas Dewey or the liberal Progressive Henry Wallace would be unappealing to whites. At the same time, the president was hoping that his civil rights moves would win him near-unanimous support from northern African Americans … and tip the scales in some of the key "battleground" states.

It was a risky maneuver, but Truman had little to lose. He was among the most unpopular presidents in history, and his campaign appeared hopelessly behind Dewey's.

Truman threw the dice.

> **On the March**
>
> In 1945, B. O. Davis became the first African American to head an armed forces base when he was promoted to commander of Goodman Field in Kentucky.

His gamble paid off. Truman defeated Dewey in the biggest upset in American political history, and his massive support from African American northern voters was a key element in the victory. For once, the prevailing winds of the national political scene had served to secure a (modest) advance for the cause of civil rights. Government-sanctioned segregation of the military was history, and desegregation in this realm helped to pave the way for advances in future areas of American society.

It would be another quarter-century, however, before African American soldiers who risked their lives in disproportionate numbers in faraway lands would be guaranteed access to the ballot box or equal access to public facilities at home.

Fighting Anyway

In 1943, an African American newspaper published a poem entitled "Draftee's Prayer." Its author asks God what, precisely, he is supposed to be fighting for. Without having received an answer, the speaker makes a vow that he has no fear of "Germans or Japs." The draftee then admits that the country he fears most is America.

He fights anyway.

The Least You Need to Know

◆ African American military sacrifices on behalf of the American republic have been immense.

◆ Most of these sacrifices were made in a segregated military system, on behalf of a social system that excluded African American, under the orders of a government that demanded loyalty without offering equal rights in return.

◆ From the time of Crispus Attucks to the time of B. O. Davis, African Americans made sacrifices for the idea of an America that had yet to come into existence.

◆ Desegregation of the American military in 1948 helped to pave the way for reforms in other areas of American society.

Part 5

The Road from Here

America in the twenty-first century offers daunting challenges to the African American community, some of which have been around for a very long time indeed. This century also offers unparalleled opportunity for growth and achievement. Here's an in-depth look at some of the obstacles, the opportunities, and the good work being done today ... and pointing us toward the future.

Supporting the Entrepreneurial Spirit

In This Chapter

- ◆ Economic progress, economic obstacles
- ◆ Expanding African American entrepreneurship
- ◆ Supporting the community

In this chapter, you find out about the movement toward economic self-determination in contemporary African American life.

Economic Progress, Economic Obstacles

Here are some snapshots from the United States Department of Commerce and the Bureau of the Census:

- ◆ In a recent five-year period, the total number of African American owned businesses rose by 60 percent—from roughly 1.3 million to roughly 2.1 million—compared to an increase of 26 percent for all businesses.

- Total number of African American–owned businesses increased by 94 percent between 1987 and 2000, advancing from roughly 424,000 to roughly 823,000.

- African American–owned businesses employed 718,300 people in the year 2000 and generated $71.2 billion in revenues.

- Median household income for African Americans in 2000: $30,439, an all-time high.

- The African American poverty rate in 2000: 22.1 percent, the lowest figure since poverty statistics were first taken in 1959.

- The percentage of African Americans 25 and over with a high school diploma in 2000: 79 percent, an all-time high.

- The percentage of African Americans 25 and over with at least a bachelor's degree in 2000: 17 percent, another record high.

Despite such encouraging signs, there are also clear signals that many African American families continue to struggle against long socioeconomic odds. Among the more sobering statistics:

- African American children in families are still significantly more likely than their white counterparts to live in poverty.

- In a recent year, unmarried African American teenagers were four times as likely as unmarried white teenagers to have had children. (This was an improvement, however, over the comparable figures from the early 1970s, when unmarried African American teenagers were 10 times more likely to have children.)

- African Americans in 1999 remained significantly less likely than whites to own the home in which they live, according to the Department of Commerce—but the rate of African American home ownership has increased steadily: 42 percent in 1992, compared with 46 percent in 1999.

One interpretation of these trends is that the economic picture for the national African American community shows both encouraging signs of improvement ... and evidence that there is still a long way to go before race-based economic obstacles are a thing of the past. If African American business ownership continues to increase—

and if middle-class and upper-class African Americans find innovative ways to support development and self-determination in inner-city communities, many of our problems may look a good deal more manageable a decade from now.

Here is information on nine creative modern programs that support and empower African American *entrepreneurship*. There are many more such initiatives, of course, but these offer examples of the kind of work being done by and for the African American business community.

What's the Word?

Entrepreneurship is the practice of organizing, running, and taking on the risks associated with operating a business.

Philadelphia United CDC

In 1999, United Bank of Philadelphia, which was named Bank of the Year by the U.S. Small Business Administration and Financial Company of the Year by *Black Enterprise* magazine, received $3 million in funding from the U.S. Treasury as part of its Community Development Financial Institution program. The bank created a Community Development Corporation (CDC) called Philadelphia United to "support the continued growth of United Bank and enable it to more effectively serve its customers in the underserved communities and stimulate local economic growth." Philadelphia United focuses on loans at the $20,000-and-upward level for local African American business owners.

Shine the spotlight on Emma C. Chappell, founder, chairman, and chief executive of United Bank of Philadelphia. She launched her bank in 1992 with investments from 3000 African American Philadelphians. Today, the bank is a $100 million asset institution, and the only African American–owned and operated FDIC-insured commercial bank in the Pennsylvania/Delaware/Southern New Jersey area. The institution prides itself on being a model "community bank."

Why It's Worth Celebrating

United Bank of Philadelphia has a deep commitment to supporting local businesses. Its work with the Treasury Department and Philadelphia United CDC is only part of the picture. Chappell estimates that her bank has created 80 local jobs directly, and something on the order of 5,000 jobs indirectly.

On the March

To learn more about United Bank of Philadelphia and its Philadelphia United program, visit www.unitedbankofphila.com, or call 215-829-BANK.

The National Foundation for Teaching Entrepreneurship

The National Foundation for Teaching Entrepreneurship (NFTE, or "nifty") teaches youth—and particularly inner-city youth—how to build businesses. Its mission is to instruct low-income youngsters between the ages of 11 and 18 in the skills of entrepreneurship. It does this by helping them upgrade their academic, technology, business, and interpersonal skills. The organization received the 2002 Esteemed Golden Lamp Award from the Association of Educational Publishers. Since 1987, NFTE has worked with over 40,000 low-income young people in underserved communities.

Shine the spotlight on Tom Brown, who won the NFTE National Teacher of the Year Award in 2002. After receiving the award, Brown, a Washington, D.C., teacher, said that getting the honor reinforced his "passion for demonstrating to at-risk youth that they have a future, and that it is possible for them to bring their dreams of escaping poverty to reality by learning how to become economically independent."

Why It's Worth Celebrating

Over a decade and a half, NFTE has secured enough funding from "corporations, foundations, and individuals" to sustain its vision and help high-risk youth improve school performance and broaden personal horizons. You can celebrate its good work—and help the organization expand its reach and influence—by donating money, volunteering your time, or sharing your own business and teaching skills. NFTE has U.S. offices in New York City; White Plains, New York; Babson Park, Massachusetts; Pittsburgh; San Francisco; and Washington, D.C. (There are also office in Argentina, Belgium, El Salvador, India, and the United Kingdom.)

 **On the March**

To learn more about the National Foundation for Teaching Entrepreneurship, visit www.nfte.com, or call 212-232-3333.

National Black Business Trade Association

The group's slogan is "Empowering Black Entrepreneurs Worldwide in a Global Marketplace," and it lives up to the idea. Established in 1993 by a group of African American business owners aiming to offer resources addressing the unique problems faced by the African American business community, the National Black Business Trade Association (NBBTA) set a number of critical long-term goals, including.

♦ Increasing the ranks of the African American entrepreneur; only 9 African Americans per 1,000 currently own businesses, whereas the comparable figure for whites is 64.

◆ Attracting the best and the brightest into the African American business community.

◆ Improving the image of the African American entrepreneur … thereby making the choice to start a business an attractive one for Africans who might otherwise embark on careers in medicine, law, or other professions.

In support of these and other goals, the NBBTA offers, among many resources, a "re-affirmative action plan" that emphasizes personal training, networking, community support, and outreach efforts designed to secure a greater portion of the African American market for African American businesses.

Shine the spotlight on Dr. Jawanza Kunjufu, whose writings and principles support the organization's intriguing "re-affirmative action plan."

Why It's Worth Celebrating

The online list of African American related business organizations alone is worth exploring closely. You can check it out at www.nbbta.com.

On the March _____

To learn more about the National Black Business Trade Association, visit www. nbbta.com.

National Black Chamber of Commerce

Incorporated in 1993, the National Black Chamber of Commerce (NBCC) represents over 64,000 African American–owned businesses nationwide. Its mission includes "empowering and sustaining African American communities through entrepreneurship and capitalistic activities within the United States." It is a nonprofit, nonsectarian, nonpartisan group committed to supporting economic growth in African American communities. NBCC is the largest African American business organization in the world.

Shine the spotlight on NBCC president and CEO Harry Alford, who recently took part in the President's Economic Forum at Baylor University as a member of the Corporate Responsibility Panel.

Why It's Worth Celebrating

NBCC's programs include extensive policy and advocacy efforts. The organization also provides legislative updates and offers members access to a variety of networking and training events. The Chamber points African American

On the March _____

To learn more about the National Black Chamber of Commerce, visit www. nationalbcc.org or call 202-466-6888.

business owners toward training on how best to win government-related business, pointing out (accurately) that "if federal dollars are involved, black businesses must be involved" under the provisions of Title VI. As if all that weren't enough, you can also download a free Small Business Financial Resource Guide—complete with federal- and state-specific financial resources—through the NBCC Web site.

African-American Women Business Owners Association

This association is a Washington, D.C.–based resource and networking group open to any type of business owned and operated by African American women.

On the March

To learn more about the African-American Women Business Owners Association, visit www.blackpgs.com/aawboa.html, or call 202-399-3645.

Shine the spotlight on Internet Black Pages (www.blackpgs.com), which sponsors the organization's online presence.

Why It's Worth Celebrating

It's a great example of a local organization supporting African American entrepreneurship on a national scale—thanks to the Internet.

Minority Business Development Agency

Sponsored by the U.S. Department of Commerce, the Minority Business Development Agency (MBDA) offers a wealth of information on access to markets, access to capital, management and technical assistance, and education and training.

Shine the spotlight on MBDA National Director Ronald N. Langston. Langston— an executive with deep experience in the real estate, financial services, and computer industries—directs the Department of Commerce's minority business development initiatives, and helps to develop strategies for serving minority business operators.

Why It's Worth Celebrating

No membership fees, no strings, no affiliations. Just great information on great programs—like the summary sheet on the MBDA's Equity Capital Access program, which offers minority entrepreneurs training in securing equity capital. Two hundred entrepreneurs will take part in the initial training and analysis phase of program; of those, 25 will be selected for a "boot camp," where they will be "drilled in the fundamentals of obtaining venture capital." It's just one of the hundreds of initiatives and information resources available through the MBDA. To learn more, check out the organization's website at www.mbda.gov.

On the March

To learn more about the Minority Business Development Agency, visit www.mbda.gov or call 202-482-0404.

Sablenet

Billing itself as "the Internet address for African American businesses," Sablenet offers a news service, a business center, a job and career center, information on international trade, free web-based e-mail accounts, a directory of African American businesses, and much more.

Shine the spotlight on H. B. Henderson, president of Sablenet, Inc., whose brainchild the site is.

Why It's Worth Celebrating

Well designed and easy to navigate, Sablenet features some great tools and access to a wealth of information of interest to African American entrepreneurs.

On the March

To learn more about Sablenet, visit www.sablenet.com or call 205-685-0184.

The Black Greek Network

No, the "Greek" in the title has nothing to do with ethnic heritage. The Black Greek Network is a group created to "encourage nepotism" in the African American community; it does so by encouraging business and social contacts among members of "important fellowship organizations" that include, but aren't limited to, African American fraternities and sororities (which, like many other fraternities and sororities, are identified by Greek letters). Other organizations whose members figure into the organization's unapologetic, informal promotion of African American talent include the Prince Hall Masons, Eastern Star, and major organizations such as the NAACP and the Urban League.

(Translation: You don't have to be in a fraternity or sorority to benefit from membership.)

Shine the spotlight on Devon Williams and Otis Collier cofounders and co-executive directors. A joint statement from the two encapsulates the group's vision: "Our goal is to help African Americans develop business socialization skills by arranging different meeting venues including business workshops, Internet communities, and networking jamborees."

Why It's Worth Celebrating

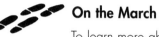

On the March _____

To learn more about the Black Greek Network, visit www.blackgreeknetwork.com or call 866-841-9139.

The organization is exclusively devoted to helping African American business people develop business social skills and high-level personal networking campaigns. It's a great contact resource for those African Americans interested in starting, financing, staffing, or running a business. If that's you, and you're willing to make the most of (or initiate) membership in one of the relevant groups, you owe it to yourself to join.

Supporting the Community

Organizations and campaigns like these are leading the way in supporting economic empowerment in the African American community. Learn more about them—and get involved in your own community by supporting African American–owned businesses!

The Least You Need to Know

- ◆ There has been significant economic progress in the African American community—but significant obstacles remain.

- ◆ Encouraging entrepreneurship in African American communities is vitally important.

- ◆ Educational initiatives that support the entrepreneurial spirit include the National Foundation for Teaching Entrepreneurship.

- ◆ Advocacy and lobbying organizations that support the entrepreneurial spirit include the National Black Chamber of Commerce.

Beyond the Rainbow: Race in American Politics

In This Chapter

♦ Racial ideologies and their consequences

♦ The fateful 1968 election

♦ The real Nixon legacy

News flash: Race is a cultural—not a genetic—phenomenon.

Biologically speaking, there is, as Dr. King suggested, one human "race," and it encompasses people of all colors and physical descriptions.

This finding, now universal among responsible scientists, puts to rest a long line of pseudoscientific nonsense about the supposed inherent inferiority of individuals based on skin color or other visible clues. Yet the scientific rejection of the idea of biological races does not change the landscape of American politics, where race—however it is defined technically—still carries immense and complicated implications.

In this chapter, you learn about some of those implications.

Racist Democracy and Its Long-Term Legacy

Race doesn't live in our genes, but racial perceptions and racial thinking do affect modern social and political institutions. This leads to a question: What are the political implications of African American identity in the United States in the early twenty-first century?

To answer that, I believe we have to look at where we're going as a nation, and where we've been. We must begin by accepting that this country, for most of its history, frequently espoused and perpetuated—and almost always left unchallenged—explicitly racist political ideologies.

In an article in the Spring 2002 *American Outlook*, Joseph L. Graves, a professor of evolutionary biology, offers an interesting explanation for the popularity of racist political ideologies—ideologies that have, as it turns out, no basis in actual biological differences between human beings.

Graves identifies three major benefits for ruling orders that appeal to (nonexistent) biological differences between groups of people:

◆ Racist ideology offers a supposedly "moral" reason for the withholding of rights and resources from groups identified as "lower" in status.

◆ Racist ideology provides a focus for social anxieties that the leadership would otherwise have to address directly.

◆ Racist ideology helps to maintain the existing social and economic system. Often, it does this by making the argument (openly or otherwise) that *all* groups would suffer horribly from a large-scale campaign of social or economic change.

Graves then cites "at least seven" serious problems with conducting a society according to racist doctrines, problems that destabilize the social system as a whole (including the dominant "race"). Racist ideologies, he points out …

◆ Promote economic inefficiency and intellectual stagnation.

◆ Tend to make social problems far worse.

◆ Cost too much to maintain.

◆ Make foreign policy needlessly difficult.

◆ Corrode communication between groups, increasing misperception and mistrust.

- ◆ Make large-scale social adjustments difficult and painful (because any change may be seen as helping a "low-status" group).

- ◆ Increase a general lack of respect for legal institutions and for broader ideas of compromise and reconciliation.

It is not hard to see how some of the hypothetical trends Graves spotlights became very real social and political problems in the second half of the twentieth century in our country. (The riots following the Rodney King verdict, for instance, offer an example of some of the consequences of the legacy of racial prejudice that had gone unchallenged for years in the Los Angeles Police Department.)

This, then, is what happened to the racist "democracy" that held the day in the United States from the end of Reconstruction in 1877 until the period of widespread social unrest that began in the 1960s.

Covert Racism

Have we as a country really grown past the period of tolerance for—or open embrace of—racist political ideologies?

From one perspective, the answer is clearly "yes." Overtly racist ideologies no longer play a leading role in American politics, and the hard-won civil rights advances of the 1950s and 1960s are established realities. But the legacy of our country's racial politics is still very much with us.

We have moved out of the era of Jim Crow and blatant civil rights abuses ... and into a stubbornly persistent period of covert racism, a period of understated, but no less exclusionary, politics. We have entered a period of code words, quiet alliances, and *de facto* separation. This brand of racial politics is indeed alive and well in the United States.

What's the Word?

De facto means "from the facts"; it reflects the actual situation encountered, and not the official or governmental pronouncements or rules concerning that situation.

Winning legal rights like the right to vote was vitally important, of course. As it turned out, however, exercising legal rights did surprisingly little to alter the many strange and subtle ways in which men or women could be kept in a predetermined socioeconomic "place"—a place defined by skin color.

Why is this so? I believe it is because large segments of white America remain deeply frightened of real-world contact with African Americans, and because irresponsible white politicians have successfully preyed upon—and, in fact, carefully broadened—this fear over the past three and a half decades.

This consciously cultivated white fear, the legacy of our long history of racially exclusionary politics, has ...

◆ Led to a destabilizing culture of (usually) unspoken racial paranoia.

◆ Helped to make African American social problems significantly worse.

◆ Made the ideal of a society where we are judged by the content of our character far more difficult to achieve than it had to be.

I also believe that the American political system could have taken a very different and more inclusive course, but that it did not do so for a number of reasons—one of which was the cynicism of a key group of white politicians.

A side note: For simplicity of illustration, I will be focusing mostly on American presidential elections in this chapter. This is because I think the patterns in those elections reflect practical political realities that have resonated in many, many other corners of the U.S. political system.

The Same Election, Again and Again

In 1968, white supremacist George Wallace and Republican Richard Nixon pulled a total of 57 percent of the popular vote for president. Nixon secured more popular votes than any other candidate, and a clear majority of electoral college votes in 1968; he defeated his Democratic opponent, Hubert Humphrey.

The 1968 election was a landmark in American political history. This was not because the segregationist George Wallace made the best third-party showing since Theodore Roosevelt, but because the election ushered in a period of racial polarization that has defined the U.S. political system ever since.

In 1968 Wallace and Nixon began a new process of speaking in code words (such as "tradition," "values," "law and order," and "neighborhood") that had the effect of attracting low-income white voters (particularly males) who were fearful of making contact with, or suffering economic losses to, African Americans. I believe the United States has been conducting essentially the same election ever since.

The surface issues change, of course, but the outcomes have, thus far, been remarkably predictable. When a white centrist southern Democrat has been able to overcome the racial anxieties and insecurities of a critical "swing" portion of middle-class and lower-middle-class white men, the Democrats have carried the day. (This happened in 1976, 1992, and 1996.)

More often, conservative candidates have successfully exploited white racial insecurities and made the most of (and, in the process, usually deepened) class divisions between whites and African Americans. The all-important middle-tier white "swing" vote has provided enough political support to provide either indisputable Republican victories (1968, 1972, 1980, 1984, 1988) or an outcome close enough to manipulate to eventual Republican advantage (2000). In the bitterly disputed 2000 election, Vice President Al Gore won roughly 90 percent of the African American vote—but failed to win enough support from white males to carry battleground states like Arkansas, his own home state of Tennessee, and the ominously unsettled state of Florida.

In presidential politics, as elsewhere in the American political system, white fear of African Americans remains a central electoral reality.

The 1968 Pattern

This state of affairs, artfully exploited in election years by careful rhetoric from white politicians, first emerged in 1968. That year marked the beginning of a long period of self-perpetuating racial polarization in this country, a cycle that produced the defecting "Reagan Democrats," the infamous Willie Horton ad campaign, and the civil rights debacle in Florida in 2000.

Obstacles and Opportunities

In 1988, the presidential campaign of Vice President George Bush successfully appealed to white racial insecurities by spotlighting the case of furloughed Massachusetts rapist Willie Horton in a prominent series of television commercials. The Bush campaign's use of Horton, an African American, convinced millions of white voters that Massachusetts governor Michael Dukakis was "soft on crime." What that phrase really meant to lower-middle-class white swing voters was a topic much debated during the campaign. Bush won handily.

Widening the Rift

In the years since 1968, when George Wallace pioneered his "politics by code word" strategy for winning the votes of alienated whites, signs of increasing racial polarization in the political life of the United States have not been hard to find.

The year 1968 was a time when, to rephrase the poet William Yeats, the center could not hold, the best did nothing—or, in the case of Dr. King, were murdered—and the worst were full of passionate intensity.

That year saw George Wallace give the Republican party a lesson in how to use racial divisions to attract white working-class voters. Four years later, President Richard Nixon showed how well he had learned that lesson, and offered an object lesson of his own to aspiring politicians across the country.

A new era began in 1968, an era of cynical political manipulation of strategically important groups of white voters. It is hard not to wonder whether some of the social problems that have worsened in the African American community in the years since could have been dealt with differently … had the American political culture only taken a different turn in that fateful year.

What If?

In April 1968, Senator Robert F. Kennedy, a surging presidential candidate, was offering a lesson of a different kind, a lesson that he would never be able to complete. He was using a message of racial *unity* to attract both disaffected whites and an overwhelming majority of African American voters.

Kennedy was not perfect, and he had had his own moments of cynical opportunism as a member of his brother's presidential administration. He had, however, developed a deep and abiding commitment to the concerns of African Americans, and he was, in 1968, the only major white politician in the country who had won the respect and admiration of large numbers of African American voters.

In the immediate aftermath of the assassination of Dr. Martin Luther King in April of 1968, Kennedy had spoken eloquently before an enraged and grief-stricken group of African Americans of his own family's loss at the hands of a white man. It was not well known at the time, but it was at the suggestion of Robert Kennedy that Martin Luther King began organizing his final campaign, the Poor People's March on Washington.

Any historical "what-if" scenario is a dangerous undertaking. All the same, it is an intriguing fact that many lower-middle-class white male *Kennedy* supporters in early 1968 turned into white male working-class *Wallace* supporters in late 1968. Both men had strong appeal to low-income whites; only one of them was alive by the time the election rolled around.

With Kennedy's death at the hands of an assassin in June of that year, did the prospect of a new coalition, of a different way of approaching racial matters in the United States, die as well?

The Nixon Legacy

Today, Richard Nixon is usually remembered in one of two ways—either as the disgraced and scandal-ridden president forced to resign the office in 1974, or as the enduring "elder statesman" who won the admiration of former adversaries in the decades following his active political career. But there is yet another Nixon who deserves to be remembered; the man who set out to attract lower-income whites in the election 1972 by deliberately following the George Wallace playbook of four years earlier.

Values

There is no reason to feel guilty about wanting to enjoy what you get and get what you earn, about wanting your children in good schools close to home, or about wanting to be judged fairly on your ability. Those are not values to be ashamed of, those are values to be proud of. Those are values that I shall always stand up for when they come under attack.

—President Richard Nixon, expertly using Wallace-minted code words to en-hance the racial divide and attract white votes during his 1972 re-election campaign

---

In taking this approach, Nixon secured for himself the largest electoral-college landslide in American history … and outlined the political strategy that has guided the Republican party ever since.

To secure his 1972 victory, Nixon played (among other dubious cards) a coded "race card" that required him to attack components of his own administration's affirmative-action initiatives. Success in politics, however, is not always logical.

The domestic Nixon legacy must be remembered, not only as one of scandal, but for the strategic encouragement of divisions between African Americans and whites, and consciously perpetuating the deep divisions that had led to "two societies, separate and unequal," as a presidential commission on race had described America in 1967.

Nixon was the first figure in the political era of nationwide African American enfranchisement to build a successful coalition that consciously *perpetuated and worsened* the "separate and unequal" society. He did it by appealing subtly to the racial fears and insecurities of whites. Robert F. Kennedy's emerging coalition, which appealed to rather different emotions and principles, never had the chance to take shape. His voice, like that of Dr. King, was silenced in 1968.

What kind of America would have emerged if those two charismatic voices had not been silenced in that fateful year?

Open Wounds

There are many open wounds in the African American community that have not healed in the years since 1968. It is an open question how these challenges would have been dealt with in an America shaped by the coalition represented in 1968 by Martin Luther King and Robert F. Kennedy, rather than that of George Wallace and Richard M. Nixon. But it is, I think, a question well worth asking.

The country as a whole has moved sharply to the right in the decades following the deaths of King and Kennedy. The Republican party, the party of Abraham Lincoln, has, in that period, formed a new governing coalition, one that has been only intermittently challenged. The foundation of that coalition remains white voters in the South and Southwest who are quite capable of decoding the underlying ideas in speeches that are supposedly about "crime" and "education" and "traditional values," but are actually about something very different.

In far too many of the federal, state, and local elections following the benchmark 1968 presidential contest, racial polarization became an essential electoral strategy. As the strategy became more formalized under Richard Nixon, three areas of racial inequality that had once been matters of deep national concern for people of all races in 1964 began to emerge as political vulnerabilities for the Democratic party. Whether the right's divisive (and successful) electoral strategy helped to cause these three social problems to worsen, or whether they would have worsened in any case, is hard to say. What is certain is that the Nixon legacy of strategic polarization and racial divisiveness has not yet solved the most pressing problems of the African American community, and it seems highly unlikely to solve them in the future.

America is still waiting for a politician capable of building an enduring national consensus whose central organizing concept is something other than racial fear.

The First Challenge: The Family Unit

Disintegration of family structures in the African American community has been a persistent problem for far too long.

High out-of-wedlock birth rates, absent fathers, and the lack of a family support network for many young African Americans have led to serious problems in America's urban areas. The persistence of these crises have helped to perpetuate negative images of African Americans, and have contributed to the increasing polarization of American social and political life along racial lines.

The Second Challenge: The Emergence of an Underclass

Despite the rise of an educated African American professional class, and despite many economic and social advances for African Americans as a whole, inner-city urban areas have remained underinspired and underdeveloped for so long that they have developed a seemingly permanent sense of despair. These areas remain stubbornly prone to epidemics of social dysfunction and particularly to problems related to crime and drug abuse.

The persistence of serious social problems in inner-city areas has led to a tragic perpetuation of racial prejudice, and to talk of a permanent African American "underclass."

White suburban flight from urban areas (which began in the 1970s) has left cities coping with huge numbers of underfunded urban schools that simply don't work for their predominantly African American and minority students. Political candidates from both parties have issued earnest calls for reform and solemn vows that the system must change, but the reality that many city school systems continue to betray their students remains.

The Third Challenge: Unequal Earning Capacity

President Lyndon Johnson's 1965 speech seeking "not just equality as a right and a theory, but equality as a fact and as a result" started a tumultuous decades-long debate over affirmative action.

FAQ

What was the origin of affirmative action? The first policies requiring clear and unmistakable actions to "level the playing field" for African Americans and other minorities in such areas as hiring, contracts, promotion, admission to educational institutions, and financial aid are associated with the Johnson administration in 1965. These policies were also supported by President Richard Nixon until he realized he could gain political advantage by running against them (and thus endearing himself to white voters).

The debates over the wisdom of these policies have become more and more bitter in recent years, and the issue remains an emotional one for the so-called "angry white men" who have viewed affirmative action programs as reverse discrimination. Many on the left have argued that aggressive affirmative action programs are the only intelligent approach given the enduring legacy of slavery and legalized discrimination faced by African Americans.

A significant dissenting voice within the African American community has been that of California educator Ward Connerly, who has helped to agitate, successfully, for the repeal of affirmative action programs in California and Washington State. Connerly has been quoted as dismissing affirmative action programs as "poisonous," in part because of their tendency to give non-minorities the impression that anything achieved by a person of color is only achieved "because of somebody giving it to us. … As long as you have this paradigm where people seem to be using race and gender as a means of making hiring decisions, as long as they keep uttering this mindless blather about 'we've got to achieve diversity,' it kind of taints the whole process."

Regardless of one's position on the question of affirmative action, its emergence as a potent and divisive contemporary political issue is hard to deny. A 1997 Gallup poll revealed that 79 percent of whites believe that African Americans have the same chance of getting a job that whites have; less than half of the African Americans polled expressed such a belief.

For the record, African American earning power remains significantly below that of whites. Recently, Ohio State University analyzed data from the Federal Reserve Board's 1998 Survey of Consumer Finances. The results: Median household income for African American families was $15,500, an increase over 1989 figures … but far below the $71,700 in income for the "typical American household" in 1998. (Source: *Chicago Tribune*, August 30, 2002, "Study Finds Blacks Earning More," Laurie Kellman.)

Beyond Politics

The fact of divisive, fear-driven racial politics remains a disturbing reality of American life. It has been a fact for so long that many people of good will have become deeply disillusioned with the prospect of working through the political system for measurable change in American society.

In the next chapter, you'll learn about some of the most promising nonviolent and inclusive campaigns for social progress that have taken root in the African American community during the long, destructive, and troubling period of "code word" racial politics in the United States.

The Least You Need to Know

♦ Racist ideologies carry consequences.

♦ The 1968 election marked a turning-point in American politics, because it showcased a new, racially divisive strategy for winning the votes of disaffected whites.

♦ Richard Nixon's true political legacy was his mastery of this strategy.

♦ Whether problems in the African American community have worsened *as a result* of this enduring and cynical political strategy, they have certainly not been helped by the emergence of the new governing coalition.

♦ No American politician has been able to fashion an enduring governing coalition that rejects (rather than exploits) racial fear.

Chapter 24

Epilogue: Beyond Race in America

In This Chapter

- ◆ Not an end but a beginning
- ◆ Examples of initiatives that can make a difference
- ◆ A final thought

The disposition of Africans in America remains the focus of national attention.

To close this book—which, unlike the saga of Africans in America, does have an ending—I offer some important examples of the work being done right now by African Americans to continue the legacy of opposing virulent racial prejudice, building coalitions, securing advances in education, developing economic opportunity, and creating enduring social change.

Build Your Own Ending

Many groups, programs, and initiatives that affect African Americans deserve recognition. Here are a few you may want to consider exploring further.

On the March

As we move confidently into the future, we choose goals to support the kinds of contributions that strengthen ourselves, our families, our neighborhoods, and our nation as a whole. Among these contributions are: equal educational opportunity; the development and support of competitive businesses; the creation of wealth for future generations; and the exercise of political and social power on behalf of our own communities. If you are inspired to get involved with any of the organizations profiled here, or any that operate in a similar vein, you will be continuing the legacy of African American self-determination and progress. Collaborative action is the best possible way to keep the tradition of growth alive.

Challenges and Opportunities

We have come to a point in history where our civil rights *must* be a given ... so that we can enter into larger issues of national and global human rights activism. And I believe that, for every challenge along the way when it comes to securing human rights, there is an equal or greater opportunity.

Consider, for example, the mission of the Southern Center for Human Rights (SCHR), an organization that has been working for over two decades to fight for the civil and human rights of "people of color, poor people, and other disadvantaged citizens facing the death penalty or confined to prisons and jails in the South." SCHR shines a spotlight on death-penalty–related abuses of the legal system that predominantly affect African Americans—such as the manipulation of jury pools; the systematic torture and abuse of minority inmates; and incompetent, drunk, or sleeping court-appointed attorneys. SCHR also challenges larger, systemic problems, such as the fact that 65 percent of victims of homicide in the state of Georgia are African American, while over 90 percent of those executed for murder in that state have been convicted of killing a white person. SCHR has been successful in a number of important legal and advocacy campaigns—securing, for instance, court decisions that struck down racially discriminatory jury selection and sentencing actions.

The organization's website includes this sobering quote from Supreme Court Justice William Brennan's dissent in the *McCleskey* v. *Kemp* case: "It is tempting to pretend that minorities on death row share a fate in no way connected to our own, that our treatment of them sounds no echoes beyond the chamber in which they die. Such an illusion is ultimately corrosive, for the reverberations of injustice are not so easily confined. ... [T]he way in which we choose those who will die reveals the depth of moral commitment among the living."

Cruel and Unusual Punishment

Spend some time on the World Wide Web to find out about The Southern Center for Human Rights, a "a non-profit, public interest legal project, founded in 1976, to enforce the constitutional protection against 'cruel and unusual punishment' by challenging excessive and degrading forms of punishment and cruel and inhuman conditions of confinement." (http://www.blackthinktank.com/)

Social Action: Protecting Civil Rights ... from Cyberspace

File under advocacy on behalf of civil rights issues in a digital age.

Where We Stand

African American advances in the area of civil rights have benefited Americans of all races and creeds. For all Americans, then, one persistent area of concern has to do with the defense of civil rights advances ... and the idea that mutual respect for the differences among groups makes our nation stronger, not weaker. And thanks to the Internet, we live in a time of unparalleled opportunity for connection, involvement, and group action in defense of civil and human rights—locally and globally.

The Big Idea

Establishing an online community specifically devoted to supporting interaction among concerned citizens committed to diversity, civil rights, and human rights issues.

The Initiative

Civilrights.org, an exciting and fast-moving virtual community with a commitment to getting important information out to its members—and building a corner of cyberspace on a solid foundation of values that support inclusion, equal opportunity, and tolerance.

Civilrights.org's mission is to empower the civil rights community to lead the fight for equality and social justice in the emerging digital society through the

On the March

To learn more about Civilrights.org, visit the organization's website at—you guessed it—www.civilrights.org.

establishment of an online social justice network. Civilrights.org leverages communications technologies to create an online society committed to the continued pursuit of equality, and to fostering greater understanding and mutual respect for difference.

—From Civilrights.org

Social Action: Supporting Tolerance and Cultural Understanding at Home—and Around the World

File under: Building bridges and opening doors is a global, neverending process.

Where We Stand

There has, we should acknowledge, been improvement since the grim days of rigid, overt racial prejudice. Today, the people of the United States face daunting issues together, and we share a mutual concern for the safety of all our citizens. While many barriers and prejudices still exist, there is now wide recognition of the social and political advances the African American community made on behalf of all Americans in the decades since the end of World War II. Demographic and social changes have slowly altered the "black-white" polarity that dominated most of America's history, and we find ourselves part of a country that has begun to embrace the diversity it has always celebrated.

The Big Idea

Develop a self-reinforcing community that supports inquiry into world cultures ... and celebrates diversity around the globe.

 On the March

To learn more about the World Cultural Foundation, visit the organization's website at www.wcf.org.

The Initiative

The World Cultural Foundation, a nonprofit group committed to encouraging communication and understanding among the world's cultures. Among the group's innovative and popular programs is its International PenFriends campaign, which allows members to correspond with people in different regions of the world.

[Our] purpose is to promote cultural understanding throughout the world. Our programs have reached into 251 countries and territories worldwide; [we have worked with] over 4 million members.

—From the World Cultural Foundation's mission statement.

On the March

The World Cultural Foundation's activities include care packages, cultural displays, educational programs, fundraising efforts, guest speakers, student exchange programs, translators, travel tours, and much more. It's a great way to learn how diverse our world really is—and how many different traditions and customs make up the human family.

Economic Action

Some of the most remarkable social advances in all of human history came about in the twentieth century, when African Americans used governmental mechanisms— namely, the courts and the ballot box—to begin the process of reversing centuries of social and legal subjugation. In the twenty-first century, the challenge is to rely less on government and more on the African American community's massive entrepreneurial potential.

Chapters 15 and 22 of this book explore the long and rich history of African American business achievement and some current resources that support business development within the community. In addition to the material in those chapters, you may also want to find out about:

- Black Think Tank, a "joint center for political and social studies" (http://www.blackthinktank.com/)

- Supporting Black Businesses, a bulletin board and article site devoted to "get(ting) involved in your own economic destiny" (www.supportblackbusiness.com)

- *Black Enterprise* magazine, which boasts a superb website that boasts "channels" covering small business, investing, personal finance, and other issues (www. blackenterprise.com)

- BlackFortune.com, "America's largest black business directory" (www.blackfortune.com)

◆ The Urban Think Tank Institute, an organization whose "an organization whose "scholarly activism gives voice to members of the Hip Hop generation." (www.blackfortune.com)

A Final Thought

In this book, I deliberately de-emphasized the mass media's favorite shorthand analyses of challenges in the African American community: cultural poverty, unreliable family structures, youth at risk, teenage pregnancy, and so on. I chose instead to focus on the resources necessary to build up our communities. I did this because what our community needs is more of the visionary, positive thinkers who are passionate about clearing the path for the new journey in the African American community—a journey guided by a vision of education, competition, technological empowerment, and business enterprise that overleaps all obstacles.

The Least You Need to Know

◆ This isn't the end, but a new beginning.

◆ You can keep the legacy of contribution alive.

◆ One of the best ways to do so is by getting involved in organizations that support the African American community and the guiding, undying vision of growth and self-determination that has sustained it through the centuries.

◆ Whether or not you get involved with one of the initiatives profiled in this chapter, you should find some way to make your own contribution to the community.

◆ In the twenty-first century, building prosperity is a major priority for the African American community.

Appendix A

Bibliography and Recommended Reading

Essential books that can take you further on the path of African American discovery.

Appiah, Kwame Anthony, and Louis Gates, eds. *Africana: The Encyclopedia of the African and African American Experience*. Basic Civitas Books, 1999.

Asante, Molefi K., and Mark T. Mattson. *Historical and Cultural Atlas of African Americans*. Macmillan Publishing Company, 1992.

Bell, Derrick A. *Faces at the Bottom of the Well: The Permanence of Racism*. Basic Books, 1993.

Bennett, Lerone Jr. *Before the Mayflower: A History of Black America*. Penguin USA, 1993.

Buckley, Gail Lumet. *American Patriots: The Story of Blacks in the Military from the Revolution to Desert Storm*. Random House, 2001.

Carson, Clayborne, ed. *Martin Luther King, Jr. The Autobiography of Martin Luther King, Jr*. Warner Books, 2001.

Cose, Ellis. *The Envy of the World: On Being a Black Man in America*. Washington Square Press, 2002.

Dray, Philip. *At the Hands of Persons Unknown: The Lynching of Black America*. Random House, 2002.

Haley, Alex, and Malcolm X. *The Autobiography of Malcolm X*. African American Images, 1969.

Hampton, Henry, and Steve Fayer. *Voices of Freedom: An Oral History of the Civil Rights Movement from the 1950s through the 1980s*. Bantam, 1990.

Haskins, Jim. *Black Stars: African American Entrepreneurs*. John Wiley & Sons, 1998.

Hine, Darlene Clark, Kathleen Thompson, and Hine Thompson. *A Shining Thread of Hope: The History of Black Women in America*. Broadway Books, 1999.

Jones, Howard. *Mutiny on the Amistad*. Oxford University Press, 1997.

Khalifah, H. Khalif, ed., Del Jones, Marva Cooper, Neal Jackson, Reda Faard Khalifah, Steven Whitehurst, Gloria Taylor-Edwards, Adib Rashad, Gregory X, Munir Muhammad, Al-Hajj Idris A. Muhammad, Lula B. Anderson-Edwards, Ras Mar-Yoi Collier. *Rodney King and the L.A. Rebellion: Analysis and Commentary by 13 Independent Black Writers*. Khalifahs Book Sellers & Associates, 1992.

Loewenberg, Bert James and Ruth Bogin, eds. *Black Women in Nineteenth-Century American Life*. Pennsylvania State University Press, 1976.

Loury, Glenn C. *The Anatomy of Racial Inequality (W.E.B. Du Bois Lectures)*. Harvard University Press, 2002.

Meier, August. *Negro Thought in America, 1880–1915*. University of Michigan Press, 1963.

Rogers, J. A. *World's Great Men of Color Pts. I & II*. Simon & Schuster (Pt. I), Touchstone Books (Pt. II), 1996.

Smith, Jessie Carney. *Black Firsts: 2,000 Years of Extraordinary Achievement*. Visible Ink Press, 1994.

Styron, William. *The Confessions of Nat Turner*. Vintage Books, 1993.

Sullivan, Ortha Richard. *Black Stars: African American Inventors.* John Wiley & Sons, 1998.

Tatum, Beverly Daniel. *Why Are All the Black Kids Sitting Together in the Cafeteria? And Other Conversations About Race.* Basic Books, 1999.

Washington, James Melvin, ed. Martin Luther King Jr., Coretta Scott King. *I Have a Dream: Writings and Speeches That Changed the World.* Harper San Francisco, 1992.

West, Cornel, and Henry Louis Gates Jr. *The African-American Century: How Black Americans Have Shaped Our Country.* Free Press, 2000.

Whitehurst, Steven. *Words from an Unchained Mind.* Khalifahs Book Sellers & Associates, 1991.

Williams, Gregory Howard. *Life on the Color Line: The True Story of a White Boy Who Discovered He Was Black.* Plume, 1996.

Woodson, Carter G. *Mis-Education of the Negro.* Africa World Press, 1990.

Wright, Bruce. *Black Robes, White Justice.* Lyle Stuart, 1990.

Zinn, Howard. *A People's History of the United States: 1492-Present.* Harper Perennial, 1980.

Recommended Websites

A representative sampling of fascinating African American-related websites:

African American Art on the Internet
www.brooklyn.liunet.edu/cwis/cwp/library/aavawww.htm

African American Biographical Database
aabd.chadwyck.com

African American Freedom Fighters—Soldiers for Liberty
www.cwpost.liunet.edu/cwis/cwp/library/aaffsfl.htm

African American History at About.com
afroamhistory.about.com

The African-American Mosaic Exhibition (Library of Congress)
www.loc.gov/exhibits/african/intro.html

African American Odyssey
memory.loc.gov/ammem/aaohtml

African American Web Connection
www.aawc.com/Zaawc0.html

African American World
www.pbs.org/wnet/aaworld/

African Americans in the Sciences
www.princeton.edu/~mcbrown/display/faces.html

Afro-American Almanac
www.toptags.com/aama/

American Holocaust
http://www.maafa.org/

American Slavery: A Composite Autobiography
www.slavenarratives.com

Archives of African American Music and Culture
www.indiana.edu/~aaamc/index2.html

Black Quest
www.blackquest.com

Black Soldiers in the Civil War
www.archives.gov/digital_classroom/lessons/blacks_in_civil_war/blacks_in_civil_war.html

Database of African American Poetry
etext.lib.virginia.edu/aapd.html

National Civil Rights Museum
www.mecca.org/~crights/cyber.html

Encyclopaedia of Slavery
www.spartacus.schoolnet.co.uk/USAslavery.htm

Gateway to African American History
usinfo.state.gov/usa/blackhis

A Tribute to Dr. Martin Luther King Jr.
www.thekingcenter.com

Index

S